Personal Finance
For Teens

A Wiley Brand

Personal Finance For Teens

by Athena Valentine Lent
(Money Smart Latina) and
Mykail James (MBA,
The Boujie Budgeter)

Personal Finance For Teens For Dummies®

Published by: **John Wiley & Sons, Inc.**, 111 River Street, Hoboken, NJ 07030-5774,
www.wiley.com

For general information on our other products and services, please contact our Customer
Care Department within the U.S. at 877-762-2974, outside the U.S. at 317-572-3993, or
fax 317-572-4002. For technical support, please visit https://hub.wiley.com/community/
support/dummies.

Wiley publishes in a variety of print and electronic formats and by print-on-demand.
Some material included with standard print versions of this book may not be included
in e-books or in print-on-demand. If this book refers to media such as a CD or DVD
that is not included in the version you purchased, you may download this material at
http://booksupport.wiley.com. For more information about Wiley products, visit
www.wiley.com.

Library of Congress Control Number: 2025933269

ISBN: 978-1-394-31573-4 (pbk); 978-1-394-31574-1 (epub); 978-1-394-31575-8 (ebk)

SKY10099737_031125

Contents at a Glance

Table of Contents

Introduction

H ey there! You've just picked up a book that could change your life in ways you never imagined. Whether it's saving for your first car, planning an epic post-graduation trip, or simply being tired of not knowing where all your money goes, we're here to help you figure it all out. Managing money might seem like something only adults need to worry about, but trust us, there's no such thing as being too young to start caring about your financial future.

We're Athena and Mykail, your co-pilots on this financial journey. Athena knows what it's like to overcome major challenges, like being homeless in high school. Now she's a financial columnist making her voice heard. Mykail, also known as The Boujie Budgeter, turned her passion for teaching young professionals into a mission to make complex money topics simple and approachable. Together, we're on a mission to empower the next generation — yes, that's you — to take control of your finances and build a future you're proud of.

Here's the good news: You don't need to be a math genius or have a ton of money to start learning about personal finance. Whether you have $5 from your allowance or you're earning your first paycheck from a summer job, you can start building healthy money habits today. Grab a notebook, set some goals, and let's start building your financial future!

About This Book

Managing money doesn't have to be scary, boring, or overwhelming. *Personal Finance for Teens For Dummies* is your go-to guide for everything you need to know about money, written in a way that's easy to understand and (dare we say it) even fun. Inside, you'll find chapters that cover budgeting, saving, investing, earning, and much more. We'll also walk you through setting goals and making smart financial decisions that align with your dreams.

Let's say you've been saving up for a new gaming console. You've got the cash but wonder, "Should I spend it all at once? When can I start investing? Am I making the best choice for my money?" Or maybe you're thinking about how to earn enough for your senior trip. We will answer those questions and more.

This book is packed with practical tools like downloadable resources, engaging videos, and clear charts to help you every step of the way. We've also included real-life stories (both our own and from people we've worked with) to show you how these tips work in real life. Whether you're building your first budget or discovering how to invest, you'll find examples and encouragement to help you take action.

Foolish Assumptions

While writing this book, we imagined you might be:

>> A teenager ready to explore financial independence for the first time.

>> Curious about how to make, save, and grow your money.

>> Looking for straightforward advice, with no boring lectures attached.

>> Hoping to achieve big dreams, whether that's going to college, starting a business, or traveling the world.

>> Someone who loves a good hack, shortcut, or actionable tip to make learning easier.

Sound like you? Then this book was made for you!

Icons Used in This Book

You don't have to read this book cover to cover (though you totally can). Think of it as your financial toolkit. You can jump straight to the chapter that answers your most pressing questions — like how to save for college or what credit cards are all about — or read it in order, to build your knowledge step by step.

We've also included special icons to help you navigate the book.

>> **Tip:** Look for these whenever you want quick, actionable advice you can use right away.

>> **Remember:** These highlight important things you shouldn't forget as you manage your money.

>> **Technical Stuff:** Indicates information that goes into a little more detail.

>> **Warning:** Watch out for common pitfalls or risks so you can steer clear of money mistakes.

Beyond the Book

In addition to the pages you're reading right now, this book comes with a free, access-anywhere online Cheat Sheet that summarizes some of our key advice at a glance. To access this Cheat Sheet, go to www.dummies.com/ and type **Personal Finance for Teens Cheat Sheet** in the search box. For more helpful tips on investing as a teen, you can find videos on topics related to the book at www.dummies.com/go/personalfinanceforteensfd.

Where to Go from Here

No matter where you are in your financial journey, this book is here to guide you. Maybe you're just starting to earn money and want to know how to save it. Maybe you're eyeing your dream college and wondering how to afford it. Or maybe you're already thinking about investing (yes, that's something teens can do!). Wherever you start, we promise to make it easy, encouraging, and even fun.

The best part? Every good habit you build today will pay off tomorrow . . . and for the rest of your life. So let's dive in, set some goals, and make the future version of you really, really proud.

1

Discover How to Build Your Financial Muscles

Understand financial planning basics.

Create a financial plan to build long-term wealth and stability.

Understand the importance of managing your money with a strategic mindset.

Find out the essentials of budgeting and setting financial goals.

Discover how credit works and why it's important for your financial health.

Explore ways to manage and reduce debt effectively.

Chapter **1**

Starting Your Financial Journey

We get it — money, that is. More importantly, we (Athena and Mykail) get how confusing and overwhelming finding out about money can be. With that in mind, we plan to give you all the tools you need to get your money started off right! Because no matter how confusing money may seem, there is always a way to figure it out.

Personal finances are so much more than spending money on all the fun and cool things that you like. Money is the resource that you can use to completely change your life. Luckily, you have not one but *two* money friends here giving you all the details on all things money.

Personal finance is a bit like mastering a complicated board game. The rules can be confusing at first, but once you get the hang of them, winning (aka reaching your goals) becomes a lot easier. Think of this chapter as your sneak peek at the game board: We'll touch on everything from budgeting to taxes, but we won't dive into the nitty-gritty just yet. By the end, you'll know exactly where to turn in this book for detailed guidance on each topic.

In this book, you'll explore why money matters at every stage of your life, especially from middle school to adulthood. But before you jump in, let's take a quick tour of what you can expect.

Mastering Your Personal Finances

Money might seem scary at first (numbers, bank accounts, taxes, oh my!), but getting a handle on your personal finances is a powerful way to take control of your life. This section explains why financial literacy matters, then guides you through the essentials of budgeting, saving, and spending.

Discovering why financial literacy matters for teens

They say, "money makes the world go 'round," and while that might be a slight exaggeration, having a solid handle on your finances definitely keeps your world from spinning out of control. When you start building healthy money habits now,

>> **You stress less:** Knowing where your cash is going (and why) can save you from late-night panic over bills.

>> **You dream bigger:** Want to save for a first car or an epic post-grad adventure? Budgeting early on makes that possible.

>> **You stay flexible:** Life changes, like going to college or starting a side hustle, feel more doable when you have a financial foundation.

REMEMBER

You don't have to master every topic right away; that's what this book is for. Take it one chapter at a time, and celebrate each win.

Exploring the basics of budgeting, saving, and spending

Think of budgeting as a roadmap for where your money goes. To build a budget, you must do the following:

1. **Track your income** from allowances, jobs, or side gigs.

2. **Plan your expenses** for essentials like food and optional fun stuff like movies.

3. **Set aside savings** for future goals or emergencies.

Saving means paying yourself first. Even setting aside a few dollars each time you earn money can grow your savings over time. Spending wisely means balancing what you want now with what your future self will need. It is crucial to practice good money habits *today* to create a foundation for lifelong financial wins.

Unlocking the Benefits of Good Financial Habits

Building strong money skills early unlocks a future filled with possibilities. Here's how good financial habits can make your life easier and more fulfilling.

Lowering financial stress through smart planning

Having a plan for your money turns chaos into clarity. By setting up a simple budget (Chapter 4 digs deeper), you know exactly where your cash is going, leaving less room for anxiety. Plus, planning helps you avoid last-minute scrambles, like struggling to pay for surprise expenses.

Improving your life with thoughtful money choices

When you make intentional spending decisions, it's easier to afford the things that truly matter, like a hobby, a trip, or an emergency fund for peace of mind. Good financial habits encourage you to say "yes" to meaningful opportunities instead of being tied down by unnecessary debt or spending. Chapters 2, 3, and 4 focus on building those good habits early.

Handling taxes and what they mean for you

Even if you're a teen, taxes can affect your paycheck or side hustle earnings. Taxes might seem boring, but they're unavoidable, so knowing the basics helps you keep more of the money you earn (turn to Chapter 22 for more tax tips). Don't be nervous about taxes; as working citizens, we have to pay them, too, and we also explain why they are required.

Saving for short- and long-term goals

Saving short-term can mean setting aside cash for things like a concert ticket or new sneakers. Long-term goals might include paying for college, starting a business, or even investing for retirement (yes, that's something teens can do!). Good habits now set you on a smooth path for later. We chat more about money for future you in Chapters 8 and 20.

Claiming your financial independence

Imagine being able to make life choices (like studying abroad or moving out) without money worries holding you back. Solid financial habits build a safety net, giving you the freedom to explore, take calculated risks, and follow your dreams. Chapters 11 and 19 focus on helping you decided what your financial independence will look like.

Confronting the Challenges of Managing Money

Nothing will come easy to anybody who is learning about money. There are so many mindset shifts and new terms you will discover to better manage your personal finances. Even with all this information, you can still make money mistakes. This is totally normal and 100 percent okay. Even as adults, we still make money mistakes. Your journey won't be perfect, and that doesn't make you a bad person.

Deciding your financial path

Financial literacy is for everyone because everyone needs to understand money. However, we all have different financial paths and goals. Your financial path is specifically for you. We all find out about and see money differently; finding what works best for you is half the battle. Throughout this book we encourage you with our advice and give you different options to tackle problems you may face.

Aiming for financial freedom

Ask yourself: Do I want to rely on others forever, or would I prefer making my own decisions with my own funds? If you're aiming for independence, a solid financial plan is your ticket to freedom. Financial freedom looks like have great credit (Chapter 5), building a solid budget (Chapter 4), destroying debt and bad habits (Chapter 6), making money (Chapters 14 and 15), paying bills (Chapter 18), and spending your money things that make you happy.

Launching your first budget or savings plan

Still on the fence? Starting small helps you see quick wins. Even a mini-budget, such as saving $5 a week, can be a game-changer. Turn to Chapter 3 to dip your toes in the water of money management or Chapter 4 for a full budget breakdown.

Mapping Out the Journey (aka This Book's Roadmap)

Here's a taste of what you'll find in each part of the book.

Part 1: Learning How to Build Your Financial Muscles. We start with the basics, like creating a financial workout plan and discovering the building blocks of budgeting. These chapters show you the value of flexing your money muscles early.

Parts 2 and 3: Money Matters for Middle Schoolers and Money Matters for High Schoolers. Whether you're just discovering how to manage lunch money or planning to find a part-time job, we've got you covered. These sections guide you through the financial challenges (and opportunities) you'll face before graduation day.

Part 4: Making Money Like an Adult. Ready to step into the working world? We'll show you how to read your paycheck, what to watch for in a job offer, and how to handle the real costs of working (such as transportation or uniforms).

Parts 5 and 6: Being an Adult the Dummies Way and Preparing for the Big Things. Now it's time to protect your money and handle those bigger life expenses, from paying monthly bills to buying your dream car. We'll also help you set long-term goals like investing and getting insurance.

Part 7: The Part of Tens. Looking for a quick reference or top tips on taxes, creating a win file (a brag-worthy record of your achievements), or other key concepts? This section's got you covered.

It might sound like a lot, but fear not! We'll tackle each subject in a fun, accessible way, giving you the confidence to take charge of your finances regardless of your age.

With a sense of what's coming, it's time to roll up your sleeves and dig into the details. Flip ahead to the chapters that pique your interest the most, or read each part in order for a complete guide to becoming a personal finance pro. Keep in mind, your money journey is yours to shape, and every bit of knowledge you pick up along the way will help you write your own success story.

Are you ready to claim your financial freedom? Let's do this!

Chapter **2**

Creating Your Financial Workout Plan

A financial workout plan is a bit like a fitness plan — but for your money. Just as you need to exercise regularly and set fitness goals to stay healthy, creating and sticking to a financial workout plan helps keep your finances in good shape. Starting early means you can build strong habits that will benefit you as your finances grow. By setting financial goals, learning to prioritize needs over wants, and managing how you spend, save, or invest, you'll gain control over your money and build a foundation for future success. Think of this as training for financial independence!

This chapter guides you in setting SMART (Specific, Measurable, Achievable, Relevant, Time frame) goals, which are essential to planning any financial journey. You also find out how to tell the difference between needs and wants — a skill that helps you focus on what really matters. Finally, you explore options for using your money wisely, whether it's for immediate spending, saving for the future, or investing to grow your wealth over time. Building a financial workout plan now gives you a head start on achieving the financial freedom you'll thank yourself for later.

Starting with Your Money Goals

Most people think that the first step to being financially successful is to create a budget. Those people would be wrong (very wrong). The first step to creating a strong financial plan is establishing strong goals. You are not creating a wish list only fairy godparents can grant. Goals need to be specific and action-able. The best goals are the ones that are clear and SMART. For every goal you have created, there needs to be an action plan to help you achieve the goal. Most people fail to have an action plan, and that's why they can't seem to reach their SMART goals. Starting with your goals gives you a clear path on what you need to focus on to win.

Everybody wants to be a winner, but few people have the action plan in place to actually make them a winner. If you aspire to have a big bank account, a nice house, and a cool car, then you need to take your goal planning very seriously. Even further, you need to have a simple action plan to make sure you win. On those days when you feel like your success isn't coming fast enough, you can review your action plan to see how far you have come. Goal setting is so important, and we can't stress it enough.

Establishing SMART goals

If you haven't realized by now, SMART goals aren't goals that make you feel like a brainiac. SMART has a secret, powerful meaning. We will spend time breaking down each one of these words and how they relate to your setting goals for your financial workout plan.

S stands for specific

A specific goal is one that clearly states what you want to achieve, so there's no confusion. Instead of a fuzzy goal like, "I want to do better in school," a specific goal would be, "I want to raise my math grade from a B to an A by the end of the semester." See the difference? The specific goal tells you exactly what you want to improve and how you want to do it and even gives a time frame (we talk more about the time frame in the section "T stands for time frame").

Having a specific goal is important because it helps you focus. When you know exactly what you're aiming for, it's easier to figure out the steps you need to take to get there. It also keeps you motivated because you can track your progress more easily.

REMEMBER

Without a specific goal, you might feel lost or unsure about how to move forward. So, making your goals specific helps you stay on track and makes success more likely!

Example:

> **Weak:** *"I am going to save some money."*
>
> **Strong:** *"I am going to save $3,000."*

M stands for measurable

A measurable goal is one where you can track your progress and know when you've achieved it. Instead of saying, "I want to exercise more," a measurable goal would be, "I want to work out for 30 minutes, 3 times a week." The key part is having something you can count or measure, like the amount of time or number of days.

When you can track your progress, it makes your goal feel more real and achievable. It also helps you stay accountable, because you know whether or not you're hitting your target.

REMEMBER

Without a measurable goal, it's hard to know if you're making progress. A measurable goal gives you a clear target and lets you celebrate small wins along the way, keeping you on track to reach your bigger goal.

Example:

Weak: *"I will see more money in my account."*

Strong: *"I will track my savings account every week."*

A stands for achievable

An achievable goal is one that is realistic and something you can actually accomplish with your current abilities. Instead of saying, "I want to become a pro basketball player by next year," an achievable goal would be, "I want to make the school basketball team this season." The goal is something you can work toward with practice, and it's possible to accomplish within a set time frame.

If your goal is too unrealistic or too big, you might get discouraged if it feels impossible to reach. Setting a goal that's challenging but possible means you can stay focused, put in the effort, and feel good about your progress. With a solid action plan, you can break your big goals into smaller, achievable steps.

REMEMBER

Achievable goals will never require you to be a completely different person to reach them. If a goal feels way too big, you can revise it to make it more manageable.

Example:

Weak: *"I will save some money every week."*

Strong: *"I will set up automatic savings to hit my goals."*

R stands for relevant

A relevant goal is one that matters to you and connects to what you really want in life. It should be something that helps you move closer to your bigger dreams or personal values. For example, if your goal is to get better grades, a relevant goal might be, "I want to spend an extra hour studying each day to improve my grades so I can get into a good college." That goal is relevant because it directly supports your future plans.

Relevant goals are important because they keep you focused on what truly matters to you. If your goal isn't something that fits with your bigger goals or interests, you're less likely to stay motivated or work hard to achieve it. It's easy to get distracted by things that seem important in the moment but don't really help you in the long run.

Setting relevant goals ensures that you're spending your time and energy on things that actually benefit you and your future. When your goals align with what's important to you, like your passions or long-term dreams, you're more likely to stick with them and feel excited when you reach them. It helps keep you on the right path toward what you really want.

REMEMBER

If your goal isn't relevant, you might end up working hard on something that doesn't benefit your bigger dreams or priorities. Relevant goals help you avoid distractions and focus on what will make the biggest impact on your future.

Example:

> **Weak:** *"I need more money in the bank."*

> **Strong:** *"I have control over my money, and this goal will help me become a financially savvy person."*

T stands for time frame

A time-framed goal is one that has a deadline or a specific date by which you want to achieve it. Instead of saying, "I want to save money," a time-framed goal would be, "I want to save $200 by the end of the month." Having a clear time frame gives you a sense of urgency and helps you stay focused.

Time-framed goals are important because they push you to take action and prevent you from putting things off. When you know exactly when you want to accomplish something, you can plan better and stay on track. For example, if you want to save $200 in a month, you might figure out how much you need to save each week to make it happen.

Without a time frame, goals can feel endless, and it's easy to get distracted or lose motivation because there's no clear finish line. A deadline gives you something to aim for and helps to ensure that you're actively working toward your goal. Setting a time-framed goal helps you stay accountable.

TIP

The time frame you set for your goal should be realistic; don't make yourself feel rushed to accomplish big goals.

Example:

Weak: *"I want to have more money soon."*

Strong: *"In 12 months, I will save $3,000 for college in the fall."*

Figuring out your reason why

Before you can call your goals final, you need to create your why. You know that these goals are important to you, but think of why they are important. Your reason why is what will make your goals more important for you to achieve. For example, maybe you want to become a dentist because you used to be scared of the dentist and you want to make sure other kids are smiling bright and happy in the dentist chair. Your why is your driving force pushing you to achieve your goals. Think about the things you love and your own values. Every goal should be related to what you want out of life.

Knowing You Don't Need It, You Want It

Ask yourself, "Do I really need this?" This is a question you will have to reflect on very often. The answer will vary each time. But the older you get, the more your priorities will change and develop. Right now, your wants might outweigh your needs, but it is important to be financially responsible even when it's easier to spend like there's no tomorrow.

There are some things that you need but not at their current price. Think about expenses like food: you definitely need food to fuel you, but maybe it's better to buy a cheaper meal or decide to cook at home instead of ordering food for delivery. The next time you are ready to spend your money, take a moment and ask yourself, "Do I really need this or do I just want it?"

Reviewing your priorities

Being financially responsible means making sure you're spending money on what you *need* before spending it on what you *want*. Needs are things that are essential for your everyday life, like food, rent, transportation, and bills. Wants are things that are nice to have but not necessary, like new clothes, the latest video game, or going out to eat all the time.

When you don't prioritize your needs first, you might end up running out of money for important things, which can cause stress or even bigger problems. For example, if you spend too much on entertainment but don't have enough for your cell phone bill, you could end up without a way to communicate. By reviewing your priorities, you make sure your essentials are covered.

This doesn't mean you can't have fun or enjoy your money. It just means making smart choices, like saving up for things you want after taking care of your needs. This helps you stay in control of your money, avoid unnecessary debt, and build good habits that will set you up for long-term success.

To help decide if something is a priority, you can follow these actions and reflections to figure out if it's something you really need or just want.

Ask yourself: "Is it essential?"

Action: Before buying something, ask yourself, "Do I need this to survive or to take care of my responsibilities?" Essentials like food, rent, transportation, and bills are priorities.

Reflection: If it's not going to affect your basic needs, it might not be a priority right now.

Check your budget first

Action: Review your budget to make sure all your important expenses are covered. If there's money left after paying for needs, you can decide how much to spend on wants.

Reflection: If you don't have a budget, create one to track where your money is going and how much you have left for non-essential items.

Think long-term

Action: Ask yourself, "Will this purchase help me in the long run?" For example, buying a laptop for school might be a good investment, while buying the latest gadget that you don't need might not be.

Reflection: If it doesn't improve your life or help with your future goals, it's probably not a priority.

Delay the purchase

Action: Wait a few days before buying something you want. This gives you time to think if it's truly important or just a short-term desire.

Reflection: If you forget about it after a few days, it probably wasn't a priority. If it's still on your mind, think about how it fits into your needs.

Consider alternatives

Action: Look for cheaper or free alternatives to the thing you want to buy. Maybe there's a way to borrow, rent, or find a discount.

Reflection: Finding alternatives helps you meet your wants without blowing your budget, allowing you to prioritize your needs.

Understanding your current habits

Habits are actions you do regularly, often without thinking about them. Some habits are good, like saving part of your paycheck, while others might not be so great, like spending money on fast food every day. Your habits, especially when it comes to spending money, play a big role in how well you manage your finances.

To become a better budgeter, the first step is to understand your current habits. Start by tracking what you're doing with your money right now. You can do the following:

>> Write down everything you buy for a week or two, no matter how small it is.

>> Use a budgeting app to automatically track your spending.

>> Review your bank and credit card statements to see where your money has been going.

This will help you get a clear picture of your spending habits. Are you spending too much on snacks? Are you saving regularly, or just when you remember? Tracking these habits gives you insight into where your money is really going.

Once you've tracked your habits, it's time to create a plan to improve them. Here's how.

1. **Identify good and bad habits:** Look at your spending. Are some habits helping you, like saving a certain amount every month? Or are some habits holding you back, like over-spending on clothes or takeout?

2. **Set specific goals:** Based on what you've learned, set clear goals. For example, if you spend too much on eating out, set a goal like, "I'll limit myself to eating out twice a week." Make sure these goals are specific and realistic.

3. **Create a budget:** Now that you know your habits, you can create a budget that works for you. List your necessary expenses (rent, groceries, transportation) first. Then, decide how much you want to spend on extras and how much you'll save each month.

4. **Develop new habits:** Replace bad habits with better ones. For instance, if you notice that you make impulse purchases online, you could create a rule to wait 24 hours before making any purchase. If you aren't saving enough, set up an automatic transfer to your savings account every time you get paid.

5. **Monitor and adjust:** Keep tracking your habits and budget regularly. If you slip up, don't stress, just get back on track. Adjust your budget if needed and continue improving your financial habits over time.

By reviewing your current habits and making small, smart changes, you'll become a much better budgeter and gain more control over your money.

Seeing the opportunity costs

Imagine you have $20, and you're deciding between going to the movies with your friends or buying a new shirt. If you choose the movies, the opportunity cost is the shirt you didn't get. If you choose the shirt, the opportunity cost is the fun time at the movies. It's about what you *could* have done with your money, time, or energy, but chose not to.

Opportunity cost is the value of what you give up when you make a choice. Every time you spend money or time on something, you're giving up the chance to spend it on something else. If you buy lunch every day, you might be missing the chance to save up for a new phone or a concert ticket.

TIP

Instead of thinking only about what you're getting, you should also think about what you're giving up. This way, you can decide if what you're choosing is really worth it, and if it helps you reach your bigger goals.

Building habits for success

Here are three keys to building habits for success, explained in a way that's simple and easy to apply.

Start small

One of the biggest keys to building successful habits is starting with something small and manageable. Trying to change everything at once can feel overwhelming, and it's easy to give up. Instead, focus on small actions that you can stick with. If you want to start saving money, don't try to save $100 a week right away. Start with $10 a week, and once that feels easy, increase the amount. Small habits add up over time and become easier to maintain.

Be consistent

Consistency is the foundation of any successful habit. It's not about doing something perfectly one day and then forgetting about it; it's about doing it regularly, even if it's in small doses. For example, if you want to get better at managing your money, commit to reviewing your budget every week. When you do something consistently, it becomes automatic, and before you know it, it turns into a habit. The key is to stay committed, even on days when you don't feel like it.

Track your progress

Tracking your progress helps you to stay motivated and see how far you've come. Whether it's checking off days on a calendar or using an app to monitor your goals, having a visual reminder keeps you focused. When you're working on building a habit of saving money, track how much you save each week. Seeing that number grow can motivate you to keep going. Tracking also helps you adjust your habits if you're not seeing the progress you want.

Deciding to Spend, Save, or Invest

For every dollar that you get, you have three options: spend it, save it, or invest it. The decision is totally up to you. We can't tell you which option is best, but we can give you the tools to help you make the tough decisions a tad easier. Since personal finance is personal and your actions have to align with your goals, let's help you understand the impacts of each action.

Imagine you just won the lottery. How would you spend, save, and invest your winnings? It is best to create guidelines for you to follow for every payday (or if you actually do win the lotto). You can keep it simple and start with this money breakdown: spend 50 percent, save 30 percent, invest 20 percent. To see this in action, if you got a paycheck worth $1,000, you would have $500 to spend, $300 transferred to your savings account, and $200 put into your investing account. These percentages can be adjusted based on your goals, values, and lifestyle.

Spending your money

We don't have to teach you how to spend your money. Spending money is easy for everybody, and thanks to the help of technology, you don't even have to leave the house to spend your money anymore. Since you know how to spend, this section will be dedicated to teaching you how to be a more informed and savvier spender.

Using debit cards

When you open a new checking account, you are provided with a debit card. When you use a debit card, it's important to remember a few things to manage your money responsibly. First, your debit card is connected directly to your checking account, so every time you swipe, the money comes out of your account right away. You have to make sure you have enough in there to cover what you're buying, or you could run into trouble with overdraft fees or even have your card declined. That's why it's super important to keep track of your spending; don't just swipe without thinking! You can easily check your account balance through your bank's app to stay on top of how much you have left.

Another thing to know is that debit cards don't help you build credit like a credit card would. While credit cards can help you build a credit history (which you'll need for bigger things later, like buying a car or renting an apartment), debit cards are different.

WARNING

Security is key. Keep your debit card and your PIN safe, and if anything looks weird on your account, like a charge you didn't make, let your bank know right away.

Using credit cards

Using a credit card can be a great tool for building your financial future, but there are some important things to keep in mind to make sure you use it wisely. First off, remember that when you swipe your credit card, you're borrowing money that you'll need to pay back later, usually with interest. If you don't pay off your balance in full each month, those interest charges can add up quickly, making things much more expensive than you planned. It's also important to keep track of your spending; just because you have a credit limit doesn't mean you should spend that much. Make a budget to help you manage how much you can afford to pay back.

Now, if you're wondering how to get a credit card, you typically need to be at least 18 years old, and some companies offer cards specifically designed for teens and young adults. You can start by checking with your bank to see if they offer a student credit card, which often has lower limits and fewer fees. Alternatively, you can ask a parent to add you as an authorized user on their credit card. This way, you can build your credit history while they're responsible for the account.

You must be responsible with your credit card to build a good credit score. Make sure to pay your bill on time, because late payments can hurt your credit score. And don't forget about security! Keep your credit card information safe, and if you notice any suspicious charges, report them to your card issuer immediately.

Credit cards vs debit cards

Just because they both are plastic does not mean the debit card and credit card are the same. These are two very different cards and are used for different reasons. Table 2-1 highlights a few differences between the two to help you understand how unalike they truly are.

TABLE 2-1   **Credit Cards vs Debit Cards**

Feature	Credit Cards	Debit Cards
Account balance	Increases with use	Decreases with use
Spending limit	Yes	No
Requires a checking account	No	Yes
Payment verification	Sign for purchases	Enter PIN code for purchases
Credit check required	Yes	No

Using buy now, pay later services

Services like Afterpay and Klarna are the new ways to spend your money. Buy Now, Pay Later (BNPL) can be really helpful or really hurtful, depending on how you use it. To get an account with a BNPL service, you usually need to sign up online or through an app. You provide some basic information, like your name, email, and sometimes your bank details, to help them verify your identity and ability to pay. We know it can be very tempting to split your $100 clothing haul into four easy payments of $25, but there is some information you need to know about BNPL.

First, while BNPL can make it easier to afford items, it's still a form of borrowing, and if you miss a payment, you might face late fees or even damage your credit score. You need to know how much you'll need to pay and when those payments are due.

Also, you need to keep track of what you buy using BNPL. It's easy to lose sight of how much you owe if you're not careful, which can lead to overspending and feeling overwhelmed. Before you use these services, make sure you have a budget in place, and only use BNPL for things you truly need or can afford to pay off quickly. Remember, just because you can buy something now doesn't mean you should.

Saving your money

Saving your money is important. There are so many great and exciting reasons to save your money. Maybe you're saving for a new video game or for tickets to see your favorite artist in concert. You can also start saving for more important and serious things like your college tuition or a house in the future.

Making your savings automatic will help you grow your money much faster. When a few dollars from your paycheck automatically transfer into your savings account, you don't have to think about saving. This is what we call "out of sight, out of mind." You can spend your money more freely when you know you paid your savings account first.

The math behind how much money to save is the same whether you are saving for emergencies, the short term, or the long term. The simple equation is as follows: total monthly savings = total savings goal / goal time frame. For example, if your goal was to save $2,500 in the next 12 months, your total monthly savings would be $208.33.

Building your short-term savings

Short-term savings are all about setting aside money for goals you want to achieve soon, usually within the next year or so. Think of it as your "spending money" for upcoming plans or fun experiences! Whether it's saving up for a new phone, a concert ticket, or even a quick getaway, having a short-term savings plan helps you reach those goals without going into debt.

So, how do you start? First, think about what you want to save for and how much it costs. Let's say you want to go to that awesome concert in three months, and tickets are $100. If you start saving now, you could set a goal to save about $33 each month. That way, by the time the concert rolls around, you'll have enough to cover the ticket!

The best part about short-term savings is that they give you the chance to enjoy things you really want without feeling guilty. Plus, achieving those goals can be super motivating and help you build good saving habits for the future.

Building your long-term savings

Long-term savings are all about putting money aside for goals that you want to achieve several years down the line: Think of things like college, a car, or even buying your first home. Unlike short-term savings, which are for things you want to buy soon (like a new video game or concert tickets), long-term savings are about dreaming big and planning for the future. So, if you're thinking of something that's going to take a few years to save for, that's where long-term savings come into play.

Now, let's talk about how long-term savings differ from emergency funds. An emergency fund is your financial safety net; it's money you set aside to cover unexpected expenses, like a car repair or a medical bill. It's all about being prepared for surprises and not having to stress about where the money will come from. Emergency funds are typically easier to access, while long-term savings are often for those bigger goals and might stay untouched for a while.

Investing your money

Investing might feel scary, but it's important to find out how to grow your money, so you will have to get over the fear of investing. When we talk about investing, it is not solely reserved for the stock market. There are so many ways to invest your money and make it work for you. We will talk more about investing in Chapter 20, but you can invest in businesses, stocks, bonds, real estate, and so much more. The important thing you must know, no matter how you like to invest, is that you must always strive to be an informed investor. Educating yourself and taking calculated risks will help you to create strong returns on your investment.

Benefits of investing early

Investing early is one of the smartest financial decisions you can make. Think of your dollars as little seedlings that will turn into a big, strong tree in the future. The sooner you plant it, the bigger and stronger it will grow. When you invest, your money has the chance to earn more money through something called *compound interest*. That's when the money you invest earns returns, and then those returns start earning returns, too.

So why should you start investing now? Time is on your side. Starting early gives your money more time to grow, and you don't need a lot to begin. Even investing small amounts can make a big difference over the years. For example, if you invest $100 and it grows 7 percent each year, in 10 years, it could almost double. Imagine if you invest even more regularly — those returns can seriously add up.

There are apps and platforms like Ellevest, Fidelity, or Acorns that make investing simple, even with small amounts. You can start with just a few dollars and buy fractional shares of big companies like Apple or Google. You can also choose low-cost options like index funds or ETFs, which let you invest in a variety of companies all at once, reducing your risk.

The key to investing is to think long-term and stay patient. You won't see huge gains overnight, but if you keep your money invested and let it grow, your future self will thank you. Plus, by finding out about investing early, you'll get comfortable making smart financial decisions that will set you up for success in the future.

Time value of money

The time value of money is a pretty cool concept that shows why saving and investing early can pay off big in the long run. Basically, it means that a dollar you have today is worth more than a dollar you'll get in the future. Why? Because that dollar today can earn interest or grow through investments.

Chapter 3

The Money Warm-up

N ow that you've created your financial workout plan, or have at least started to, it's time to be basic (about money skills). If you haven't started a financial workout plan, see Chapter 2. We know, we know. No one wants to be basic, but when it comes to your money, you need key basic skills that will help you manage your money correctly. Managing your money is a good way to achieve those financial goals you want, such as maybe a new car or bike. It's also a great way to help you get ready for the real world since it's easy to experience a hurdle right after starting.

Athena experienced a hurdle to her money journey when opening her first checking account at age 18. She mistook her debit card (the card assigned to her checking account for spending) as a credit card and consistently thought that going negative in her account was borrowing money. Going negative in your checking account is not the same as borrowing money on a credit card, and after a few months of Athena using her checking account inappropriately, the bank decided it would be best to close her account and try again later.

Understanding money skills is key to starting your money journey off on the right foot, and the earlier you start, the more that time is on your side. As you find out in Chapter 20, where we talk about investing, you want time to help your money make money. First things first, though: Let's find out about banking and how you can use your checking account correctly.

Finding a Trusted Adult

Many banks require you to be at least 18 to open your own checking account; however, some banks allow you to be a co-owner of one with the help of a trusted adult. Since finding out about checking accounts is so crucial to starting your money journey, we know you might not want to wait that long. In this case, we suggest finding a trusted adult to help you open your first checking or savings account (we talk about these account types in the section, "Exploring the differences between checking and savings accounts," later in this chapter).

A trusted adult is someone you feel comfortable with, can share important things with, and can ask for advice. For example, a trusted adult can be your parent or guardian, and also another relative such as your grandma, grandpa, aunt, uncle, cousin, or even an older sibling. A trusted adult can also be a teacher, a coach, a counselor, a neighbor, a mentor, or a clergy member. Having a trusted adult is important for any area of your life and can also be important when it comes to helping you manage your money.

WARNING It's important to know that a trusted adult should never be inappropriate in any way or make you feel uncomfortable, or bully you into doing things you don't want to do. If this is happening, let someone know who can help you get out of this situation.

Thinking about money attitudes

If you need to find a trusted adult who can help you open a checking account, you'll want to think about their money attitudes. What's a money attitude?

A money attitude is how you view and how you act about, and toward, money. For example, someone who finds it important to save might have a good attitude toward money. In the same way, someone who spends all their money without contributing to their financial goals might have a bad attitude toward money. When it comes to money, it's important to have a balance of both spending and saving. Money should be not only enjoyed, but used as a way to help you become a responsible adult.

If you're unsure of your trusted adult's money attitude, you can try asking them the following questions to see how they respond:

>> How old were you when you got your first checking account?

>> Do you think it's important to save money or more important to spend?

>> When I get my first paycheck, how do you think I should spend it?

>> Did you work when you were my age?

>> Do you have a budget?

>> I want to save up for a car. How do you think I could do that?

>> Do you think I'll need student loans if I go to college?

>> Are you saving up for a big financial goal?

>> What did you wish you did differently about money when you were my age?

>> Is investing important?

It's important to know that there are many ways a trusted adult can manage their own money. We all know adults who prefer to save all of their paycheck and adults who prefer to spend carelessly. One of us has even had a parent ask to borrow money because they weren't very responsible with paying their bills first.

It's hard to know what adults do with their money, but if you see an adult complaining about not having enough, or saying they maxed out their credit cards, they might not have a money attitude you want to be around. For example, are you going to pick Aunt Maggie who buys too much stuff at the dollar store, or will you choose Uncle Ben who saves up all year so that he can take a nice summer vacation?

REMEMBER

Some adults find it hard to talk about money. If your trusted adult doesn't want to answer any questions, or gets upset or mad when discussing money, do not take it personally. It just means that they aren't the trusted adult you want to talk to about money, and you should maybe think about someone else.

Understanding bank requirements

All banks have requirements when it comes to opening a checking account. Some are national, while others may be specific to the state you're living in or the company you (or your trusted adult) work for. It is important to know the rules and requirements for the bank you are opening an account with.

These requirements also apply to who can open a checking account with you if you are under 18 years old. Sometimes a bank will allow you to open an account with a trusted adult who can be anyone, as mentioned previously; other times, it must be a parent or guardian you live with or who is legally responsible for you. Some banks may also let you open a checking account on your own starting at age 16!

A bank will also require identification to make sure it's really you and your trusted adult opening the new checking account. Identification is anything that can help prove who you are.

There are different types of identification that both you and your trusted adult may need to share with the bank to help keep you safe:

For teens

>> **School ID:** If your school provides student identification cards, this may be accepted.

>> **Birth certificate:** Helps verify your identity and age.

- **»** **Social Security card (U.S.) or national insurance number:** Some banks require this for tax purposes.

- **»** **Passport (if you have one):** A government-issued ID that proves your identity.

For your trusted adult (parent/guardian)

- **»** **Driver's license or state/national ID card:** A government-issued photo ID is typically required.

- **»** **Passport:** Another option for proving identity.

Knowing a trusted adult is available when you need them

The last thing to think about when choosing a trusted adult to help you with your finances is how often you'll have access to them. Depending on which bank you go with, and how old you are, you may need your trusted adult to go to the bank with you to make any deposits or withdrawals. Last but not least, your trusted adult should also be able to help answer any questions you might have when it comes to your finances. And if they don't know the answer, that's okay! They just need to point you in the right direction.

Opening Your First Checking Account

A checking account is a key money basic and a must-have once you reach adulthood. As you get older, you will realize (or maybe you do now!) that almost everything money related involves some of the accounts we mention in this chapter. That's why it's so important to start off on the right foot when it comes to banking. Banking involves managing the money in your checking or savings account.

Exploring the differences between checking and savings accounts

It's important to know the difference between a checking and savings account. A checking account is for everyday money management. Everyday money management involves things you do frequently, such as paying a bill or buying groceries. Everyday money management can also involve paying for transportation like gas money or going out to eat with your friends.

A savings account, on the other hand, is for (you guessed it!) saving toward your financial goals, like a piggy bank. A savings account is also a great place to put money aside for future emergencies or expenses that may be coming up but aren't here yet, such as tires for a car. Another cool feature of a savings account is that it pays you interest. Remember from earlier in the chapter that since time is on your side, your money can make more money for you. A savings account is one simple way your money does just that.

You can access both checking and savings accounts online with a computer, and most now come with their own apps for your phone! We love the fact that you can review your checking account balance anytime you want to go shopping so that you can make sure you are staying under budget when it comes to your fun money! (For more on budgeting, check out Chapter 4.) You can also sign up to have your paycheck deposited automatically so that you have money in your checking account right away instead of having to deposit a paycheck.

TIP

You can find out if your new bank account has an app by checking their website or asking someone who works at the bank when you set up your new account.

REMEMBER

Some banks require a minimum deposit in your checking or savings account to avoid a monthly fee. Double-check to make sure that you keep a minimum amount in your account at all times, or instead, you can find a different bank that doesn't require a minimum balance.

Unlocking the features
of a checking account

A checking account is primarily used for everyday money management, which includes spending your money. Since a checking account is used to spend money, there are usually a few different ways you can access it as well as making withdrawals. Checking accounts come with a debit card that you can use where credit cards are accepted, and you can also use it at an ATM to get cash out. You can also make payments with a checking account by using the identification numbers assigned by your bank, transferring money online to someone else's bank, or using a check.

REMEMBER

Money-transferring apps like Venmo, Cash App, and PayPal are not the same as a checking or savings account. In fact, it's a good idea to not keep a lot of cash in those types of apps. These apps are not regulated by the Federal Deposit Insurance Corporation (FDIC). The FDIC is an organization that helps protect your money in a checking or savings account.

Your bank uses identification numbers called account numbers and routing numbers. Your account number is unique to you and stores all of your information, which you can access at any time. Everyone has their own account number that belongs to them and only them. This is how banks can keep all of your money separate and safe from other bank members, along with your own personal information.

A routing number is kind of like a bank's own account number. Out of all of the banks in the world, each one has their own individual number to help keep them separate. For example, Wells Fargo and Capital One are both banks, but they have different routing numbers. This is why you need both a routing number and an account number to use your checking account when paying a bill or setting up a money transfer. The routing number lets someone know which bank you have your checking account at, and the account number lets people find your actual personal information.

Once you turn 18 (or 21 depending on your state), you will no longer be required to have a trusted adult to help you with your checking account. Ask your bank how to remove your trusted adult as an account owner. We think that it's important to have your own checking account in your own name since it can help you practice being responsible.

Don't bounce checks. When you spend money you don't have, and your checking account goes into the negative, this is commonly known as *bouncing a check*. A bank will charge what is called an *overdraft fee*, which means that not only do you have to pay the money you spent, but you also have to pay the bank for causing your account to go into the negative. This is what happened to Athena and why she couldn't get a regular checking account until she was 21!

Savings account features

A savings account is designed to help you save your money instead of spending it. Since it's designed for savings, its set up a bit different from your checking account. One of the biggest differences between these two types of accounts is how often you can make withdrawals.

Most savings accounts will limit you to how many times you can withdraw your money (usually no more than five to six times) in one month. Savings accounts also come with an ATM (automated teller machine) card to use instead of a debit card. An ATM card does not have a chip in it that will allow you to make purchases at a store; instead, it can only be used at an actual ATM.

Another major difference between a checking and savings account is interest. Interest is what a bank will pay you to save your money with them instead of somewhere else. The more money you save, the more interest you can collect from the bank, which also encourages you to save more.

Some bank accounts may require you to have both a checking and savings account with them. Other banks will let you transfer money from other checking accounts at different banks. Either way, it's important to know this so that you can make sure your accounts are at the best place that makes sense for you!

Knowing Your Options at Financial Institutions

Just like there are different types of accounts to manage your money, there are also other places to manage your money than just banks. The two most common financial institutions that people use when it comes to managing their money are a bank or a credit union. There are a few key differences between them.

Storing your money in a bank the traditional way

Banks are for-profit financial institutions that are privately owned by people called *shareholders*. Since banks are for-profit, their main goal is to make money for their shareholders. This is done through a variety of different services and financial products that you will find out about throughout this book. Almost anyone can open a checking account at a bank, and you often do not need to live near the bank to become a customer. There are usually two different types of banks you can choose from.

Using brick-and-mortar banks

When a bank has a physical building you can visit in person, it's called a *brick-and-mortar bank*. Brick and mortar is used to describe an in-person bank, even if it's not made out of these materials. With an in-person bank, you can go inside and speak with employees to help you with a question or issue about your checking or savings account instead of relying on online banking. You can also access money at your bank by walking up to the tellers, using an ATM, or going through a drive-through like you do for fast food. Some banks also allow you to keep a safe deposit box there to store your valuables.

TIP

If you're unsure which bank is closest to you, open the internet browser on your phone or computer and type **bank** + your zip code. This should give you a list of what banks are closest to you. You can do the same thing to find your local credit unions!

Banking on your phone

Along with in-person banking, you can also bank online! While online banks are still owned by shareholders, you may get better deals with an online bank since they have no brick-and-mortar locations for which they have to pay. Online banks save money when they operate fully online and can offer the same customer support over the phone as well as online. Some people feel comfortable keeping their money only online, while other people feel comfortable knowing there is a building they can go to anytime to access their money when they need it.

TIP

You can link your debit card to Apple Pay and Google Wallet so that you don't need to keep your debit card on you. This means you're less likely to lose it! Check out `https://www.apple.com/apple-pay/` and `https://wallet.google/` to find out more.

Staying local with a credit union

Credit unions are another type of financial institution that are similar to banks, with a few key differences. Credit unions are considered non-profit financial institutions. Instead of being owned by shareholders, they are owned by the people who use the credit union as a customer, also known as a member.

If you are a member, a credit union usually requires you to live in a designated area, such as a city or state. For example, a credit union in Texas may require you to live in Texas if you want to open a checking account with them. Just like a regular bank, credit unions offer in-person service at brick-and-mortar locations as well as online checking.

Credit unions may also offer better interest rates for financial products and savings accounts for their members. Since credit union members are locally based, with a smaller customer base, they might also have more flexibility when it comes to their members' needs. This means that if you have extra questions or concerns, they can take more time to work with you, unlike a bank, which most likely has customers waiting in line.

TIP

Join a community bank. Community banks operate like regular banks in some ways, except they are traditionally smaller and put part of the profits back into the community by investing in local projects and businesses. Since they are smaller, they can feel friendlier than a traditional bank and can help you have a more personalized experience, like a credit union but with bank features.

Looking at other banking alternatives

There are a few other banking alternatives that can help you make money faster but don't offer the same type of account features. We feel it's still important to cover these alternatives so you know about all the options that are available to you as a young consumer.

Using high-yield savings accounts

A high-yield savings account (HYSA) is a type of savings account that earns more interest than a regular savings account. More interest means that your money will be able to not only make money faster, but will also be able to make more of it. These types of accounts are offered by online-only banks and credit unions. Because these financial institutions usually have less administration costs, they can give you a higher interest rate.

High-yield savings accounts are usually connected to your checking account so that you can transfer the money to and from your account pretty easily. If your high-yield savings account isn't at the same financial institution as your checking account, the transfers may take a few days to be available instead of instantly.

We love high-yield savings accounts to help our money grow while still being able to access our money quickly in case something happens. Mykail just bought a new house and Athena has an older pet: These are both instances where they may need to access their cash quickly! It's also fun to watch your money grow and work for you even if it's little by little.

REMEMBER

Your money needs time to grow. Although being patient can be hard, this is a great time to practice for things you'll need to deal with as you get older, or even now!

Some banks, like Capital One, allow you to open multiple savings accounts. For example, Athena does this and can easily separate her money into different savings buckets for emergencies, for important purchases, and for her business expenses.

Thoughts on brokerages

Despite having *broke* in its name, a brokerage account is the exact opposite. In fact, a brokerage account is one of the things that can help you get rich, especially when you're younger. That's because you have the power of compound interest on your side.

You use a brokerage account to buy investments like stocks, ETFs, and mutual funds held at a financial institution known as a brokerage firm. We'll be diving deeper into investing in Chapter 20, but for now, we'll keep it pretty basic. You can buy the investments yourself or you can ask someone at the brokerage firm to help you pick the right ones for you and your financial goals.

While you can get money in and out of your account, it's not like a checking or savings account where you can have immediate access to your funds. Brokerage accounts are meant to not be touched until later on, preferably after your money has had enough time to make you money. Even though these aren't the types of account you'll be using every day for managing your money, we still feel it's important for you to know about so that you can make informed choices with your money.

REMEMBER

A brokerage account is not the same thing as a checking account!

You'll hear this throughout the book, but personal finance is personal, which means that what may make sense for you might not make sense for your friend or coworker, and that's okay. At the end of the day, this is your money journey and it's up to you to decide what that looks like.

Chapter **4**

Budgeting Basics

O ne of the most important parts of building your financial workout muscles is finding out how to keep track of your money. Along with that, you need to be able to tell your money where to go so that you can hit all the financial goals you dream about and more. That's what a budget does.

A budget is a plan that tells you where to spend (and save!) your money. Not only can a budget help you save for your financial goals, but it can also help you save for emergencies and allow you to spend money on things that you want and are fun.

For example, our budgets let us eat out every month. Mykail's budget helps her travel to cool places like Thailand, while Athena's budget allowed her to have a llama at her wedding (yes, wedding llamas are a thing!). Our budgets also help us take care of our financial responsibilities, such as owning a house and putting money away to help pay our bills when we are sick and can't work.

This chapter will help you understand how to set up a budget and keep to it, as well as the importance of budgeting. Doing this now is a gift that you are giving yourself, and even if you don't have any money coming in right away, knowing what to do when you do get it will help you get that much farther!

Budgeting: The Money Comes in, Then the Money Goes out

A budget is you telling your money where to go. It's covering the important stuff like your bills and letting you spend on fun stuff, like the newest phone, and hanging out with your friends. A budget is one of the most important money tools there is. Two main factors of your budget are your income and your expenses. Let's get started with those.

Defining income

Income is money that you have coming in. It's also the money that you use to pay for your expenses, saving goals, and that cool coffee place you want to check out with your friends. You can earn three main types of income: active, passive, and portfolio. All income is good income, and the more income you have, the more you can create a really cool life that you like.

Active

Active income is any income that you get by providing a good or service (working). For example, working a job on the weekends at a grocery store or restaurant is considered active income. Active income is also money you earn from doing chores around the house, services around the neighborhood, and other types of fun side-hustles, like babysitting or selling stuff you find for more than what you paid.

Passive

Passive income is money you can make without having to work. For example, benefits someone can get from the government are usually considered passive income. You can also get passive income from work you do once and then receive profits from. For example, many authors and musicians create a book or song and then collect royalties when someone new reads their book or listens to their song!

TIP

We also like to think of money we get for gifts as passive income. Using money you receive for your birthday, a holiday, or other type of gift is called a *windfall*. By using your windfalls smartly, you can hit those financial goals even sooner!

Portfolio

Portfolio income is anything you make from your investments. For example, money earned from interest in a high-yield savings account would be considered portfolio income. So would money from retirement accounts and money you earn from stocks and mutual funds in a brokerage account. You can also earn portfolio income when you sell your investments for more than you originally paid for them.

REMEMBER

The more income sources you have, the better. That means you not only have more money, but you can also be prepared in case something should happen, like a job opportunity not working out or an emergency car repair you weren't expecting.

Determining expenses

If income is money that comes in, then expenses are (you guessed it!) money that goes out — that you are spending. Not all expenses are the same, and here are a few of the different names you'll hear people commonly reference them by.

Fixed

Fixed expenses are something you pay frequently that is the same amount of money every time. Most fixed expenses are paid monthly (like bills), but some can be every few months, once a year, or even weekly, depending on what type of service or good you are paying for. For example, I (Athena) make my car payment every month, and it's the same amount every time. My car payment is considered a fixed expense. So is stuff like my rent, cell phone, and car insurance.

Here are some examples of fixed expenses:

>> Rent or mortgage (if you own a house)

>> Car payments

- » Insurance
- » Streaming services to watch TV and movies, or listen to music
- » Child care
- » Internet
- » Cell phone
- » Utilities
- » Doctor appointments
- » Medicine
- » College classes if you are in school
- » Student loan payments

Fixed expenses are sometimes the easiest expenses because you know it's always going to be the same as what you paid last time.

WARNING

Always try to make sure you are spending less on your expenses than the amount of income you bring in. If you spend more than your income allows, you can end up in debt with serious (and pricey!) consequences.

Variable

Variable expenses are ones that change every time you spend money. Groceries, gas, eating out, and buying makeup are all examples of variable spending. So is spending money on stuff like fun activities.

Here are some examples of variable expenses:

- » Groceries
- » Eating out with friends and family
- » Getting food delivered
- » Buying lunch at school
- » Paying for parking
- » Filling up your gas tank

- » Taking care of your car — think oil changes and new tires
- » Taking an Uber, Lyft, or Waymo
- » Purchasing items for your favorite hobby
- » Going to concerts
- » Playing video games
- » Buying makeup and beauty products
- » Getting supplies for taking care of your pet
- » Shopping for room décor

In some ways, variable expenses are easier to cut back than fixed expenses because you usually have more control over how often you buy something or leave the house.

Needs versus wants

An expense that is a need is something you must pay for as it is essential to your everyday life. Think about what you do every day and all of the things that get you there. Food is a need because you should eat breakfast, and so is a place to sleep. You need clothes and a ride to and from school and work. You also need supplies for school and then a place to come home to at night.

An expense that is a want is something you do not have to spend money on but want to anyways. For example, food is a need but eating out isn't. You need to wear clothes, but you don't need a hundred pairs of shoes. You need a ride to the store or school, but you don't need a brand new car to do so. Wants can also be fun things like going out with your friends or buying video games and expensive makeup.

TIP

It's okay to want nice things! That's the thing about budgets: You can save up and buy them later on while still paying your bills!

Fixed and variable expenses can both be needs and wants. Groceries are a variable expense, but they are also something you need. You need might need milk, eggs, and butter to make dinner, however you don't need most expensive brand of milk, eggs, and butter. By having a budget, you can meet your expenses in the middle.

Spending categories

A way to keep track of all of your expenses is by putting them into spending categories. A *spending category* is what you call a group of expenses gathered together and put into one area. For example, in a category called transportation, you would put your car payment, money you need for gas, and car maintenance all into one area in your budget. This can help you see how much something is really costing you.

A lot of the time, you may forget smaller expenses that can add up into one bigger expense. For example, getting oil changes and new tires or registering your car aren't things that happen every month, but you should still remember these expenses so that you can plan for them. This happened to Athena earlier this summer. On top of making her car payments, she had to fix her air conditioner, which was an additional $1,000 that she had to find room for in her budget.

Here are some common spending categories:

» Home

- Rent or mortgage
- Property taxes
- Insurance
- House mainte-nance (where you spend money to fix something around your house or yard)
- Furniture
- Cleaning supplies
- Home decorations
- Pet food
- Pet medication
- Items needed for pets, like cat litter and collars

» Utilities

- Internet
- Electricity
- Gas
- Trash (yes, you have to pay to get your trash picked up!)
- Cell phone

» Transportation

- Car payment
- Gas
- Insurance
- Oil changes and tires
- Ubers and Lyfts
- Bus and subway passes

» Food

- Groceries
- Eating out with friends and family
- Fast food
- Uber Eats and DoorDash

» Entertainment

- Streaming services like Disney+ and Spotify
- Movies
- Concerts
- Video games and consoles
- Going places with friends
- Gifts for friends and family
- Items you need for a hobby

» Professional

- Work clothes and shoes
- Certifications
- Education classes for school or work
- Supplies for school and work
- Parking

» Personal

- Doctor visits
- Medicine and vitamins
- Health insurance
- Watches
- Exercise equipment
- Hygiene products
- Haircuts, manicures, and pedicures
- Makeup
- Clothing
- Shoes
- Purses, wallets, and sunglasses

» Financial goals

- Vacation costs, such as airplane tickets and hotels
- Retirement
- Investing (for more information about investing for your future, see Chapter 20)
- Saving for a future car or house
- College
- Emergency fund
- Paying off debt (for more about paying off debt, go to Chapter 6)

Budgeting Styles

Now it's time to find out how to create a budget so that you don't spend more money than you bring in. By budgeting, you'll know how much money you have at the end of the day to put toward your financial goals and dreams! These are the four main types of budgeting styles.

For all of the following budgeting sections, we will be using an income of $1,000 to demonstrate how each style looks in action. We will also say you have the following expenses:

>> Bus pass ($100)

>> Cell phone ($75)

>> Groceries ($75)

>> Rent ($200)

This means that you have an income of $1,000 and expenses of $450. After your expenses have been paid, you have $550 left to be spent or saved in your budget.

Budgeting the zero-based way

A *zero-based budget* is one where you account for every dollar of income you bring in. That means if you earned $200, all $200 is going to have a job that you've already assigned. This budget is one way to find out the basics of money management and how powerful it is to make sure every dollar you have is working for you.

With these scenarios, you have $550 that needs to be assigned a job. The $550 can be for something that is both a want and a need; it just needs to be told what to do so that you don't spend it by accident if you were counting on it being available somewhere else.

For now, let's split the money and put some toward a financial goal and some toward fun. The point is to assign every dollar a job.

In addition to accounting for every dollar you bring in, the second goal of the zero-based budget is to make sure you only spend the money you put aside for it. So the $100 you put aside for eating out is the only money you should be spending for the entire month in that category. Once that money is spent, it's officially gone and you will have to wait until next time you make a new budget.

TIP

If you have money left over in a category, you can use that money in your next budget or put it toward a financial goal you're working on to help you achieve it faster. It's okay to not spend every dollar just because. It's all about making your money work for you!

Budgeting the 50/30/20 way

The 50/30/20 method is a bit more flexible than the zero-based budgeting method. For this method, you divide your money into three different sections and then assign your spending to those. The three sections are as follows:

» 50 percent needs

» 30 percent wants

» 20 percent financial goals

By dividing your money up into certain percentages, you are giving yourself space to not only be careful with your expenses, but also have room to work on your financial goals. If all of your expenses were a need, they would take up 45 percent of your income.

Using these percentages, you would still have another 5 percent ($50) that you could use for a need. You'd have 30 percent ($300) left for wants (anything you don't need but still want to buy) and 20 percent ($200) for your financial goals, like saving up for a graduation trip with your good friends.

TIP

It's okay if all of your needs are less than 50 percent. That means you have more money to put toward your wants, financial goals, or both! When Athena has extra money left over, she puts half of it into a high-yield savings account (HYSA) for one of her financial goals and she leaves the rest in her checking account for extra fun!

Using cash envelopes (cash stuffing)

A *cash-envelope budget* consists of using cash to pay for items by physically handing over money instead of using your debit card or transferring money. Each spending category you have gets its own envelope that you put cash into, and you then spend the money you put aside in that cash envelope for that expense. Here's how it works.

1. **Figure out your income, expenses, and spending categories for the month.**

2. **Write out a category on each envelope, along with the amount you want to spend on it.** Expenses you already have scheduled to come out of your checking account or pay online do not need to have an envelope. However, you need to remember them so that you don't end up in the negative by assigning money to spend that you won't have.

3. **After you know how much cash to withdraw, visit an ATM or bank to withdraw the exact amount.** ATMs are easier to access but only allow you to withdraw $20 and $50 bills. If you visit a brick-and-mortar bank, you can get direct cash but it might not be an option if you have an online only bank.

4. **Stuff your envelopes.** Place the exact cash amount you've assigned into its corresponding envelope.

5. **Spend your cash.** Like zero-based budgeting, you can have exact cash to do what you want. But it's up to you to only spend from that envelope. If I put aside $50 for eating out, then I only get to spend $50 for that month. It's up to me to make it last however long I need it to. Once it's spent, I need to make sure I am now making meals from the groceries I have at home.

This budgeting method might seem strict to some and freeing to others. Seeing money physically can help you save it since you are actually seeing the cash leaving your wallet! It also allows you to quickly know if you are overspending, unlike using a debit or credit card. For example, do you really need to ask yourself how much money you have left over if there is nothing in that envelope to spend?

Athena loves this budgeting method the most, as it has helped her cut back on her random spending the most. In college, Athena had an especially hard time knowing where her money went. By using cash and taking a set amount of money every week, Athena knew she had to make the money last, and it helped her to be more mindful with her spending habits.

Cash envelopes can also encourage you to save money. There is nothing like having money left over after your budget is up, especially seeing it in cash. You can roll this money over into another goal, or you can add it to a category you want to spend more in for the next budgeting cycle, like going out with friends.

Paying yourself first

The last method of budgeting we want to share is called the "pay yourself first" budget. This budget is often called the "anti-budget" because it doesn't involve putting money aside into a million categories or involve tracking where every single penny goes. Instead, this method forces you to make your financial goals your main priority by putting aside 10 percent of your income first and then being flexible with the remaining 90 percent. You can save more, which people usually do, but most start off with 10 percent.

If you started with $1,000 a month, you would be saving $100 (10 percent) first, and then you would cover your expenses with the remaining $900. A certain percentage doesn't need to cover your needs or wants, nor do you have a set limit of how much you can spend. This is why it doesn't feel like a budget to a lot of people who use this budgeting method.

One of the drawbacks of this method is that it can encourage wasteful spending just because you have the money put aside to spend. Another drawback could be how much you designate to hit your goals and how much even 10 percent of your income is. For example, 10 percent might feel more drastic for someone with a lower income than a higher one.

TIP

If you want to try this budgeting method and are scared of starting at 10 percent, consider starting at just 1 percent. Then, after a couple of months, you can bump it up to 2 percent and so on until you hit either the 10 percent marker or an amount you feel comfortable with. This is how we started saving for retirement, and then gradually increased the percentage over time.

Budgeting in Action

Budgeting can be overwhelming when you're first getting started, but here are some helpful tips and apps that can keep you on track.

>> **Don't be afraid to dream big.** There is a saying that if you shoot for the moon, you'll at least land upon the stars, and we couldn't agree more. Even if you don't hit a huge goal, you will still have achieved progress and that's something.

>> **Let people know.** The topic of budgeting trends on TikTok and Insta all the time. People think it's cool, and duh, it is.

>> **Be honest with your spending.** If you spend a lot at Starbucks or on Call of Duty, that's okay. It's about making room in your budget to spend on what you feel is important while taking care of your responsibilities, and only you get to decide that.

>> **Don't forget to shop around.** Target and Walmart aren't always cheaper. Try to check out at least three stores for an item you want to find at a cheaper price. The less you pay, the more you have to spend somewhere else.

>> **Have fun.** Keep trying until you find the method that works for you. If one works for a while and stops, switch it up. The important thing is to not give up. But above all remember to find the fun and joy in budgeting.

TIP

Don't forget to check to see if your bank has their own app. Most financial institutions do, and this is an easy way to keep track of not only your budget, but also your incoming and outgoing cash flow and all purchases you have made.

Budgeting Apps

A lot of apps require you to be 18 or older to use for your finances, but here are a few that you can use with help from your parents.

>> **Acorns early** (`https://www.acorns.com/kids-learn/`): This app lets your parents contribute to your savings goals while helping you see how investing works over time. Acorns Early also features fun money quizzes and videos, allowing you to explore different financial topics based on your interests.

>> **Goodbudget** (`https://goodbudget.com/`): This app mimics the cash envelope method by letting you use virtual envelopes to help see where your money goes. You can use this app to play around with what your spending categories would look like with different amounts of money.

>> **Greenlight** (`https://greenlight.com/`): This is a banking app that allows you and your parents to monitor your spending while you find out about money basics that we cover in this book. This app comes with your own debit card so that you can practice card transactions and get experience handling a checking account firsthand.

If you are 18 or over, check out these apps.

>> **Oportun** (`https://oportun.com/`): This app allows you to set up savings goals and then save for them by using the power of rounding up your purchases to the nearest dollar and then depositing the difference. So, if a purchase is $2.75, Oportun will round it up to $3.00 and then send that $0.25 to your savings account. Every little bit adds up, and this is a great way to start saving with smaller amounts.

>> **Qapital** (`https://www.qapital.com/`): This is an all-in-one app when it comes to managing your money. Not only does it help you budget, but it also helps you save and invest along the way. The app is colorful, offers easy-to-set goals, and allows you to follow along. For managing your money without a lot of fuss, this app is it.

>> **PocketGuard** (https://pocketguard.com/): If you are ready to jump all the way in to managing your finances with the best of them, this app will help you do just that. Not only does it help you budget, but it also helps you see your cash flow and net worth, pay your bills, and keep track of any future debt you might have.

Chapter 5

Everybody Needs a Little Credit

B uilding a solid credit profile is a crucial step toward financial independence and stability. Whether you're preparing for a major purchase like a car or trying to secure your first apartment, understanding how credit works is essential.

A strong credit score can open doors to better rates and opportunities, while a weak one can create obstacles. In this chapter, we will break down the basics of personal credit, explaining the components that make up your FICO score and how they impact your financial life.

Mastering Personal Credit 101

Credit is kind of like the scary monster in your closet. You have heard about the monster from everyone else, so you're scared it might ruin your life like it did theirs. However, when you actually find out about credit, you realize it's not a scary monster in the closet, but instead it's your favorite fuzzy sweater that protects you when it gets cold outside.

While you don't wear your big fuzzy sweater every day of the year, there are times when you need it, and you will be glad that you kept it in your closet. That's exactly how you should feel about credit: While you don't need to use credit every day, it's best to keep your credit healthy and ready to use when it's needed. Having good credit helps when you need money to purchase big things like a car or rent your first apartment (see Chapter 19), but sometimes it's also needed when you are applying for a job or trying to go to college.

We want you to understand how to improve and maintain your credit, so you have no trouble getting the things you want (and need) in life. We promise it's not as scary as some people make it seem.

Exploring where you can use credit

Credit is basically borrowed money that you can use to buy things now and pay for them later. You can use credit in all sorts of places, and it's important to find out about it because your credit history will impact your financial life down the road. Good credit can make it easier to borrow money with lower interest rates, which means you'll pay less to borrow that money.

There are two common examples where your credit history will come into play: renting an apartment and buying a car. When you're looking to rent, landlords often check your credit score to make sure you're financially reliable. And if you want to buy a car and need a loan, lenders use your credit score to decide if they'll lend to you and what interest rate they'll charge.

Here's a less obvious example: applying for certain jobs. Some employers check credit history as part of the hiring process, especially in jobs that deal with money or sensitive information. They want to know if you're responsible with your own finances before handling theirs.

Knowing how to build and maintain good credit now helps set you up for success in these areas and others down the line. Your credit profile is more than just your credit score, and we discuss this in the section, "Keeping Score: Your Credit Profile," later in this chapter.

Finding out who is checking your credit report

There are many people (and organizations) who are interested in your credit profile, and many of your potential creditors are looking for different red flags when making their final decision to grant you credit access. You find out more about your credit score and credit report features in the section, "Deciphering the credit score," later in this chapter.

Here are five different types of people and organizations that might check your credit profile, along with their reasons for doing so and what they're looking for.

Landlords and property managers

Who they are: These are the people or companies who rent out apartments or houses.

Why they pull credit: They want to make sure you're likely to pay your rent on time.

What they're looking for: They look for consistent, on-time payments and a solid credit score to feel confident you'll be a responsible tenant.

Banks and lenders

Who they are: These include banks, credit card companies, and other lenders.

Why they pull credit: They pull your credit when you apply for loans, like for a car, home, or credit card, to evaluate how likely you are to repay what you borrow.

What they're looking for: They look for a strong credit history, low debt levels, and a good credit score to decide if they'll lend you money and, if so, at what interest rate.

Employers

Who they are: Certain employers, especially those in finance or sensitive fields, may pull your credit.

Why they pull credit: Employers may check your financial habits to determine if you're responsible and trustworthy.

What they're looking for: Employers aren't looking at your credit score but are looking for any red flags, like high debt or issues like unpaid bills, to assess your reliability.

Insurance companies

Who they are: These are companies that provide coverage for things like your car, home, or even life.

Why they pull credit: Some insurers use credit history to determine your "risk level" when setting your premiums.

What they're looking for: They want to see a responsible credit history, as some studies suggest people with good credit may file fewer insurance claims.

Government agencies

Who they are: These are different agencies (state, federal, and local) that help with public goods and services like food, housing, and medical coverage.

Why they pull credit: They want to ensure that the requester meets criteria to be approved for assistance and how much assistance they qualify for.

What they're looking for: They want to verify basic information, such as name, address, and income, to appropriately help applicants receive proper assistance.

Understanding the benefits of good credit

Having a good credit profile is like having a golden ticket in the world of personal finance. When you build up good credit, it shows lenders, landlords, and even some employers that you're responsible with money and can be trusted to pay things back on time. The stronger your credit profile is, the more people and companies feel confident that you're a safe bet.

When I (Mykail) was 19, my good credit score got me approved for a Victoria's Secret store credit card with a $2,000 limit! This was a big deal because, at the time, my friends who applied were only approved for $300 or $500 limits. My mom had helped me build my credit profile over the years, and when I applied for my first credit card, I had a 750 credit score. Because I had a good credit score, the credit card company felt confident giving me a higher limit, which gave me more flexibility (though I had to be careful not to overspend). That experience really showed me how powerful good credit can be even at a young age.

Here are three key benefits of having good credit.

1. **Better approval odds:** Good credit makes it easier to get approved for loans, credit cards, and even apartments.

2. **Lower interest rates:** A strong credit score often means lower interest rates, saving you money over time when you borrow.

3. **Higher credit limits:** With good credit, you're more likely to qualify for higher credit limits, giving you more flexibility with purchases if you need it.

Avoiding the penalties of bad credit

A bad credit profile can seriously limit your options and make everyday financial steps harder. When your credit score is low, it signals to lenders, landlords, and even employers that you might be a risky borrower, which can lead to higher costs and fewer opportunities.

Remember that Victoria's Secret credit card I was approved for? Here's the rest of that story, I (Mykail) ended up getting fired from my internship that helped me pay off my credit card, so I didn't have enough money to pay off the full $600 balance. At the time, I didn't realize I could have just paid the $25 minimum payment to stay in good standing. Instead, I didn't make any payments for two months while I tried to save up for the full amount. Those missed payments tanked my credit score by 200 points! When I later tried to buy my first car, my credit score was so low that I couldn't get approved on my own and had to ask my dad to co-sign for me. That experience taught me that even small missteps can have a big impact on credit.

TIP

A *co-signer* is someone who agrees to take responsibility for a loan or credit card if the primary borrower can't make payments. They're often needed when a person has little or poor credit history, as their stronger credit profile reassures the lender that the loan will be repaid.

Here are three penalties you might face for having a bad credit profile.

1. **Higher interest rates:** Bad credit usually means higher interest rates on loans, which can cost you more money in the long run.

2. **Difficulty getting approved:** A low credit score can make it hard to get approved for loans, credit cards, or even apartments.

3. **Lower credit limits:** With bad credit, you may only qualify for low credit limits, which restricts your ability to use credit when you need it.

Keeping up with payments and building good credit habits early can help you avoid these financial headaches.

REMEMBER

For every negative mark on your credit, it will take about seven years for those blemishes to get dropped from your credit report. Be mindful of your actions to keep your credit healthy and strong.

Keeping Score: Your Credit Profile

A good credit profile is essential to your financial health, and a bad credit profile can hurt your finances. In this section, we discuss your credit score. It might get confusing, but your credit report is *not* the same as your credit score. They are two very different things, even though many people try to use them interchangeably.

A *credit score* is a three-digit number that represents your credit-worthiness, or how likely you are to pay back borrowed money. It's calculated based on information in your credit report and ranges from 300 to 850, with higher scores indicating better credit.

The credit report provides the full picture of your financial behavior, while the credit score is just a summary number created from a financial model using the information from your credit report (we talk more about your credit report in the section, "Obtaining your credit report," later in this chapter). These terms shouldn't be used interchangeably because they describe different aspects of your credit.

REMEMBER

Your credit report does not change depending on the credit bureau; they should all have the exact same information. However, your credit score will be different depending on the financial model being used.

Decoding the credit score

Fun fact: Hundreds of different credit score financial models are used to determine your credit-worthiness. Depending on what you are interested in buying (a home, car, or apartment), a lender will contact different credit bureaus that provide different credit scores. Oftentimes lenders will use the median score or the lowest score from the different reporting models for your loan approval and processing.

The FICO score is the most widely recognized model, used by over 90 percent of lenders. FICO has various models (such as FICO 8 and FICO 9) and newer versions that can focus more on specific aspects of credit (medical debt is weighted differently in FICO 9).

Here's a breakdown of how it works.

300–579: Poor. This range often means you'll be denied for many types of credit or offered very high interest rates.

580–669: Fair. You might be able to get credit, but the interest rates will still be high.

670–739: Good. This is where most people fall; you'll usually get approved for loans with fair rates.

740–799: Very Good. You'll have more options and better rates on loans and credit.

800–850: Excellent. This is the best range. You'll qualify for the best rates and credit offers.

The FICO 8 credit score model is based on five main parts, with each affecting your score in different ways. Understanding the FICO score breakdown is very important. Figure 5-1 gives you a visual breakdown of how each part of your habits are weighted using the FICO model. The better money habits you maintain the higher your credit score will remain.

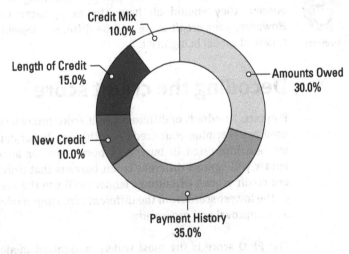

FIGURE 5-1:
FICO credit score range diagram.

Payment history (35 percent): This is the most important part of your score and is all about whether you pay your bills on time. Lenders want to see that you're reliable, so even one late payment can hurt your score. A simple way to keep this part strong is to always pay at least the minimum balance due each month, even if you can't pay the full amount. Setting up automatic payments is a great way to make sure you never miss one.

Credit utilization (30 percent): This part looks at how much of your available credit you're using. Lower utilization is better, as it shows lenders you're not relying too heavily on borrowed money. For example, if you have a $1,000 credit limit, keeping your balance below $300 (or 30 percent) can help boost your score. Staying under this percentage shows responsible credit usage.

Length of credit history (15 percent): Lenders like to see a longer credit history, as it shows you have more experience managing credit. Starting to build credit early (even with a low-limit credit card) can help you in the long run. The longer you keep accounts open, the better it reflects on your score.

Credit mix (10 percent): This part looks at the variety of credit types you have, like credit cards, student loans, or car loans. Having a mix shows you can handle different types of credit responsibly. So, if you only have a credit card, taking out a small, manageable loan (such as a student loan) could help diversify your credit profile.

New credit inquiries (10 percent): Applying for a lot of new credit in a short time can make lenders think you're taking on too much too quickly, which can slightly hurt your score. Each application triggers a "hard inquiry," which can temporarily lower your score. To keep this part strong, try to apply for credit only when you really need it, like when you are opening your first credit card account or buying a car.

The two most important actions you can take to keep a high credit score are paying your bills on time and keeping your credit utilization low. Those two categories are 65 percent of your total credit score.

Looking at the big three credit bureaus

The credit bureaus are the folks that keep all your credit data organized and in their database for lenders to request. Once you open your first credit account, your information is stored. Each month, your creditors will report to the credit bureaus any changes to your account (payments, balances, and inquiries). Hundreds of companies provide consumer reporting services; however, there are three big guys that everyone should know.

The big three credit bureaus are Experian, Equifax, and TransUnion. These three nationwide companies collect and keep track of your credit information. Each one has a unique way of gathering data about your financial habits, which helps them create a credit report that potential lenders use to gauge your reliability with credit. Here's a breakdown of each credit bureau.

>> **Experian:** Experian collects information from your lenders and creditors and focuses on making sure the data in your credit report is accurate. It offers a variety of tools to help you manage your credit, including score tracking and alerts.

>> **Equifax:** Equifax provides similar services but also focuses heavily on security, especially after a major data breach a few years ago. They've put new safeguards in place to protect your information and offer resources to help you keep your credit secure.

>> **TransUnion:** TransUnion works with lenders to help them make decisions and provides a lot of educational content for consumers. They offer resources to help you better understand your credit and how you can work on improving it.

Each of these credit bureaus creates its own credit report on you based on information they gather from your financial activities, such as credit card use, loans, and payment history. While your credit report from each bureau should be similar, they may have slight differences because not all lenders report to all three bureaus.

To access your credit report, you can go online to Annual CreditReport.com, a government-authorized site where you can view each of your credit reports for free once a week.

Beyond the basics: other credit scores explained

Credit scores can vary because they're based on different scoring models, each of which is designed for specific purposes. While all scoring models assess your financial behavior, some are better suited for certain situations. Here's an overview of the main types of credit score models, when they might be pulled, and what they're typically used for.

>> **VantageScore:** This is a commonly used score that was created by the big three credit bureaus as an alternative to FICO. The VantageScore model considers similar factors but may treat them a bit differently. For instance, it might consider utility or rental payment history more significantly if that information is available. This score is often pulled by landlords, some credit card companies, and online lenders.

>> **Industry-specific FICO scores:** Besides the general FICO score, there are specific versions for different types of lending, like FICO Auto Score for car loans and FICO Bankcard Score for credit cards. These specialized scores weigh factors in a way that's relevant to the type of credit you're applying for. So, if you're trying to buy a car, a lender might look at your FICO Auto Score to predict how likely you are to make timely car loan payments based on past behaviors.

>> **Insurance scores:** Some insurance companies use credit-based insurance scores to decide what rate to offer you for car or home insurance. These scores aren't exactly the same as your FICO or VantageScore, but they are calculated based on similar credit data, focusing on elements that statistically relate to risk for insurance purposes.

The type of score they pull depends on what you're applying for. Here's a quick breakdown.

>> **Credit cards:** Lenders typically use the general FICO Score or sometimes the FICO Bankcard Score.

>> **Mortgages:** Mortgage lenders usually rely on older versions of the FICO model, like FICO 2, 4, and 5, because they're standardized by federal mortgage guidelines.

>> **Car loans:** Lenders might check your FICO Auto Score, which specifically evaluates your risk level for auto financing.

>> **Insurance rates:** For setting premiums, some insurers use their own credit-based insurance score models.

By understanding these different types of scores, you can get a clearer picture of how your credit habits might be viewed in different situations, making it easier to manage your credit profile wisely.

Digging Into Your Credit Report

Your credit score and your credit report are *not* the same thing, and these two terms should not be used interchangeably. We mentioned this already, but it's worth mentioning again (and maybe 100 times more). This section is all about getting access to your credit report, reading your credit report, and disputing any discrepancies you find on your credit report.

Obtaining your credit report

Here's a quick story about our friend Jayden. When Jayden turned 18, he was ready to buy his first car. He'd saved up from his part-time job, and with his friend Mateo tagging along for support, he felt confident he could snag a small loan. But after the test drive and some paperwork, the salesperson returned with unexpected news: Jayden didn't qualify for the loan. His credit score was way too low. Jayden was confused; he hadn't even started using credit yet, so how could his score be in bad shape?

When he got home, Jayden checked his credit report online for the first time, only to discover that someone had stolen his personal information and opened a credit card in his name months ago. That mystery balance had been growing all this time, and Jayden's credit score had taken a serious hit. It took him weeks to clear things up, but he learned his lesson: Keeping an eye on his credit report could save him from this mess in the future. Now, Jayden regularly checks his report, knowing he'll be better prepared for big purchases.

Jayden should serve as a warning that you don't know what is on your credit report until you get a copy of it. Take the time to review your credit report before you decide to make any big purchases, and even if you aren't planning on a big purchase anytime soon, you should get into the habit of checking your credit report at least twice a year. March and September are our favorite times to review.

Viewing your credit report for free

There are a few safe and reliable places where you can check your credit report for free. The main site is AnnualCredit Report.com, which gives you access to your reports from all three major credit bureaus (Equifax, Experian, and TransUnion) once a week. This site is government-authorized, so it's trust-worthy and completely free.

You can also create an account directly on each of the big three websites to get alerts and dispute inaccurate information. While it's not required, it can be helpful to select one of the three and create an online account.

Many credit card companies and banks now offer free access to your credit score and sometimes even credit report updates. It's a convenient way to stay on top of changes in your credit profile, especially if you check your banking app regularly. They even have credit monitoring features that will alert you when there are any changes to your credit.

Lastly, there are free credit monitoring apps like Credit Karma and Credit Sesame. While they might not always have your exact score from every bureau, they're great for getting a general idea of where you stand and tracking any big changes. Just keep in mind that while these apps are free, they may show you ads or offers for financial products, so don't feel pressured to sign up for anything unless you're interested.

Paying to get your credit report

If you're looking for more frequent updates or detailed credit monitoring, there are paid options to consider. Some services, like Experian, Equifax, and TransUnion, offer direct access to your credit reports and scores more than once a year, along with tools to track your credit in real-time. Paid credit monitoring can be a good idea if you're especially focused on building or protecting your credit, because it alerts you to changes, like new accounts opened in your name, which could signal identity theft.

Credit monitoring services are also useful if you're planning to apply for a big loan soon, like a car loan or a mortgage, and want to keep a close eye on your score. When you're paying for credit monitoring, you usually get access to detailed insights on what's affecting your score the most and tips on how to improve it. Plus, these services often include identity theft protection and insurance, which can help cover costs if someone does manage to steal your info. Just be sure to read the fine print and only pay for what you need.

Making your credit report make sense

When you're looking at your credit report, it's kind of like going through a "report card" for your finances. But instead of grades, it shows how responsible you've been with borrowing money and paying it back. If you've never looked at one before, it can seem like a lot of information. But don't worry, knowing what to look for will make it easier.

>> **Personal information:** Start by checking that all the basic info is correct (such as your name, address, birthdate, and Social Security number). Mistakes here are rare but can happen, and they might cause problems with your credit. If anything looks off, make a note to contact the credit bureau and get it corrected.

TIP

Always double-check that your current address is accurate on your report. Incorrect addresses could mean someone else's info got mixed in, or it could even hint at identity theft!

>> **Account history:** This part shows all your credit accounts, like credit cards, car loans, or student loans, and whether you've been paying on time. If there are any accounts you don't recognize, it might be a sign that someone has opened an account in your name or an indication of a

possible banking error. Also, look at the payment history; late payments can drop your score, so make sure this info is right.

TIP

If you spot a late payment that you know you didn't make, you can dispute it. Fixing errors like this can quickly boost your score if it was negatively impacted by a mistake.

>> **Credit inquiries:** Every time you apply for credit, like a new credit card or a loan, it shows up as an "inquiry." Too many inquiries in a short period can hurt your score, so try to space out applications if possible. Reviewing this section lets you see who has checked your credit recently and why.

>> **Public records and collections:** This section includes things like bankruptcies, foreclosures, and accounts that were sent to collections if you missed payments. Ideally, this section will be empty. But if there's anything here, make sure it's accurate, since negative marks can seriously impact your credit.

Taking the time to look at these areas will help you make sure your report is accurate and protect your credit score. Check for anything unexpected, and if something doesn't look right, don't hesitate to follow up. Regularly reviewing your report is a great habit that can prevent surprises and keep your credit strong.

Reporting incorrect information

If you find something on your credit report that doesn't look right, it's important to know that you have the power to correct it. Taking action to fix mistakes on your report can protect your credit score and ensure that your financial "report card" reflects the real you. Here's a breakdown of the steps to get those errors fixed.

1. **Gather evidence:** Before you do anything, make sure you have proof of the error. Look for things like bank statements, receipts, or email confirmations that can back you up. You want to be able to show exactly why the information is wrong.

TIP

Keep copies of everything! Even if you're emailing, make sure to save any attachments and messages in case you need them later.

2. **Contact the credit bureau:** It's best to focus on the three main credit bureaus (Experian, Equifax, and TransUnion). If you find an error, you need to reach out to the bureau that's reporting the incorrect information. Most bureaus let you file a dispute online, which is the fastest way. Clearly explain what's wrong and attach any evidence to support your case.

REMEMBER

If you see the same mistake on multiple credit reports, you'll need to dispute it with each bureau separately. Fixing it with one bureau won't automatically fix it at the others.

3. **Notify the creditor:** If the mistake involves a specific lender (like a bank or credit card company), it's a good idea to contact them directly. Explain the issue and ask them to correct it on their end, too. Sometimes, credit bureaus need confirmation from creditors to make changes, so this step can speed things up.

4. **Follow up:** The credit bureau should respond to your dispute within 30 days, but sometimes they take longer or might need more information. Check in if you don't hear back, and keep an eye out for any updates to your report. Once the dispute is resolved, you'll get a response explaining the decision, and if the error was corrected, it'll show up in your credit report.

5. **Get a free updated report:** After the dispute is settled, you're entitled to a free copy of your corrected credit report from the bureau. This way, you can confirm that everything has been updated. This is the final step to make sure your credit report looks accurate.

Correcting errors on your credit report can seem like a lot of work, but taking these steps can save you from the headaches of a lower credit score or denied applications. Plus, it feels great to know your credit report reflects the real you and your current positive money habits.

REMEMBER

Without a successful dispute, negative marks on your credit typically take seven years to "fall off" of your credit report.

Building Your Credit to 800+

Remember our friend Jayden? Well, Jayden never really thought much about his credit score until that first time he checked his report. Seeing that number hit him hard, and it was a little rough, with a couple of dings he hadn't even realized were there. But instead of ignoring it, he decided to take control. He read up on credit and disputes, found out how things like on-time payments and keeping balances low could work in his favor, and set a goal: By the time he was 21, he wanted an 800 credit score. That number felt almost legendary, like the credit equivalent of a perfect GPA.

Over the next few years, Jayden stayed on top of things. First, he made sure to get all the false charges removed. He only used a small portion of his credit limit and paid off his balance every month, even if it meant skipping a night out here and there. When he got his first job, he kept things consistent, checking his report annually and watching his score climb steadily. Finally, by the time he hit 21, Jayden was looking at an impressive 803. He didn't really brag about it, but he knew the perks: His credit score meant he could qualify for some pretty cool things, like lower interest rates on loans and even premium credit cards with travel rewards. He could rent an apartment without needing a co-signer and get approved for the best financing options on a car. That solid score didn't just make him feel responsible, it was actually opening doors he hadn't even imagined when he'd first checked his credit report at 18.

Jayden is a great example of putting in the work for your credit score, but remember that credit is a range and while an 800+ is amazing, any credit score over a 750 can get you some of the best rates and show lenders you are trustworthy.

Increasing your credit-worthiness

When it comes to building good credit, think of it like training for a sport or leveling up in a game: it takes practice, consistency, and knowing the right moves. Building up your credit might not feel exciting now, but trust us: The future you will be so grateful you put in the effort. Here are a few actions you can take to boost your credit-worthiness and get yourself closer to those credit score goals.

» **Always pay on time.** Your payment history is the biggest part of your credit score. Paying your bills on time, even the minimum, makes a huge difference. Late payments can bring down your score fast, so set reminders or automate payments if you can. Even small steps like these show lenders you're dependable.

» **Keep balances low on credit cards.** Another big part of your score is *credit utilization*, or how much of your credit limit you're actually using. Keeping your balance under 30 percent of your credit limit is ideal (but the lower the better), so if you have a $1,000 limit, aim to keep your balance below $300. This helps show you can handle credit responsibly.

TIP

You can request a credit limit increase on your credit cards every six to nine months. It is important to keep your spending habits the same, as this will help lower your credit utilization.

» **Avoid opening too many accounts at once.** Each time you apply for credit, like a credit card or loan, it counts as a "hard inquiry" and can slightly impact your score. Opening too many accounts too quickly can look risky to lenders, so be selective and only open accounts you need.

» **Build a credit history.** Length of credit history matters, too. The longer your credit accounts have been open, the better it reflects on your report. If you're just starting, keep that first credit card open and in good standing; it'll grow with you over time and help strengthen your history.

» **Keep your credit mix balanced.** Credit scores also consider the types of credit you have. A mix of credit, like a credit card and a small student loan, shows that you can manage different kinds of debt. But this doesn't mean you should rush to open new accounts; only do it if you need them.

Monitoring your credit

Keeping an eye on your credit is like watching your back in a video game: It's all about staying alert to avoid any sneaky surprises that could mess up your progress. Credit monitoring helps you make sure your credit stays strong and alerts you if something's off. Here's how to set yourself up to monitor your credit in a way that works for you.

>> Start with free platforms. Websites and apps like Credit Karma and Credit Sesame offer free access to your credit reports and scores, plus alerts for any big changes. Many banks and credit card companies offer free credit monitoring as well. While they don't cover every single detail, they're a great way to check in regularly without spending money.

>> Explore paid platforms for extra protection. If you want a deeper level of monitoring, you can go with paid services like Experian CreditWorks or myFICO. These platforms offer more frequent updates and sometimes include identity theft protection. If you're serious about tracking every change or have had issues with identity theft before, paying a little extra for these services might be worth it.

>> Consider freezing your credit. If you're not planning to apply for new credit anytime soon, consider freezing your credit. A freeze stops anyone (including you) from opening new credit in your name, so it's a great way to block fraud. You can set up a freeze with each of the three credit bureaus (Experian, Equifax, and TransUnion) for free. Just remember, you'll need to unfreeze it when you're ready to apply for something.

>> Set up notifications. Many credit platforms (both free and paid) let you set up notifications for new activity, like newly opened accounts or a big change in your balance. These alerts are super helpful for catching any suspicious actions quickly. You can also set notifications to remind you of bill payments, which helps protect your score and keeps you on track.

Monitoring your credit doesn't have to be complicated, but it's key to keeping your financial life secure and healthy. By staying on top of your credit activity, you can make sure that nothing slips through the cracks and get a heads-up on any issues before they become major problems.

Keeping your credit score strong

Keeping your credit score strong is like taking care of a plant: you don't have to obsess over it every day, but a little attention now and then helps it grow into something solid. Credit is only one piece of your financial plan, so don't feel pressured to make it "perfect." The truth is, even a great credit score will have some ups and downs along the way, and that's completely normal. Life happens; sometimes you'll take on a loan, pay it off, maybe even run up a little extra on your credit card during tough months. Those changes can temporarily affect your score, but they're part of building your credit story.

Instead of aiming for a specific number, think of credit as part of a bigger financial picture that includes budgeting, saving, investing, and setting goals for your future. Focus on establishing good habits, like paying bills on time, keeping balances manageable, and checking in on your credit report every once in a while. These steps build a solid foundation for long-term financial success.

Remember, the goal isn't to reach "perfect" credit, it's to stay responsible with credit over time. Your credit score is just one indicator of financial health, and as long as you're working to keep it strong, you're on the right track. Keep at it, stay patient, and let your smart decisions take you where you want to go.

Chapter **6**

Breaking Down Debt

Y
ou already know this (or else you wouldn't have grabbed this book!), but life costs money. The amount of money you'll need in life depends on several different factors. One of them is called the cost of living.

The *cost of living* (COL) is how much money you need to support your lifestyle. Along with bills, your COL includes things such as food and transportation, which can be higher or lower depending on where you live. For example, it typically costs more money to live in a bigger city than it does in a smaller town. Some states, like California and New York, are more expensive to live in than states like Kansas and South Dakota. Your COL can also be influenced by your hobbies, responsibilities, and random life events.

Another factor that can determine how much money you'll need is the amount of debt you carry. *Debt* is the money you owe a person or institution that you must pay back. Not all debt is considered the same. Some debt is commonly referred to as "good" debt, while other debt is referred to as "bad." But guess what? Debt is actually neither good nor bad.

You can look at debt as a financial tool that can help you invest in your future, purchase a home, and cover car repairs. Debt can also help cover you if your expenses are more than your income in a month. We don't ever want you to feel bad when it comes to talking about personal finance. Instead, we want you to feel empowered.

As we go deeper into this chapter, we will discuss the various types of debt and how they work. We'll also go more in depth on how you can pay your debt off, as well as make it work for you as a tool in your money management warm-up plan.

Looking at Different Types of Debt

In order to use debt to your advantage, you need to understand the different types of debt that you can take on. While debt isn't good or bad, there are differences that can make debt more reasonable when it comes to paying it off. First, let's go over some key finance terms that will help you to understand how debt works.

>> **Lender:** The business or organization that lends the money.

>> **Borrower:** The person who borrows the money.

>> **Loan:** The amount of money that is lent to the borrower. In this chapter, we also refer to loans as *lines of credit*.

>> **Interest:** The amount of money or fees a lender charges you for borrowing money. For example, a $5,000 car loan may have a 6 percent interest rate.

>> **Payment:** The amount of money and interest you must pay back according to the lender.

>> **Terms and conditions:** The rules a lender gives to the borrower when it comes to paying back the loan. The amount of your payment and how often you must pay it in order to pay back the loan are examples of terms and conditions.

Now that we've discussed some terms, we're going to cover three main things you need to know when it comes to debt: whether your loan is secured or unsecured, whether it's revolving or fixed credit, and what is your interest rate.

Borrowing Basics: Secured and Unsecured Debt Explained

Do you ever borrow something from a friend with the intention to pay them back and they ask to hang on to something of yours to make sure you bring their stuff back? Let's say Athena's phone stopped working one day and buying a brand new one wasn't in her budget, but she then remembered Mykail had an extra phone she was no longer using. Mykail agreed to allow Athena to borrow her phone, but she asked Athena if she could borrow her laptop until Athena returned her phone.

Collateral is something you can exchange when borrowing something so that the other person feels better about lending you that thing. An item that has value to you and others is called an *asset*. In the scenario we just shared, Athena's laptop and Mykail's phone are both considered assets; however, Athena's laptop is being used as collateral since she will get it back when she returns Mykail's phone.

Collateral can also come in handy when it comes to borrowing money. A *secured loan* is one where you promise to give someone an asset of yours as collateral if you aren't able to pay back the loan as agreed upon. Most secured debt comes in the form of auto loans and mortgages, which you'll find out more about in the later section, "Understanding Specific Loans." With both of these types of debt, the bank can take control of the item you *financed* (borrowed money for).

TIP

It can be easier to get a secured loan because the business you borrow from knows that you have an item that can be sold if you don't pay your loan back. Secured debt may also have a lower interest rate since there is collateral.

An *unsecured loan* is one where you borrow money without having to offer an asset as collateral. If you are unable to pay your debt according to the agreement you had previously decided on, the business can't make their money back by keeping your assets. Instead, they will have to go through other ways to get the money back that they lent you, sometimes in the form of making you go before a judge in court or sending your debt to an agency known as a *debt collector*. This can also tank your credit score, which can affect the financial products you can get later.

It is easier for people with a higher credit score to get an unsecured loan. The higher your credit score, the more trustworthy a lender finds you, which can result in better terms and conditions. This is why it's so important to make sure you keep your credit in good standing.

Examples of unsecured loans and debt are credit card debt, medical bills, and personal loans. They can also be things like owing money for a driving ticket or forgetting to pay back a Buy Now, Pay Later service (more on that in the section, "Buy Now, Pay Later").

Revolving and fixed lines of credit

The next thing to learn about debt is whether it's a revolving line of credit or a fixed line of credit. There are a few key differences between these two different credit types.

A *revolving line of credit* is an approved amount of money that a lender has agreed to let you borrow when and as often as you need it. The amount of money you are allowed to borrow is preset by the lender and available to you whenever you decide you'd like to access the funds.

A credit card is a good example of a line of credit. You're given a predetermined limit of how much you can borrow at any given time, and you can access the funds all at once or little by little. Once it's paid back, you can borrow it again. Many people use revolving credit to help cover emergencies and unexpected expenses. But you can also use your revolving lines of credit to cover your everyday expenses to earn what are called credit card points. Usually, people who use their credit cards for this purpose can pay off the balance in full every month.

If you cannot pay your balance off in full every month, it doesn't make sense to do this. Any points and rewards can be canceled out by you having to pay interest.

Revolving credit has flexible payment terms, which reflect the amount of your payments. These payments are based upon your interest rate and the amount of money you are currently borrowing. You may avoid interest altogether if you pay off your balance before your bill's due date.

A *fixed line of credit* is money you receive all at once; this is also called a lump sum. After you receive the lump sum, you must repay it in accordance with a predetermined set of terms and conditions that you and your lender have agreed upon. After you borrow the money, you cannot ask for more or pay some of it back and then borrow it again, like you can with a revolving line of credit. Fixed lines of credit are usually used for bigger and more substantial purchases, such as a house or a car.

A fixed line of credit has payments that are the same amount every time you pay. Fixed lines of credit have a set interest rate, and revolving lines of credit typically offer flexible ones. (We discuss interest rates in the next section, "Understanding your interest rate.") Because the payment is the same amount no matter what, it can be easier to budget for since you always know what to expect.

It's important to always read the fine print when it comes to borrowing. A fixed line of credit, like an auto loan, may have an early termination fee. *Early termination fees* mean that you have to pay additional money if you pay off your loan sooner than the due date, since you will no longer be paying interest. Interest is how your lender makes their money, so watch out! When used correctly, both revolving and fixed lines of credit can be useful to you on your personal finance journey.

Understanding your interest rate

Last but not least, it's important to know what your interest rate is when it comes to your debt. Fixed and variable interest rates operate very differently and can affect how you repay your debt.

Fixed

A *fixed interest rate* means that the interest on your debt stays the same for the entire time you pay back your loan. Fixed rates are usually attached to fixed lines of credit, which is one of the main reasons why your payment is the same amount and easier to budget for. Fixed rates are also typically much lower than variable interest rates, which can mean you save additional money.

Choosing fixed interest rates can help you budget for your future and hit your financial goals since you know exactly what to expect.

REMEMBER

Just as the market goes up and down, so do interest rates. If interest rates go down after you make your purchase, you can try to get an even lower rate by refinancing. *Refinancing* means that another lender buys your original loan and then you pay them back instead.

Variable

A *variable rate* is the opposite of fixed, which means it fluctuates. The rate is usually based off of the stock market and goes up and down accordingly. This means that your payments can also go up and down, depending on how much interest you are paying at that time.

The main risk with variable rates is not knowing if your interest rates will rise one day and go down the next (see Figure 6-1). If the interest rate goes up, your payment goes up. This can cost you more money in the end. But if your interest rate goes down, you can save money. This is why a variable rate is so tricky: There are both pros and cons to it.

WARNING

Some lenders will offer a low variable or even fixed interest rate for a few months, and then charge you significantly more. This is often known as an introductory rate. It's always important to read the fine print, and if something seems too good to be true, it usually is.

A fluctuating payment can be harder to plan for, especially when you are just starting out on your money journey. One month, your payment may be reasonable, and the next you could be struggling to cover it.

A $10,000 36-month auto loan payment at three different interest rates

7.41% interest rate
Payment $330.84
Total Payment after 36 months $11,910.28

9.63% interest rate
Payment $341.80
Total payment after 36 months $12,304.75

14.07% interest rate
Payment $365.35
Total payment after 36 months $13,116.74

FIGURE 6-1: An example of how different interest rates can affect a monthly payment.

* Average used car interest rates Source: Experian Information Solutions, 3rd quarter 2024

TIP

If you prefer knowing that your payment is the same amount every month, a fixed interest rate may be the way to go when you finance something.

In a nutshell, it really comes down to whether you prefer the peace of mind that comes with fixed payments or the potential savings (and risks) of a variable rate. It's all about finding what works best for you! Fixed and variable interest rates are two different ways in which interest can affect how much and how long you pay off your debt.

Applying for Specific Loans

Now that we've covered the basics of debt, let's talk about specific types of loans that you'll most likely take out in your lifetime.

Auto Loans

An auto loan is a type of financing that allows you to purchase a vehicle by taking out a loan from a lender. The loan is usually the money needed to cover the cost of the vehicle plus any taxes and fees after you make a down payment on a car. The higher the down payment, the less money you'll need to borrow for the loan. However, if you have really good credit or the car dealership is having a sale, sometimes you can purchase a car with no money down.

An auto loan is a fixed line of credit, which means that you can only borrow the amount you need for the car at one time. You then pay back this loan over a predetermined period of time in installments. A lender usually gives you up to six years or 72 months to pay off your loan. Your credit score and how much money you put as a down payment will determine the length and amount your loan payment will be.

An auto loan is a secured loan because your lender will use your car for collateral if you don't make your payments. They use it as collateral by taking it back from you. This is called *repossession*.

An auto loan is a practical way to finance a vehicle purchase, making it more accessible to buy a car without paying the full price upfront. The loan payment is also budget friendly by being the same amount every month, which can be easier to plan your living expenses.

TIP Always try to shop around when taking out a loan. Check out not only your current bank, but also a credit union. Sometimes credit unions have much better terms and conditions that can make owning your dream car more affordable!

Student Loans

Student loans are unsecured loans that students can borrow to help pay for expenses related to their higher education. These loans can help students pay for their tuition, fees for classes, and books and supplies needed for each class. Student loans can also help cover living expenses such as room, board, and transportation.

Student loans can come from the government or from private lenders like banks and other financial institutions that offer these types of loans. The two main types of student loans are federal student loans that come from the government and private student loans that come from financial institutions.

Federal student loans are usually the preferred type of loan when borrowing for your education because they typically have a lower interest rate and more favorable repayment terms and conditions. Federal loans also offer what's called a *grace period*, which means they allow you a certain amount of time (typically six months) after you finish school to find a job and figure out payment arrangements. Private student loans are less flexible when it comes to repayment schedules and can have a much higher interest rate.

Since student loans are unsecured, no collateral is involved. However, if you do not pay back your government loan, the government can then garnish your paycheck to get their money back. Garnishing a paycheck means that they take a certain amount of money directly from your paycheck with your employer's knowledge, and you get what's left after taxes.

Based on the amount you borrow for school, you can end up paying a lot of money for a long period of time. It's important to borrow only what you need and to avoid any extra unnecessary college expenses. Student loans are important for many students in order to help them pursue higher education, but they come with responsibilities that need careful thought.

Mortgage

A *mortgage* is a loan that is used to purchase a home. When you take out a mortgage, you borrow money from a bank or lender and agree to pay it back over a period of time, which is usually between 15 to 30 years (a long time!). A mortgage is paid back in installments that are the same amount of money every time, which can make it much easier to budget for. However, your payment can fluctuate tremendously if you choose a variable interest rate instead of a fixed interest rate.

The amount of a mortgage depends on several key factors:

>> The amount of money needed to purchase the house

>> The interest rate on the loan

> » The amount of money you are putting as a down payment (just like a car)
>
> » The property taxes owed every year
>
> » The insurance to protect your home

TIP

Most mortgages require a down payment, which is a percentage of the price of the home that you pay upfront. A larger down payment can lead to better loan terms and conditions, including a lower interest rate and smaller installment payments.

WARNING

Like an auto loan, you are borrowing a secured debt because the house is considered collateral. When a lender takes back a house, it's called foreclosure, and that can affect your ability to buy another home for a very long time.

REMEMBER

We'll discuss mortgages in Chapter 19, but remember: There are always more expenses besides just a mortgage when it comes to buying a home. Homes require lots of care and extra money for repairs and upgrades, just to name a few things you'll have to pay for once you're a homeowner.

Revolving debt

Revolving debt is a type of credit that lets you borrow money up to a set limit and use it multiple times as long as you pay it off. You can choose how much to pay back and when, which can add flexibility to your budget. It is common to carry a balance, but it's always best to pay it down as soon as you can because otherwise, you'll start paying interest.

If you don't pay off the full amount, interest is charged on the remaining balance, and you must make a minimum monthly payment. This type of debt offers flexibility but can lead to high interest costs if not managed well.

Credit cards

The most common example of revolving debt is a credit card. A credit card usually has a predetermined amount of money that you can borrow up to, along with an interest rate that is variable.

This means that while it can stay the same, it can also change, affecting how much you end up owing.

The debt you charge to a credit card is called the *balance*. Once you pay down the balance, you can borrow more. If your balance hits the limit the credit card company has given you, you won't be able to borrow more until the remaining balance is lowered. Any balance you carry over from the previous month is charged the interest rate, and this is then factored into your credit card payment. You are also required to make a minimum monthly payment.

REMEMBER

It's easier to spend money using a credit or debit card than it is using cash. Not using physical money can trick your brain into spending more.

WARNING

Do not borrow more than you can afford to pay back. This is how people can end up with credit card debt.

Try to get a credit card that offers incentives. A lot of credit cards not only offer points to help you travel for less, but they also offer cash back for everyday spending.

Buy Now, Pay Later

Buy Now, Pay Later (BNPL) financing has become very popular in recent years. While it's not a completely new way of paying for items you purchase, it is offered now more than ever before, along with affordable terms that may differ from a credit card.

Companies such as Klarna and Affirm allow customers to apply to use their buy now, pay later financing. If the loan is approved, the company will purchase the item on your behalf and instead of paying the store directly, you pay back the company that financed your purchase. The company will most likely take the amount you owe and divide it into four "easy" payments. One payment is due at the time of purchase, and the other three payments are on a schedule until the item is paid off.

This payment option allows you to purchase products and services immediately while deferring payment over time, often with little to no interest if you pay on time and in accordance with the terms and conditions you agreed to. Because of its flexibility, BNPL can seem like a more affordable way to buy items you want, especially when you're younger and you may not have enough money to purchase an item at its full price. For example, buying a pair of Nikes for $150 seems like a lot, but breaking it down into smaller payments of $37.50 can seem more doable.

BNPL can seem like a better alternative than a credit card, and for a lot of people it is. Even we use this option when making purchases to help our cash flow last longer without needing to rely on a credit card. But because BNPL is so easy to get, it's also easy to use too often. When you use something more than you should, it's often referred to as abusing it. And if you have too much freedom and flexibility with your purchase power, it's easy to abuse that, too.

It's easy to not realize how much you are buying when your payments are spread out over time. This can lead to overspending, which can jeopardize the rest of your financial goals. If you miss payments, you can be charged late fees and also cause damage to your credit scores. This can affect your eligibility later on when you may need it most.

WARNING

Always keep track of the future payments you owe so that you can double-check your budget later on. If you don't have the wiggle room for even smaller payments, BNPL may be something that you can't afford and should save up for instead!

TIP

If you find yourself using BNPL a lot more than you feel you should, you may need to add more fun money into your budget to help you cover purchases you'd like to make. You can always allocate money in categories differently to help you live the lifestyle you want. That's what a budget is for!

Paying Down Your Debt

Now that you've found out about the different types of debt you may come across, it's important that you know how to pay that debt off.

REMEMBER

The longer you hold onto debt, the more money you pay in interest and fees, which takes away from the money you could be saving and using elsewhere.

Paying down your debt is important for a few reasons. The more money you have going toward debt, the less money you have to spend in other areas of your life for fun and other financial goals that you'd like to accomplish, like traveling or buying your first home. Having more debt can also mean potentially throwing away more money toward interest.

It can also be harder to finance other things if you already have a ton of debt. For example, a lender looks at your current debt and compares it against your income to see if you can even afford taking on more debt. The more debt you have, the less likely a lender is to feel comfortable lending you more, since they assume you may have trouble paying it off later on.

There is no right or wrong way to pay down debt, as you will discover in the next section. The number one thing you need to remember is to just keep trying.

There are two main methods to pay down your debt: the snowball method and the avalanche method. Both work in different ways, which can motivate different people depending on what they prefer.

Snowball method

The snowball debt method focuses on quick wins to help keep you motivated. First, you make a list of your debts from the smallest amount of debt you have all the way to the largest amount of debt you have. (The amount is how much you owe.) For example, if you owed your credit card $300, that's how much the amount would be on your list. Next, write out your minimum payments that you must make each month to keep your debt current.

It would look something like the illustration in Figure 6-2.

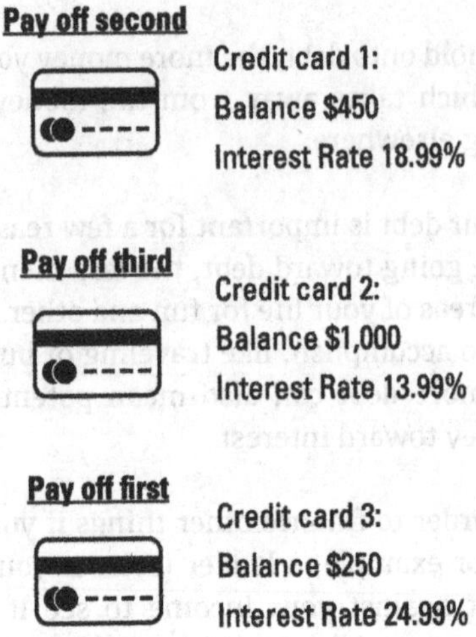

Pay off second

Credit card 1:

Balance $450

Interest Rate 18.99%

Pay off third

Credit card 2:

Balance $1,000

Interest Rate 13.99%

FIGURE 6-2:
Planning
debt
repayment
using the
snowball
method.

Pay off first

Credit card 3:

Balance $250

Interest Rate 24.99%

After you have paid all of the minimum amounts on your debt, you will start to pay off the smallest debt first using any extra money you come across during that month. This could be money you freed up from revising your budgeting, income from side gigs, or cash gifts and bonuses.

Once you pay off the smallest debt, you then take the amount you were paying on that debt plus any extra money and start putting it toward your next-smallest debt. Then, wash and repeat, doing the same thing over and over while making your minimum payments until all of your debt is paid off. This creates a snowball effect that helps you pay off debts faster.

The snowball method leaves you feeling positive and happy, which can help you stay motivated when paying down your debt.

TIP

While you may end up paying more interest later on, you'll still pay way less than you would have originally if you had kept to your minimum payments.

Avalanche method

This debt payoff method focuses on you paying off your debt based on the accounts that have the highest interest rates. Higher interest rates mean that you are spending more money holding onto that debt.

You make a list similar to how you would with the snowball method, but instead of organizing your debt from the smallest to largest payment, you organize your debt from the largest to smallest amount of interest, as shown in Figure 6-3.

Pay off second

Credit card 1:

Balance $450

Interest Rate 18.99%

Pay off first

Credit card 2:

Balance $1,000

Interest Rate 13.99%

Pay off third

Credit card 3:

Balance $250

Interest Rate 24.99%

FIGURE 6-3: Using the avalanche method to organize debt by interest rate.

After you've made your list, continue to make the minimum payment amounts on all of your debt that you are currently making. Any extra money you come up with can be used as an extra payment toward the debt with the highest interest amount. By putting extra money toward your debt with the most interest, you end up paying less over time than you would using the snowball method.

Once your debt with the largest interest rate is paid off, you'll continue putting extra money toward your debt with the next-largest interest rate and continue until you have paid off all of your debt.

Fireball method

The fireball method is a mix of both the snowball and avalanche methods. With this technique, you first pay off the debt you dislike the most. For many, this is credit card debt. The debt that has an asset attached, such as an auto loan or your mortgage, is saved for last. This method can help you feel motivated while taking care of the debt that bothers you the most.

Debt pay-off tips

Paying off your debt can take a long time and can often seem hard to do. That's why it's so important to set yourself up for success. The following tips can help.

>> **Make a budget.** Understanding how much money you have coming in and matching it up to your expenses lets you know how much money you can realistically put toward your debt. There is almost nothing that hurts as much as breaking a promise to yourself with unrealistic expectations regarding yourself and your money.

>> **Decide which debt to pay off first.** This can help you prioritize what's important, whether it's paying off your credit cards, student loans, or money borrowed from a relative. By deciding what should come first, you'll make sure that you are directing the funds accordingly.

>> **Find extra money to use for debt repayment.** You can find money in a few different ways: by making more income, cutting back on your expenses, or doing a combination of both. We prefer a mix of both to help us hit our financial goals, but sometimes it's a lot easier to do one or the other and build from there. Even if it's cutting back on something that's $5 here or $10 there, that will always add up to something bigger. If you decide to earn more, plan how much you'll be putting toward your debt repayment and other expenses.

>> **Earn money from a side gig.** This work can be flexible so that you can do it around school time and other commitments. Mykail likes to teach classes sometimes after work, and Athena likes to deliver for Uber Eats during the lunch rush. Athena also made money from pet sitting while she was writing this book!

The longer you hold onto extra money, the more likely you are to spend it, so make extra payments as soon as you can. It may seem silly making small payments here and there, but trust us, it adds up!

>> **Ask your lender about your interest rate.** Many lenders have phone numbers that you can call to speak to customer service about your current rate. Sometimes they can lower it, saving you lots of money in the long run. Athena has called her credit card company before to schedule a payment plan when she couldn't make her full payment, they were helpful and helped her create a payment plan that fit better into her budget.

>> **Sell stuff from around the house.** Athena loves to declutter every few months, and she tries to sell what she can for extra money. Sometimes this goes toward buying new home décor she has her eye on, and other times it goes to help her pay her loan down even faster. Either way, she is making her home clean and tidy while making some extra cash. You can sell stuff on Facebook Marketplace and apps like OfferUp. If you are under 18, ask your trusted adult to help you!

Keep your eyes on the prize. It's hard to stay focused, but one thing that will help you hit your goals is to set not only realistic ones, but also goals that you can practice self-discipline achieving. Working hard can be tiring at times, but it can also be rewarding. This is how Mykail has accomplished so much, all before age 30!

Remember, you aren't a bad person if you have debt. When used correctly, debt can be a useful tool in your financial toolbox that can help you hit all the financial goals you set for yourself.

2

Money Matters for Middle Schoolers

Understand your personal finances and how to make informed decisions.

Discover the importance of saving for your future and setting financial goals.

Manage your money effectively while balancing school and daily life.

Chapter 7

My Money and Me

One of the things most grown-ups regret is not being taught about money when they were young. To a student in junior high, that might sound silly, but it's true. A lot of adults start off in life having a hard time with their finances because they didn't learn about managing money while in school.

In life, it's a good idea to get informed about something before you try it for yourself. Even if you discover just one new thing about a topic beforehand, it can help you have a better outcome. This includes personal finances.

Knowing about money before you have a job and are old enough to open up your own checking account is important. The more you know now, the less likely that you'll make mistakes later, when it matters most.

Understanding Money Basics as a Middle Schooler

When was the last time you bought something? When was the last time you saved up to buy something? Obviously, both of those things have to do with money.

Money makes the world go round. From paying for the food you eat, to purchasing the book you are reading now, things cost money! And knowing how to earn, save, invest, and spend money is important when you're just starting out on your own money journey.

If you're new to these concepts about money, don't worry! In this chapter, you'll find out the basics of incoming money and then outgoing money.

Incoming money

Think about a time when you wanted to purchase something. Were you able to purchase it outright? Or, did you have to save up to buy it? Or, are you still wondering how you'll get the money you need to buy it?

Incoming money is money that you receive (to spend or save) that's exchanged for time you work or a service you perform. This is called *income*. Here are some different examples of activities that can help you generate income:

>> Babysitting your siblings

>> Getting an allowance from doing chores around the house

>> Doing yard work for a neighbor

>> Pet sitting

>> Collecting cans and trading them for money at a recycling center

>> Selling items at a lemonade stand or bake sale

>> Tutoring people who are younger than you or who need help in a subject you are really good at

>> Helping out at a family-owned business

All of these are ways that you can exchange your time and service for money as a middle schooler. When you are older, you can get a part-time job, depending on the state where you live. Most states require you to be at least 16 years old and to only work part time if you are still going to high school.

Income is important because it pays for your bills (when you eventually get them) and allows you to have fun and save for the future.

It's okay to have a small income as a middle schooler. Your earning potential will increase as you get older, so don't fret!

Outgoing money

Outgoing money is any money you have going out that you are responsible for. You can both spend money on your expenses and save money for financial goals and emergencies. Outgoing expenses are what you spend on things that you use or buy. Think of it as the money that leaves your wallet or bank account. Whether you are an adult or a middle schooler, here are some examples of expenses you may have.

>> **Food.** This includes groceries you buy to eat at home and food you eat at restaurants.

>> **Transportation.** This includes using a bus or train, or getting rides from someone. Even gas for a car is an outgoing expense. Along with gas, cars need to be registered every year so that they can be on the road; they also need insurance and maintenance. Some may even have a car payment!

>> **Housing costs.** This is the money you use to pay for where you live. If you pay rent or a mortgage, that's a big outgoing expense.

>> **Utilities.** These are the services you need every day to help you live in your home. Electricity, water, gas, trash, and internet access are all things you pay for each month to use while you are at home. Sometimes people have even more utilities depending on where they live.

>> **Clothing.** This is any money spent buying new clothes, shoes, or accessories, yes even if it is thrifted.

>> **Hygiene products.** These are items, like soap, that you use to stay clean and to feel, look, and smell your best.

>> **School supplies.** These are items like books, notebooks, and pens for school. Other school supplies may include a

computer and a backpack to help you carry everything to and from class.

>> **Entertainment.** This includes money you spend on movies, video games, and activities with friends.

>> **Pets.** This includes food, toys, and medical care. Some animals even require additional supplies; for example, cats also need litter.

Understanding outgoing expenses is important because it helps you to manage your money better and to make sure you don't spend more than you have. It's like keeping track of how many snacks you eat; if you have only a few, you need to be careful not to eat too many!

Discovering Where Your Money Goes

Knowing where your money goes can help you to not only budget, but also to plan better for the future. It's important to know how much money you have coming in versus how much money you have going out; this enables you to allocate funds properly as well as not spend money that you have put aside for something else.

Spending your hard-earned money

When it comes to knowing where your money is going, it's important to know a few key terms.

Fixed expenses

These are costs that stay the same each month. You can count on them being a regular part of your budget or spending plan. Examples include rent or mortgage payments, car payments, and car insurance. No matter what you have to pay, these amounts are the same and go out at the same time every month.

Variable expenses

These costs can change from month to month. They aren't the same every time, and you may or may not have control over them. Examples include groceries, entertainment, and utility bills. For example, one month you might spend more on food, and the next month you might spend less on food but more on entertainment.

Needs and wants

Needs are items that you require every day to function. Wants are things you don't need to function. A want can even be a need, but one that costs more than another item that fulfills the same need.

Here are some examples of items that you need.

>> **Food:** Nutritional items necessary for your health.

>> **Shelter:** A place to live, whether it's rented or mortgaged.

>> **Clothing:** Basic clothing required for protection and comfort.

>> **Utilities:** Essential services like electricity, water, and heating.

>> **Healthcare:** Medical care and prescriptions that you need for your health.

Here are some examples of wants.

>> **Entertainment:** Movies, concerts, and hobbies, as well as video games and subscriptions to streaming services like YouTube or Netflix.

>> **Dining out:** Eating at restaurants instead of preparing meals at home. This also includes food delivery and food you pick up from fast-food chains.

>> **Luxury items for clothes:** Designer clothing, gadgets, or accessories that are not necessary. This can also include expensive items like makeup, wallets, watches, jewelry.

>> **Taking trips:** Vacations and trips that are fun rather than necessary.

Needs are the things you require to live and to function, while wants are additional comforts and pleasures that enhance your quality of life. Understanding this difference can help you to spend on the things that matter to you and to budget effectively.

Saving money for the future

Close your eyes and imagine yourself when you're 30. (We know, this may sound silly, but just do it for us!) Think about where you live. What does your house look like? Do you get up every day and go to work? Where do you work? Do you drive to get there? What do you do every day?

We talk more about visualizing your future self in the next chapter, but it's important to think about your future, even as a middle schooler. Everything you do in the future will cost money, so, setting yourself up with a future you can afford is important.

Along with your everyday life, you'll need money to do things you want to do, like travel, buy a house, get a new car, and one day, stop working altogether because you'll be retired. Saving money as soon as you can will help you take advantage of something called compound interest.

Using the power of compound interest

Compound interest is the interest added to the original amount of money you invest or borrow, plus any interest that has already been added. This means your money grows faster because you earn interest on both the initial amount and the interest it has already earned. This is often called *interest on interest*. This is what we mean when we say your money makes money.

Compound interest includes the following.

>> **Principal:** This is the original amount of money you start with (in the following example, this is $1,000).

>> **Interest rate:** This is the percentage that shows how much your money will grow each year (in the following example, this is 5 percent per year).

>> **Time invested:** This is how long you keep your money invested or borrowed.

For example, if you invest $1,000 at a 5 percent interest rate compounded yearly, you will earn $50 in interest after the first year. Your total will then be $1,050. In the second year, you will earn interest on not just the $1,000, but also on the $50 of interest from the first year, leading to even more interest earned.

It's important to understand compound interest when it comes to saving your money and investing it for your future. It can help you earn more from your savings or investments, which means you hit your financial goals even faster.

Chapter 8

Money for the Future

Begin with the end in mind.

—STEPHEN COVEY

When Athena was in her senior year of high school, she was given an assignment in her psychology class that forever changed her life: reading the book *The 7 Habits For Highly Effective Teens* by Sean's father. This book is based on the best-selling book for adults called *The 7 Habits For Highly Effective People* by Sean's father.

What was so life-changing about it? Well, it was about planning for the future. Athena knew she wanted a lot in her life and had a lot of ideas for how it would look. But she wasn't entirely sure how to get there.

Back then, she lived in a small town without many resources. The internet was nothing like it is today, and so it wasn't easy to research and gather resources, including tapping into the knowledge of others. Feeling frustrated, she had only taken psychology as a way to get further ahead in her college classes so she would have a better chance of getting accepted into her dream school, Arizona State University.

Being a bookworm, Athena knew she would most likely find the book she was reading enjoyable, but it also turned out to be a book that she would repeatedly reference when it came to planning her future. The book was broken up into several chapters that each covered a habit that you could implement to be successful in your future. The one that resonated the most (and still does to this day) was about planning with your future in mind.

It might sound backwards, but planning with the future in mind is a great way to get started with living the life you want. We're going to show you how to plan for your future and how you can also use planning with your personal finances.

Imagining Your Future Self

Beginning with the end in mind is about first imagining your future self. Knowing where you want to be in the future is a great first step to creating what can end up being your dream life. And you're never too young to get started.

REMEMBER

Every single action you take is going to have an outcome that affects your future, even if the action doesn't seem important at that time or place.

One example is eating breakfast. Sure, missing breakfast once or twice isn't going to hurt you. But missing breakfast every day can change your digestive system and can lead to you not getting enough nutrients. Not getting enough nutrients can affect your health and mental well-being.

This is just like not getting enough sleep. It's okay to stay up late once in a while, but a lack of sleep can create a poor sleep schedule that makes you tired.

By imagining your dream life, you can start to take action and create habits that can make it a reality. For example, if you want to become an athlete in high school, you should probably play a sport and work out now so that you're ready when the time comes. If you want to save a ton of money to see the world, you need to find out how to save and possibly even earn money now.

Getting started creating your plan

Building a plan for the future you requires some research, self-reflection, and time with yourself to figure out what you really want. A future plan can include your career, where you want to live, what you want your family to look like, and even things you want to do for fun. It can be as far away as when you're a senior citizen, or it could be who you want to be by the time you graduate high school.

Here are some ways you can start creating your future plan now.

>> **Self-reflection:** Take time to assess your current situation, values, and what you truly want in life. What are your passions, strengths, and weaknesses? Understanding yourself is crucial for making informed decisions.

>> **Set clear goals:** Define what success means to you. Set specific, measurable, achievable, relevant, and time-bound (SMART) goals. Consider different aspects of your life: career, health, relationships, and personal growth. Setting goals in different areas of your life can help you to think outside the box and to become a well-rounded person, which is great!

>> **Research and explore:** Gather information about the paths you're interested in. This could involve exploring different career fields, educational opportunities, or lifestyle choices. Talk to people who are in roles or situations you aspire to. You can also talk to teachers, watch documentaries, and check out books suggested by your local librarian.

>> **Create a roadmap:** Create a timeline for when you want to achieve these milestones, and include deadlines to keep yourself accountable. Break down your goals into smaller, actionable steps, and give yourself flexibility when you set them. For example, don't try to master shooting free throws in a day if you've never played basketball before.

>> **Pick your goals:** Determine which goals are most important and begin taking action on them. This might mean enrolling in a course, networking, or starting a new hobby that aligns with your goals.

>> **Stay flexible:** Be open to adjusting your plan as needed. Life can be unpredictable, and being adaptable is key to navigating changes and challenges. Life doesn't always work out as expected, and you may need to change a few things to accomplish what you set out to do.

>> **Practice the three Rs (regularly review and revise):** Set aside time to regularly assess your progress. Are you on track to meet your goals? What obstacles are you facing? Be honest, as honesty helps you get where you need to be faster. Also, use this time to celebrate your achievements and adjust your plans accordingly.

>> **Stay committed:** Keep your motivation high by reminding yourself of your long-term vision. Surround yourself with supportive people who encourage your growth. They can be friends, family members, mentors, people you meet at church, your trusted adult, or a teacher. It's important to grow as a person, especially during the time you have now.

By following these steps, you can create a practical and motivating plan for your future self that evolves as you grow and change.

Setting financial goals for the future you

Once you know what you want your future to look like, you have to think about the money you're going to need to help get you there. Creating future financial goals involves several steps.

>> **Check out your finances:** Take a moment to look at your current financial picture. What's coming in? What's going out? Knowing your income, expenses, savings, and debts is the first step. Because you are young, there may be some items that you don't have yet, and that's okay. What's important is to just know where you currently stand.

>> **Dream big:** Think about what you really want to achieve financially. Do you want to save for a cozy home, build an

emergency fund, pay off debt, or perhaps save for that dream vacation? Again, you might not have debt, but if you are going to college, will you be acquiring debt such as student loans? That may be a future goal of yours that you want to take action on.

>> **Get specific:** Once you have your dreams in mind, make them specific. If a new home is on your list, figure out how much you'll need for a down payment and when you'd like to buy. You can do this by going online and finding your dream home in your dream neighborhood. You can also get specific on trips or schools you'd like to attend.

>> **Plan to save and invest in your future:** Decide how much you want to save each month to reach those dreams. Once you get a checking account, setting up automatic transfers to your savings or investment accounts can make this super easy!

>> **Celebrate your progress:** Don't forget to check in on how you're doing! Keeping track of your progress can boost your motivation and help you stay on course.

>> **Stay flexible:** Life is full of surprises, so be ready to adjust your goals if needed. It's all part of the journey!

>> **Don't stop learning:** The more you know about personal finance, the better! Learning can open up new paths and ways for you to reach your goals.

By following these steps, you can set fun and achievable financial goals that will lead you to a bright future.

Financial Goals As a Middle Schooler

Here are a few financial goals you can set in middle school to help you get started on your personal finance journey.

>> **Open up a checking and savings account.** You'll need a trusted adult to help you do this. You can find out more about choosing a trusted adult in Chapter 3.

>> **Practice with your debit card.** Use your own debit card to make a purchase to practice for when you get older.

>> **Find out how to read and write a check.**

>> **Set a goal.** Do this for something small and then achieve it.

>> **Earn part-time income.** Figure out if there is a way to start earning an income either after school or during the weekend.

>> **Save money.** Put aside money for your savings whenever you come into extra cash or income.

>> **Try out a budget.** There are a lot of different budgeting methods for everyone. We talk more about budgeting in Chapters 4 and 9.

>> **Keep track of any money you wasted on stuff you really didn't want.** This way, you can figure out how to avoid wasting money in the future.

>> **Put money toward a bike or car.** The time when you need transportation will be here before you know it!

>> **Read books on finances.** Books like this one can help you find out more about planning and looking after your finances.

>> **Make a donation.** Donating to a organization fighting for causes you care about is investing in the future you want to see.

Future Financial Goals As an Adult

Here are a few ideas for goals that you can dream about later as an adult:

>> Saving for emergencies

>> Paying off student loans

>> Saving up for a house

>> Taking a big trip somewhere

>> **Getting married or starting a family**

>> **Retiring early**

>> **Buying a brand new car**

WARNING

It's a good idea to know what you can save for in the future because it will be here before you know it. It's important to enjoy being a kid, but it's also important to know the things that you can one day accomplish by getting a head start.

Earning Money in the Future

Earning money is one of the most important parts of your personal finance journey. You need to earn money; there is no way around that. As we expressed before, everything in life costs money. You have living expenses to pay for and financial goals to accomplish. That's why it's important to know about your income and future earning potential.

There are two main types of income: active and passive. Each type has its own place and vibes, and can help you get ahead financially.

Active income

Active income is when you trade a service, your time, or a product for money on a regular basis. For example, you actively go to work every day if you have a full-time job and exchange your time for a paycheck. If you deliver for DoorDash or give rides through an app like Uber, you are exchanging your time and service for tips. If you make stuff to sell or you help a neighbor out with their yard, you're actively involved in making an income. Active income stops if you stop.

Examples of active income include the following:

>> Wages from a full- or part-time job

>> Bonuses and tips

>> Money you receive from chores

Examples of *how* you make active income include the following:

>> Side gigs like shopping for others, delivering food, or giving rides for a rideshare service

>> Freelancing

>> Making items to sell

>> Babysitting and pet sitting

>> Selling items online for more than you paid for them, like clothes

>> Cleaning someone's yard

Passive income

Passive income is the opposite of active income. Instead of doing something over and over again, you usually do something or set something up once and then collect money from. A lot of people say that passive income requires no effort, and that's not true. Everything requires some effort on your part; some things just require more than others.

Examples of passive income include the following:

>> Earned interest and dividends on investments

>> Bonds

>> Ad revenue from social media content

>> Renting out a room in home or renting a home to others

>> Selling products that you create once (such as download-able graphic design kit)

>> Royalties from songs or books

>> Affiliate marketing (links to different products online that someone can buy, where you get a commission from the sale)

>> Making an app

Active income requires your attention and effort on a consistent basis, while passive income flows in after you've done the initial work. Both of these types of income can help you hit the financial goals you set for yourself and help you be more financially stable.

Considering Your Future Career Options

While all income is important, one of the biggest factors in your finances that will affect you over the long term is your career.

A career is the series of jobs you'll have over your lifetime. A lot of people have careers where they work in one area known as a sector or field. Other people have their career split into two different areas over their lifetime, and still others have careers that are all over the place in different areas.

The time to research careers is now, while you don't have to work full-time. It will be harder to take this time when you're older and you need to make money.

So what goes into a career? And how do you find the best one? Here are some tips to help get you started.

Developing crucial skills

A skill is something that you can do well or are at least proficient in. Proficient means that while you aren't the best at it, you can still get it done and in a timely manner. Skills are usually broken into two different categories: hard skills and soft skills.

Hard skills are actions that are tied to your job or career. For example, having experience taking care of animals as a vet assistant is something you can apply to other jobs that involve animals. But that skill really wouldn't come in handy if you were to start being a chef. Hard skills belong to a specific job or sector.

Soft skills, on the other hand, can come in handy regardless of the career or job. Sometimes, soft skills can even be more important because it's easier to train someone a hard skill than it is a soft skill. That's because soft skills require time, effort, and sometimes a certain personality.

Examples of soft skills you can practice include the following:

>> Answering the phone in a professional way

>> Saying please and thank you

>> Checking your email on time

>> Knowing how to apply for a job professionally

>> Being on time to classes and meetings

>> Letting other people speak without talking over them

>> Being patient

>> Following rules that have previously been set

>> Following a dress code

>> Not giving up on a school project even if it gets hard

>> Practicing being fair

>> Learning to plan ahead (proactively) versus dealing with things after they happen (reactively)

Planning your educational path

Different careers require different levels and types of education. For example, some careers require you to go to college; others require you to go to a trade school or the military; and others allow you to pick up skills on the job.

Knowing what education you need is important because you can actually start preparing for it now. For example, getting into a college may require you to take classes known as prerequisites in high school. If you will need to take a lot of math in high school, you should make sure now that you are caught up on math and not behind your peers. The same goes for subjects like

English and science. If you are behind now, you'll get even more behind later if you don't catch up.

Some careers may also require you to be in school for a prolonged period of time, like being a doctor or a lawyer as well as various internships and additional programs that involve licensing.

Taking your values into account

Think about something that is important to you. Now, ask yourself why it's important. It might be because of a value you have.

Values are sort of like an internal compass. Instead of telling you north and south, your compass can tell you whether you feel strongly about something or whether you think it's right or wrong. You may think that being fair is really important, and that can be considered a value. Other values that people have may include family, friends, education, having a safe home to sleep, or even personality traits, like being considerate.

When choosing a career, it's important to think about what values you have. This is because your career could either go along with your values or go against it. For example, following rules at all times might be a value that's needed to be a police officer who upholds the law. If you don't always follow the rules, or have a hard time when others do, then being a police officer might not be for you. Instead, you might want something more flexible, such as a job that allows you to be creative, like an artist.

Pondering your interests

Finding your career interesting is important. If you don't like what you're doing, or are consistently bored, you're not going to want to be the best employee you can be. So, if you don't like being in the kitchen, then you probably shouldn't be a chef. If you don't like exercising, then you probably shouldn't be a physical trainer. Doing something you like is the dream, but doing something you're interested or good at is a close second.

Considering your salary

Also known as compensation, salary is important to consider when picking your career. The level of education you need to achieve, and the career or field you are considering, can all affect your salary. Compensation can also be influenced by where you live, how long you are with your employer, and even what your schedule looks like. Some doctors make more money by working nights, and some teachers earn more by teaching extra classes.

CAREER EXPLORATION WEBSITES

Here is a list of different websites you can use to help you get started on your career today.

- CareerOneStop (www.careeronestop.org/): This website includes different assessments to find out your skills and interests as well as what career would be a good fit for you. It also helps you find training programs, develop your resume, and conduct your job search.

- O*NET OnLine (www.onetonline.org/): This website offers you a chance to look directly at careers within various fields. It also helps you find a career based on what level of education you want or certifications you currently have. You can also narrow down the pay to your current location or where you one day want to live.

- U.S. Bureau of Labor Statistics (www.bls.gov/k12/students/careers/career-exploration.htm):The U.S Department of Labor offers this website to help you find careers based on your skills and interests. This is a great place to start if you already know what you are really passionate about!

Chapter 9

Managing Money in Middle School

People may say you're too young to learn about money, but we know you obviously aren't listening because you picked up this book. Middle and high school is actually the best time to learn about money. Here's why.

In the United States, rules around working are made by an organization called the United States Department of Labor, or the U.S. Department of Labor for short. Along with deciding rules about safety and how much someone should be paid, they also determine what age you can be to legally start working, which is typically 14. In addition to the rules set out by the Department of Labor, there are also laws that determine how old you must be to work for an employer that isn't your family.

While the national law says you can legally start working in certain jurisdictions at age 14, there are still certain things you can do if you are 13 and younger, such as babysit or work for a business your family runs. This is why it's important to learn about money as soon as you can. Knowing about money before you get a regular paycheck can help you start off on the right foot with good money habits, which will help you hit your financial goals even faster.

In this chapter we discuss money management basics, such as finding out more about banks, checking accounts, debt, budgeting, and more. You can also discover more about these topics in Chapters 3, 4, 5, and 6.

TIP

To find out more about the rules regarding your age, how many hours you can work, and other questions, check out the Youth Rules.gov website at www.dol.gov/agencies/whd/youthrules.

Visiting the Bank

Growing up, we would watch family members interact with money in many different ways. One unique way Athena frequently saw was her grandma hiding money under her mattress in a cookie tin. While Athena still keeps a few dollars around her house in random places, she knows now that her money can work best for her in a bank.

Financial institutions are places where you can store your money safely to be used when you need it. They can also help you save for your financial goals, help you plan for retirement as you get older, and help you invest so you can take advantage of compound interest. The two main types of financial institutions most people use are banks and credit unions.

Using banks and credit unions

Banks are for-profit financial institutions that are privately owned by people known as shareholders. Banks make money by offering you different financial services, such as checking and savings accounts, loans, and credit cards. Almost anyone can open a checking account if they are age 18 and up, which means these types of accounts are readily available.

Credit unions are non-profit financial institutions, which means they are owned by the customers who use the credit union, known as members. Credit unions offer the same financial products that regular banks do, but they can also be more flexible to help their members when they need additional assistance with their money. To be a credit union member, you may need to live in a certain area or be part of an affiliation, such as having a family member who has served in the military.

You can access both banks and credit unions in person and through mobile apps on your phone. Thanks to the internet and technology, you can do most of your banking online or over the phone, making it easier than ever to manage your money. It's up to you and how you feel most comfortable when accessing your money.

Checking accounts and debit cards

A *checking account* is used to store your money for everyday use. Everyday use would be something you do a lot of, such as buying groceries or shopping for necessities. You can also use this account to pay bills, like rent and car insurance. Since you use your checking account to spend money as opposed to saving or investing it, you can withdraw your money in various ways, such as by using a debit card to make purchases or checks to pay bills.

Your account will also have its own individual number, known as your account number. This is so the bank knows who the money belongs to.

Savings accounts

A *savings account* is used for saving toward your financial goals. It's also where you store money to be used for future expenses, like gifts, and for emergencies such as a car repair or a sick pet that needs to go to the vet. Since savings accounts aren't made for spending, you usually have to transfer the funds to a checking account if you need to access the cash. Certain savings accounts also pay you interest to motivate you to save even more.

REMEMBER Always look at the bank's age requirements when opening an account. Some financial institutions will let you open an account if you are as young as 8, but you will still need an adult to help you open it. Once you turn 18, you can have your own account with no one else needed to help you maintain it.

Understanding Credit in Middle School

One of the most important financial tools when you get older will be your ability to get credit. Credit is when someone lends you money to make a purchase with the understanding that you will pay them back later in a timely manner.

Let's take buying a new phone, for example. A new phone can be expensive, often hundreds of dollars. Say, you find one that's $300 on sale but you only have $200. The phone company can decide to still let you have the phone if you promise to pay them back over time. You do this every month when you pay your phone bill. This is an example of buying something with credit and is one of the most common ways to buy a new phone.

You can use credit to buy almost anything by taking out a loan or a credit card, which you'll find out more about in the next section. For now, just know that your credit is important and that you must always pay back money you owe on time. Eventually, you'll have borrowed money often enough where you'll have what's called a credit score. A *credit score* is a report card for your money habits that's based on how responsible you've been at paying back loans.

If you always pay back what you owe on time, your credit score can go up. This makes it easier for you to borrow money in the future or to get better deals. But if you don't pay back what you owe, your credit score can go down, and people may not want to lend you money next time. So, it's important to be responsible with credit!

earn an allowance or do chores for neighbors and get paid, that's your income. It can also come from other sources, like gifts or interest from a bank account. In simple terms, income is the money that comes in, which you can use to buy things, save, or spend on fun activities. See more about types of income in Chapter 8.

Expenses

Expenses are the money you spend to buy stuff or pay for a service. Think of your life as a business and the expenses as the costs of running your business. For example, if you buy snacks, pay for a movie, or even put gas in a car, those are all expenses. They can be planned, like when you save up for something special like a car, or unexpected, like if you need to fix your car.

REMEMBER

It's important to keep track of your expenses so you don't spend more money than you have, because this is how you get into debt.

Money left over

While this isn't technically part of a budget, we still think it's important to explain what it is. After you take your income and subtract the money you've spent (expenses), you can see what money you have left over. It's with this money that you can save for your future and pay down debt.

REMEMBER

The more money you have left over, the more money you can put toward making your financial dreams a reality.

TIP

Budgeting is about tradeoffs. You might be able to afford something but you're not always able to afford whatever you want. It's okay to have stuff to look forward to!

TECHNICAL STUFF

Always look for coupons online! We love apps that help lower our spending by providing discounts and cash back, just for shopping we were going to do anyways!

SMART SPENDING

One way you can make your budget work for you is to learn how to spend smart. Smart spending can help you stretch your money so you can use it for more important things later on. Here are a few questions you can ask yourself when you want to buy a product or service to see if you're spending smart:

- Is this something you need, or is it something you want? Remember the difference between wants and needs like this: "I need shoes but I don't need Nike Airs. I need a phone but not an iPhone."

- Is this available at a better price somewhere else? Not everything is the same price at different stores. In fact, stores depend on having a price difference so that you will hopefully shop there instead.

- Do you own something like this already? You might want a new T-shirt, but you already have a T-shirt that you haven't worn a lot collecting dust in your closet.

- Is there a better way to spend your money? Most of the time, there will be a better way to spend your money. For example, it's probably a better idea to buy a box of six ice cream sandwiches for $3.99 at the grocery store rather than buying one ice cream sandwich for $1.75 at the ice cream truck every day.

- How can you budget your money to afford what you want? If you still want something after asking the previous questions, figure out a way to make it happen in your budget. When Athena wants new makeup or skincare, she makes sure to increase her spending category so she can buy those items when they are on sale.

Discovering Different Ways to Budget

Now that we've covered the different parts of your budget, it's time to go over the different ways you can budget. There are four main budgeting methods. For all of these scenarios, we will pretend you are earning $100 every week by babysitting your siblings after school.

Zero-based

A zero-based budget is when you give every dollar of your income a job and put it to work! That means if you babysat your siblings and earned $100, you already have an idea of how you can make that $100 work best for you. This helps you to not spend money you don't have or on something you don't need. With this scenario, you have $100 that needs to be assigned a job based upon your income and expenses.

50-30-20

A more flexible way to budget is with the 50/30/20 method. This method involves splitting your money into different buckets and then matching your expenses from there. The different buckets are as follows.

>> **Needs (50 percent of your income):** Based on your $100 income, your expenses for things you need, like gas to get to your job or lunch money for school, should be no more than $50 for the week.

>> **Wants (30 percent of your income):** With $30 of your weekly paycheck, you should be able to buy stuff you want, such as an app for your phone or a video game you saw someone mention on YouTube. This is for fun and fun only!

>> **Financial goals (20 percent of your income):** The remaining $20 of your weekly pay should go toward your financial goals. So, it could go toward saving for something cool that you really want or are hoping to one day buy, like a new phone or car.

Cash envelope

Cash envelope budgeting is when you pay for your expenses in cash that comes from envelopes. It works like this: Each envelope has one of your expenses written on it, or maybe a category of your spending, like fun. You then divide your paycheck into different amounts and then spend what's in your envelopes. Then, once it's gone, it's gone.

Pay yourself first

The last method of budgeting is called the "pay yourself first" budget. People also call this the "anti-budget" because you don't put money aside into a million categories or track your money. Instead, this method forces you to make your financial goals a priority by putting aside 10 percent of your income first and then being flexible with the remaining 90 percent. You can save more, but most people start off with 10 percent. With $100, you would save $10 and then spend the rest.

REMEMBER

Budgeting is different for everyone, but that's what's fun. You can keep trying until you get the hang of it and flex those financial muscles.

3

Money Matters for High Schoolers

Balance work and studying for academic success.

Explore your options after high school and plan your next steps.

Understand the process of getting into your dream college.

Discover how to secure financial aid and scholarships for college.

Chapter **10**

Work Hard, Study Hard

There are perks to being a student. Don't believe me? Go to your favorite store and ask them if they have a student discount; chances are, they do. Lots of cool technology and innovation launch on college campuses and are exclusive to students before being introduced to a wider audience. Facebook originally required an .edu email address. Tinder marketed exclusively to college students to get off the ground. Banks have special checking accounts exclusively for students. In other words, being a student can be really beneficial to you.

In this chapter, we will look at some of the perks of student life, and how you can use this time in your life to build savings as well as work experience that will give you a strong head start into life after college.

Making the Most of Student Discounts

Being a student doesn't just mean you're studying algebra and writing essays; it also means you've got a golden ticket to some serious perks. No, your school ID isn't just a hall pass — it's a passport to savings. Let's dive into why student discounts are your new best friend and how you can make the most of them.

"Do you offer a student discount?" should be your favorite new question. You'd be surprised at how often the answer is "yes." From movie theaters to museums, local restaurants, and even big-name brands, companies love students (and their spending power). The secret? You have to ask. Whether you're buying a new hoodie, grabbing coffee, or signing up for a streaming service, make it a habit to flash your student ID or drop the magical "student discount" line. Worst case? They say no. Best case? You save enough to splurge on something else.

TIP

Websites and apps designed specifically for students are like treasure chests of deals. Platforms like these often partner with brands to offer exclusive discounts and freebies just for showing proof of enrollment. Think of them as VIP clubs, but instead of bottle service, you're scoring discounts on laptops, software, clothes, and even travel. Signing up for student discount platforms takes minutes, but the perks? Endless.

Your ID is a golden ticket. That little card with your awkward photo can unlock more than classroom doors. Colleges often partner with local businesses, so check out what's near you. Some schools even negotiate perks like free bus rides, discounted gym memberships, or special student nights at local hotspots. Don't leave money on the table — explore what's already baked into your student status.

Lastly, think long-term, not just immediate goodies. Yes, that 10 percent off at your favorite pizza spot is amazing, but student perks go beyond food and fashion. Imagine saving hundreds of dollars on travel, software for school projects, or even memberships to career-building organizations. By strategically using these discounts, you're not just saving pocket change; you're laying the foundation for smarter spending habits.

Finding Work-Study Programs in College

Many students need to maintain a part-time or full-time job while attending school. In a 2020 study, the National Center for Education Statistics reported that about 40 percent of full-time undergraduate students held a job at the same time and about 73 percent of part-time college students held a job at the same time. So, if you are considering college and you know that you might need to earn money to get through, just know you are not alone.

Thinking back to my (Mykail) time in college, I was not eligible for work-study. I wish I was because that would have saved me from calling my parents every three days asking for money to help me with books, supplies, and the occasional party.

FAFSA: Signing up for work-study jobs

Picture this: You're in college, juggling classes and homework, and figuring out how to pay for everything. Enter work-study jobs, your potential lifesaver. The Federal Work-Study program is designed to help students earn money to pay for school while gaining valuable work experience. You get cash for your bills and a job that fits your busy college schedule.

The Federal Work-Study program is a part-time job funded by the government, specifically for college students with financial need. Unlike a regular job, work-study positions are designed to be flexible around your class schedule. These jobs are typically on-campus (think library assistant, tutor, or admissions tour guide), but there are also off-campus options in certain fields.

It all starts with the Free Application for Federal Student Aid (FAFSA). When filling out your FAFSA, make sure to check the box indicating that you're interested in work-study. This helps your college's financial aid office determine if you qualify. If you're eligible, your school will include work-study as part of your financial aid package.

Here's the process in a nutshell:

1. **Fill out your FAFSA.** Check the work-study checkbox!

2. **Review your financial aid award.** See if work-study is listed.

3. **Secure a position.** Once on campus, search your school's job board or ask the financial aid office about openings.

Work-study is based on financial need, so your eligibility depends on the information you provide in your FAFSA. Not everyone qualifies, but if you're unsure, your school's financial aid office can help clarify this for you. Even if you don't qualify, other part-time job options are often available on campus! (We discuss part-time jobs in the next section.)

Work-study jobs are tailor-made for college students, offering flexibility that a typical part-time job might not. Your supervisors know your classes come first, so your work schedule can easily adapt to your academic needs. Most of these positions are conveniently located on campus, which means no long commutes. Beyond convenience, work-study jobs provide invaluable career skills. Whether you're shelving books in the library, assisting a professor, or working as a lab tech, you'll gain experience that looks great on your resume and can help you explore potential career paths. Plus, the money you earn through the work-study program can go a long way toward covering essentials like tuition, textbooks, or even your favorite snacks. The best part? Work-study earnings typically don't count against you when filling out next year's FAFSA, so you get the financial boost without it impacting your future aid eligibility. It's a win-win: practical experience, extra cash, and a job that fits your schedule.

Balancing your workload with your study schedule

Balancing work and study schedules, as well as everything else college throws your way, can feel like juggling flaming torches — but don't worry, it's totally doable! The first thing to remember is that studying comes first. College is your chance to build the future you want, and your coursework is the foundation for that. Treat your study schedule like it's non-negotiable; after all, that's what you're in college to do. Block off time for classes, assignments, and test prep before adding anything else to your calendar.

Once your study schedule is locked in, it's time to build around it. Start by writing down all your commitments: work hours, classes, and study blocks. Then, add in other priorities, like exercise, hobbies, or a much-needed coffee catch-up with friends. Use tools like a digital planner, color-coded calendar apps, or even good old-fashioned sticky notes to keep everything organized. When creating your schedule, aim for realistic time slots for each task (don't book a two-hour study block when you know your focus will fade after 45 minutes). Include breaks to recharge and keep yourself on track.

Fitting in social activities can be tricky, but it's also essential for your mental health and overall college experience. The key is prioritizing. Say yes to the events that matter most and skip the ones that don't add value to your life or that leave you feeling drained. A little planning goes a long way when scheduling hangouts after work or study sessions, so you don't feel torn between obligations.

TIP

Communicate. Professors and supervisors are often more understanding than you might think, especially if you're proactive about discussing your workload. If your work-study job has you swamped during midterms, let your supervisor know early and see if you can adjust your hours. Similarly, if a professor has a strict deadline that clashes with other responsibilities, ask politely if extensions or alternative options are available.

REMEMBER

The goal isn't perfection; it's finding a system that works for you. Balancing work, study, and fun is a learning curve that you will need to consistently reassess and tweak your schedule as needed.

Working Non-Campus Jobs While Studying

When I (Mykail) was working on my graduate degree for business administration, I worked as an online tutor and a wedding dress consultant at a popular wedding dress chain. An interesting mashup for sure, but it helped me afford my daily expenses. Non-campus jobs can be part-time or full-time. These are for students who don't qualify for work-study or didn't get selected for a graduate assistant job. Finding work as a college student can be simple when you understand your schedule and properly communicate with your professors and supervisors.

Finding flexible jobs in school

Part of the reason why I (Mykail) ended up selling wedding dresses in college was because this was a super-flexible position. The shifts were only four hours, four days a week, and we closed at eight p.m., so it was easy to fit around my class schedule and still have time to party *and* study in the evenings.

REMEMBER

When you are considering an off-campus part-time job, the main requirements are that the job is flexible and the supervisor understands that you are in college. It's worth mentioning in the interview that you are in college and you will need to create shifts around your school schedule. Any good hiring manager will respect that and work with you to ensure everything is well balanced.

Here are some useful questions to ask during an interview to determine if a job will accommodate your college class and study schedule:

- >> "What does a typical work schedule look like for this position?"

- >> "Are employees able to adjust their schedules during exam weeks or heavy coursework periods?"

- >> "Does the company allow shift swapping or trading with other employees if scheduling conflicts arise?"

- >> "How do you prefer employees communicate if they need to adjust their work schedule?"

- >> "Are other student employees in this position, and how do they manage their schedules?"

- >> "If my class schedule changes each semester, is it possible to adjust my work hours accordingly?"

- >> "Do you see this position as a good fit for a full-time student?"

By asking these questions, you'll not only gain insight into whether the role fits your needs, but also demonstrate to the employer that you're proactive and committed to managing both responsibilities effectively.

Creating your own income

If the old-fashioned way of earning money in college doesn't appeal to you, why not think outside the box? Gig work and entrepreneurship are excellent alternatives that allow you to build an income on your own terms. Whether you're delivering coffee to caffeine-deprived students or launching a TikTok-worthy jewelry business, there are countless ways to make money that fit your unique skills and schedule. When I (Mykail) worked as an online tutor, it was the best because I could pick up shifts whenever I needed extra cash without strict obligations.

Why consider gig work?

Gig work is perfect for students because it offers flexibility. Need to study for an exam? Simply block off your availability. Got a free weekend? Take on a few extra gigs to bulk up your savings. Many gig platforms allow you to set your own hours, so you're in control of when and how much you work. Plus, gig jobs often require minimal training, so you can start earning quickly.

Beyond the paycheck, gig work can help you build soft skills like time management, communication, and problem-solving, which are qualities that look great on your resume. It's also a low-risk way to experiment with work environments and discover what you enjoy before committing to a long-term job.

Twenty gig-work platforms to check out

Here's a list of platforms to get started with gig work.

>> **Uber Eats:** Deliver food.

>> **DoorDash:** Another food delivery option.

>> **Instacart:** Deliver groceries.

>> **Fiverr:** Offer freelance services like writing, graphic design, or video editing.

>> **Upwork:** Connect with businesses looking for freelancers.

>> **TaskRabbit:** Help with tasks like moving, cleaning, or assembling furniture.

>> **Tutor.com:** Tutor students online in various subjects.

>> **Chegg Tutors:** Provide academic help to other students.

>> **VIPKid:** Teach English online to kids overseas.

>> **Amazon Flex Delivery:** Deliver Amazon packages in your area.

>> **Rover.com:** Offer dog-walking or pet-sitting services.

>> **Care.com:** Find babysitting, housekeeping, or elder-care gigs.

>> **Shipt:** Deliver groceries and essentials.

>> **Secret Shopper:** Become a secret shopper for retail and food companies.

>> **Poshmark:** Resell clothing or accessories.

>> **Depop:** Another great platform for reselling items.

- **Airbnb Experiences:** Offer tours, classes, or unique experiences in your area.

- **NotaryCam:** Become an online notary.

- **Thumbtack:** Offer professional services like photography or event planning.

- **Survey Junkie:** Earn money by taking online surveys.

One of the best perks of gig work is its adaptability. You can pick up gigs in your downtime, like driving for Uber Eats between classes or selling handmade crafts on Etsy over the weekend. Plan your work hours around your class and study schedules, and don't forget to take breaks when you need them.

TIP

Use a calendar app to block off time for gigs, so you can stay organized and avoid overcommitting.

Why consider entrepreneurship?

Starting a small business while in college might sound intimidating, but it's one of the most rewarding ways to earn an income. You can turn your hobbies or talents into cash while building skills in marketing, finance, and leadership. Plus, being your own boss means you can set your own schedule, choose your workload, and grow your income potential over time. Bonus: It looks amazing on grad school applications or in future job interviews.

There used to be so many people on campus who made their own money in so many different ways, selling clothes, creating makeup brands, doing hair — there was even a girl who had a really profitable button-making business. It's cool because your customers are all on campus, so word can get around really fast.

Entrepreneurship also helps you think creatively and can open doors to scholarships or grants for student entrepreneurs. You might even qualify for campus resources, like incubators or mentorship programs, to help launch your idea.

Whether you're earning tips delivering food or launching a thriving side hustle, creating your own income in college is empowering. Not only can it ease the financial strain of tuition and living expenses, but it also gives you the freedom to prioritize your education and personal goals. Who knows? Your gig or business might be the start of something much bigger.

Becoming the Intern

Besides studying, we think the next most important thing you need to do in college (or high school) is getting good internships. Internships are basically your taste-test of the real corporate world. Your goal should be to land an internship at least every summer. This is where you will get real-world experience and you can decide if the industry or career is right for you. You can do an internship and truly love it, or you can be living your worst nightmare. You won't know until you get to dip your toe into the real working world.

TIP

Your goal for a summer internship is to get an offer from a company, either another summer internship or a full-time job offer after graduation.

Applying for internships

Internships are the golden ticket to building real-world experience, boosting your resume, and figuring out if your dream job is actually dreamy. But landing an internship isn't just about luck, it's about strategy.

Where to find internships

The first step is knowing where to find the opportunities. Start with your college's career center website, which often has a job board tailored to your school's connections. Next, create profile platforms on Handshake, RippleMatch, and WayUp, which are goldmines for student-friendly internships. If you want a more targeted approach, talk to on-campus recruiters when they have events or check company websites for direct postings. Don't overlook social media — many companies post openings on their Instagram or LinkedIn accounts.

And don't be shy about networking. Let professors, classmates, and family members know you're on the hunt. Sometimes, the best internships aren't listed online; they're handed to people who ask.

Update your LinkedIn profile

Your LinkedIn profile is like your digital handshake with recruiters. Make sure it's polished! Use a professional headshot, write a compelling summary that highlights your skills and career goals, and showcase your experience, whether it's part-time jobs, volunteer work, or projects. Don't forget to add relevant keywords to attract recruiters — think *social media management*, *data analysis*, or *graphic design*. And turn on the Open to Work feature to let employers know you're ready to dive in.

TIP

Post a brief update about your internship search — something like, "Excited to explore internship opportunities in marketing this summer! Open to connecting with professionals in the field." It's subtle but effective.

Polish your resume

Your resume is your personal highlight reel. Keep it concise — one page max — and make sure it's tailored to the internship you're applying for. Use strong action verbs like *managed*, *created*, or *analyzed* to describe your achievements, and quantify them when possible. For example, "Increased social media engagement by 30 percent over three months" sounds way more impressive than "Ran the Instagram account."

If you're struggling, head to your college's career center for help. Many offer free resume reviews and templates to make your application stand out.

When applying, make sure your cover letter and resume aren't just a copy-paste job. Tailor them to the company and the role, and use them to show why you're passionate about the internship. Before hitting submit, double-check your application for errors. It's a small step that goes a long way in showing professionalism.

Utilizing the career center

Your career center is the crown jewel of resources, and they are happy (and paid) to help you on your mission to land a rockstar internship. Yes, they can help you perfect your resume, but that's just the start. Sign up for mock interviews to practice answering tough questions in a low-pressure environment. Nervous about networking? Attend a career fair hosted by your school. These events are an excellent way to meet recruiters face-to-face, ask questions about their companies, and even secure interviews on the spot.

Career centers often have connections with alumni who love to give back. Don't hesitate to ask if there's a mentorship program or alumni network you can tap into.

TIP

Landing an internship takes effort, but every application, mock interview, and LinkedIn update is a step closer to your dream opportunity. Start early, stay organized, and remember that every "no" is just practice for your eventual "yes."

Internship alternatives

Get creative with your internship search. Everyone's journey will look a little different, and even if you don't land your dream internship with a dream company your first summer, you can use this year's experience to get you closer to your dream. Our friend Jason did just that! He was having a hard time finding a summer internship and then remembered that his uncle had a small business. So, he asked if he could be his uncle's executive assistant intern for the summer to get experience, and then the next summer, he used that to land an internship with a Fortune 100 company.

Co-ops

A *co-op*, short for cooperative education program, is an opportunity to blend academic learning with real-world work experience. Unlike internships, co-ops are typically longer, lasting multiple semesters, and they alternate between full-time work and full-time study. You'll work with a company in your field, gaining hands-on experience while still earning college credits.

Co-ops are a fantastic choice if you want to immerse yourself in a specific industry and build deep connections within a company. They often pay more than traditional internships and provide a structured learning environment. Plus, the extended time with an employer can lead to a full-time job offer after graduation. If your goal is to graduate with both a degree and significant work experience, a co-op might be the perfect fit.

Apprenticeships

An *apprenticeship* is a training program where you learn a trade or profession directly from experienced mentors. They are more common in technical fields like healthcare, technology, and skilled trades, although they're growing in popularity for roles like digital marketing and software development. Apprenticeships often combine hands-on work with classroom instruction.

Apprenticeships are ideal if you're looking to gain practical, in-demand skills and earn a paycheck while you learn. Many apprenticeships lead directly to a job offer, making them a great alternative to internships if you want a clear path into a specific career. They're particularly beneficial if you prefer learning by doing rather than sitting in a classroom.

Fellowships

Fellowships are short-term opportunities, usually tied to a specific project or research focus. These programs are often funded, providing a stipend or salary to participants. Fellowships can range from academic research roles to hands-on work in industries like public policy, education, and non-profits.

If you're passionate about a particular field or project, a fellowship offers the chance to dive deep into meaningful work. They're especially useful for building expertise and networking with leaders in your chosen area. Fellowships can also be an excellent stepping stone to graduate school or specialized careers. Unlike internships, which may involve more general tasks, fellowships often allow you to contribute directly to impactful projects.

Paid versus non-paid internships

Let's be clear: we 100 percent believe that you should be getting paid a fair wage for the work you do for a business (for-profit *and* not-for-profit). However, while some fields require paid internships, in other fields it is common that internships are unpaid. Depending on the requirement, you will know what route you must take for your internship. If you are required to take an unpaid internship, make sure that your supervisor will provide you with feedback to fulfill your credit requirements.

If you are getting paid for your internship, there are two common ways in which internship programs typically pay:

>> **Stipend.** This is a lump sum payment that is disbursed on a set day, usually at the end of the internship but sometimes on a monthly basis.

>> **Hourly.** Payment is based on how many hours you worked and is recorded on timesheets.

Making your mark at your internship

Internships aren't just about showing up — they're about showing out. Meet Taylor, a sophomore majoring in marketing, who landed a dream internship at a boutique advertising firm. They were over the moon, but when they stepped into their first meeting, the room full of seasoned professionals and slick PowerPoint decks felt intimidating. Taylor knew they needed a game plan, not just to survive but to thrive. Here's how they made their mark, and how you can, too.

Setting your goals

Taylor started by setting clear, actionable goals for their internship. They didn't just want to "learn stuff" or "do a good job." Instead, they got specific:

>> Understand the basics of digital ad campaigns.

>> Create a portfolio piece by the end of the internship.

>> Build relationships with at least five team members.

Setting goals gave Taylor a sense of purpose. They didn't wait for their manager to tell them what to do, they asked questions like, "What does success look like in this role?" and "How can I best support the team?"

TIP

Define what success means for your internship. Break it down into learning goals (what you want to know), performance goals (what you want to achieve), and networking goals (who you want to meet). Write them down and share them with your supervisor during your first week.

Building your team of mentors and sponsors

Taylor quickly realized that succeeding in the workplace wasn't a solo mission. They observed that the most successful interns weren't just good at their jobs, they were also great at building relationships. During their first month, they identified potential mentors — people whose work inspired her or who seemed approachable and supportive. They scheduled quick coffee chats with them, asking about their career paths and advice for success in the industry.

But Taylor also kept an eye out for sponsors: people who could advocate for them when they weren't in the room. Taylor's direct supervisor became one of their biggest allies, recommending them for a high-profile project that became a turning point in their internship.

TIP

Mentors guide you, but sponsors open doors for you. Build relationships with both by being genuine, curious, and willing to learn. Don't just focus on the highest-ranking person; find allies at all levels.

REMEMBER

Networking isn't just about what people can do for you; it's also about how you can contribute to their success. Be helpful, reliable, and engaged in team projects.

Tracking your progress and achievements

By the midpoint of their internship, Taylor faced the classic "What have I actually accomplished?" crisis. They started keeping a weekly journal, noting every task they completed, every skill they learned, and every piece of feedback they received. By the end of the summer, Taylor had a full list of achievements, from successfully running a team meeting to creating a report that impressed the department director. The director was so impressed Taylor was offered a job for the next summer at the end of Taylor's summer internship.

TIP

Create a "brag file" to document your progress. Use a simple notebook, a digital spreadsheet, or even a notes app and include the following info:

>> Specific tasks you completed

>> Positive feedback you received

>> New skills you learned

>> Quantifiable results (such as "Improved engagement by 20 percent on social media posts")

REMEMBER

Celebrate small wins, too. Finding out how to navigate workplace dynamics, mastering new software, or even surviving your first team presentation are all achievements worth acknowledging.

IN THIS CHAPTER

» **Exploring a gap year**

» **Looking at two-year and four-year colleges**

» **Checking out trade schools**

» **Joining the military**

» **Signing up for AmeriCorps VISTA**

Chapter **11**

Getting Ready for Life After High School

A fter high school, your life changes considerably. This sounds dramatic, but it's true! Although those days leading up to your high school graduation can be exciting and fun — and also overwhelmingly emotional and stressful — you actually need to start thinking about life after high school much earlier than graduation time.

While the ideal time to start preparing for life after high school can be as early as freshman year, most people start getting really serious in their junior year.

There are so *many* options once high school ends — and while college is one excellent route, remember that it is not your only option. There are many ways to earn money and develop skills that are not connected to the traditional college route.

This might feel like a heavy load for a 17- or 18-year-old, hope-fully, this chapter can help you to discover what path you want your life to take after you earn that diploma.

Weighing Your Options After High School

As we said, college is an option, but it's not the *only* option. If you're not sure college is for you, you should research and consider other options. If you are unsure about what you want to do after leaving high school, doing this research will offer you some great ways to discover more about yourself and your strengths.

Taking personality quizzes

Personality tests are like a mirror for your brain and heart. They're designed to help you figure out your strengths, weaknesses, and natural tendencies. Tests like the Myers-Briggs Type Indicator (MBTI), Enneagram, and the Big Five personality traits are popular options, but there are tons of them out there.

If you know you thrive in creative environments, maybe a career in graphic design or writing is your jam. If you love logic and order, engineering or accounting might be more your speed. Rihanna, for instance, likely used her bold creativity to become both a music star and a beauty mogul. You can do the same; use your traits to guide your choices.

TIP

When looking for answers, be sure to find a reliable test. Free options include 16Personalities or Truity; for deeper insights, try Gallup's Clifton StrengthsFinder. Take it seriously, but not too seriously; the results are a guide, not a rulebook. Match traits to possibilities. Use what you find out to research college majors, trade programs, and careers.

Your personality can guide more than your career; it can shape how you balance hobbies, relationships, and even part-time jobs. Introverts might thrive in independent or remote work.

Extroverts might love team-oriented or public-facing roles. Detail-oriented people could explore technical fields. The key is starting with what feels natural and building from there.

Researching job requirements

Planning life after high school can feel overwhelming, but researching job requirements is like drawing a map for your journey. It helps you to understand what's ahead, focus your efforts, and make informed decisions. Plus, knowing what's expected gives you confidence and eases the stress of stepping into the unknown.

Start by exploring jobs that align with your interests, skills, or hobbies. For example, if you love building things, careers in construction or engineering might excite you. Enjoy connecting with others? Healthcare or teaching could be a great fit. From there, dive into resources like O*NET OnLine or the U.S. Bureau of Labor Statistics to find details about required education and skills, as well as salary expectations. Checking company websites and job postings on LinkedIn can also give you a clearer picture of what employers are looking for.

TIP

When researching, pay attention to key details like education requirements (high school diploma, trade certification, or degree), necessary skills (technical or soft skills), and experience levels (internships or apprenticeships). It's also smart to consider practical factors like salary, job outlook, and location to see if the role matches your lifestyle goals.

If you're still unsure, connect with people in the field. Attend career fairs, ask questions at info sessions, or reach out to professionals online to hear firsthand about their experiences. Their insights can help you understand what the day-to-day job looks like and whether it's something you'd enjoy.

Taking time to research job requirements not only clarifies what steps you need to take, but also helps you feel prepared and motivated. Whether you're planning to enter the workforce, go to a trade school, or pursue a degree, this groundwork can make all the difference.

Considering a Gap Year

Not everyone knows exactly what they want to do after high school. Some people feel pressure to jump straight into college, while others aren't so sure. If you're feeling stuck, taking a gap year might be worth considering.

A gap year is when you take a year off between high school and your next step. It can be a chance to figure out what you really want out of life, gain new experiences, and prepare for what comes next. But like any major decision, it's not all sunshine and Instagram-worthy travel photos.

Taking a gap year — benefits

Emma Watson — yes, Hermione Granger herself — is an example. She took a gap year before attending Brown University to focus on acting and promoting women's rights. Her time off allowed her to explore her passions and return to school more focused and driven. While your gap year might not include Hollywood premieres, it can still be life-changing.

Giving yourself time to explore your interests

Taking a gap year gives you the freedom to explore your interests before committing to a college major or career path. Whether it's volunteering abroad, taking on a job, or trying a new hobby, this year can be all about you figuring out what makes you excited to get out of bed in the morning. It's like giving yourself a personal reset button.

Developing valuable skills

During a gap year, you're not just sitting around. Many people use this time to build soft skills like independence, adaptability, and problem-solving. These qualities are not only helpful in life, but they also look great on a college application or resume. Imagine walking into college already knowing how to manage your time, budget your money, or even speak a second language.

Easing the transition to college

For students who feel burned out after high school, a gap year can be helpful. Taking a break can recharge your batteries and prepare you mentally for the challenges of college. Studies show that students who take a gap year often perform better academically because they enter school with a clearer sense of purpose.

Taking a gap year — downsides

Gap years aren't all good. There are some huge downsides and barriers to exercising the option to take a gap year. The best way to make a good decision is to weigh the pros and cons of your option. Let's talk about some of the downsides of taking a gap year.

Looking at financial barriers

Let's be real: Taking a gap year can cost money. Traveling, volunteering, or even living at home while working requires some level of financial planning. Without a clear budget, you could end up spending more than you can afford. That's why it's important to plan ahead and consider affordable options like local internships or part-time jobs.

TIP

To avoid financial stress, look for programs with scholarships or consider working part of the year to save money. To combat social pressures, stay in touch with friends and remind yourself why you chose this path. Communicating your plans to supportive friends and family can help you feel less isolated.

Facing social pressures

There's also the fear of falling behind. Watching your friends head off to college while you're still figuring things out can be tough. But remember, life isn't a race. Taking the time to make the right decision for you is more important than keeping up with anyone else's timeline.

REMEMBER

The gap year is intended to only be one year and to use to plan and prepare for your next step. If you are able to take a gap year, be sure to have a plan — without one, a year can go by very quickly without your coming closer to figuring out what you want to do next.

Attending Community College

Starting your college journey at a community college can be a smart and empowering choice, even if it doesn't seem like the traditional path. About 41 percent of all undergraduates in the U.S. attend community colleges, so you're in good company. These schools often offer flexible class schedules, lower tuition costs, and smaller class sizes, making them a great option for students easing into college life.

Let's say you're unsure of your major or want to save money while deciding. Attending community college can save you thousands of dollars. On average, tuition and fees at public community colleges are around $3,860 annually, compared to $10,950 at public four-year institutions (according to College Board Research). That's money you can save or use to transfer to your dream school later on. Plus, many community colleges have articulation agreements with four-year universities, which makes transferring your credits much easier.

TIP

Before committing, check out the transfer policies of any four-year colleges you're considering. Planning ahead ensures your hard work will count toward your bachelor's degree.

If your plan is to start at a community college and transfer to a four-year school (see the next section for more on four-year colleges), you're not alone. Roughly 80 percent of community college students aim to transfer to a four-year school, and many succeed according to the National Center for Education Statistics (NCES). Starting small can help you build confidence, save money, and explore your options before committing to a four-year institution.

Think about it this way: You spend two years acing your classes at community college, then transfer to your dream school as a junior. You've got fewer loans and just as much campus spirit. It's a win-win!

TIP

Meet with your academic advisor regularly to ensure you're on track with transfer requirements. Missing a detail could cost you time or credits.

STARTING COLLEGE WHILE STILL IN HIGH SCHOOL

Dual enrollment programs give high school students the chance to earn college credits early. It's like a two-for-one deal on college courses without full college costs! Beyond the cost savings, dual enrollment can help you adjust to college-level work while still having the safety net of high school.

Imagine leaving high school already halfway done with an associate degree or skipping some intro courses when you eventually transfer. That's a time- and money-saver. Just make sure the credits you earn align with your future academic goals.

Talk to your school counselor about dual enrollment options and how they fit into your plans for college or career training.

Looking at community college — the benefits

Community colleges shine when it comes to accessibility, flexibility, and affordability. Whether you're balancing a part-time job or exploring a career change, community colleges provide the wiggle room you need.

They also offer hands-on training in fields like nursing, tech, and trades, so if you're eager to dive into a career, this might be your best bet. Plus, smaller class sizes mean you'll get to know your professors, and that can translate into better mentorship and guidance.

Looking at community college — the downsides

Of course, it's not all sunshine and tuition savings. One downside is the stigma some people attach to community colleges. But let's be real: Anyone judging you for making smart financial choices isn't paying your bills.

Another challenge can be the lack of a "traditional" college experience. If you're looking for football games and Greek life, that's harder to find at a community college. And for transfer students, navigating the transfer process can feel overwhelming without the right guidance.

Attending a Four-Year College

Choosing a four-year college can feel like the ultimate rite of passage after high school, but it's not a one-size-fits-all decision. Whether you're thinking about living on a picturesque campus, diving into rigorous academics, or joining an epic intramural frisbee team, let's explore the world of traditional four-year colleges to help you make an informed choice.

Don't worry, we give more detailed information about getting into your dream college in Chapter 12.

Examining private versus public colleges

Private and public colleges may seem like they belong in completely different worlds, but the reality is a bit more nuanced. Public colleges are often state-funded and typically offer lower tuition rates for in-state students. They also tend to have larger campuses and more diverse academic programs. On the flip side, private colleges often boast smaller class sizes, which can mean more personalized attention from professors (often at a higher price tag).

TIP

Don't just focus on the sticker price. Both public and private colleges offer financial aid, and private institutions sometimes have more generous scholarships. Research your options thoroughly before ruling anything out.

Looking at traditional colleges — the benefits

Four-year colleges offer more than just a degree. You'll get access to on-campus resources, such as libraries, career centers, and networking opportunities. You'll also be surrounded by peers, which can make it easier to form connections and create lifelong friendships. It's like an exclusive incubator where you grow and develop into an adult.

Another major perk? Many careers require a bachelor's degree as a minimum qualification. By attending a four-year college, you may open doors to job opportunities that might otherwise be out of reach. According to the National Center for Education Statistics (NCES), individuals with bachelor's degrees earn an average of $26,000 more annually than those with only a high school diploma.

TIP

Join clubs, attend campus events, and get to know your professors. These experiences are just as valuable as your classes when building your future.

Looking at traditional colleges — the downsides

Traditional colleges aren't without their challenges. Cost is a significant factor, with the average yearly tuition for a public four-year college being $10,740 for in-state students and $27,560 for out-of-state students. Private college tuition averages $38,070 per year. These numbers don't even include housing, meal plans, or textbooks.

Additionally, the transition to college life can be overwhelming. Balancing a full course load, extracurriculars, and a social life takes practice. Some students may also feel pressured to choose a major before they're ready, which can lead to unnecessary stress.

REMEMBER

Take the time to explore your interests before committing to a major. Many colleges offer first-year programs designed to help you discover what excites you.

Attending a Trade School

Not everyone's post-high-school journey needs to include dorm rooms, lectures, and endless papers. Trade schools, also known as vocational or technical schools, offer a direct path into specific careers that often come with job security and solid paychecks. These schools focus on teaching practical skills, whether you're interested in becoming a mechanic, dental hygienist, electrician, or chef.

Trade schools stand out because of their shorter timelines. Many programs take two years or less to complete, which means you can start earning a paycheck faster than your peers who are heading to traditional colleges. Plus, these careers often align with high-demand fields, so finding a job after graduation is usually straightforward.

Researching different trades

Choosing a trade that aligns with your skills and interests is the first step. If you enjoy working with technology, consider paths like IT technician or auto mechanic. Creative minds might thrive in fields like cosmetology or culinary arts, while those seeking job stability could explore healthcare or skilled trades such as HVAC technician or electrician.

To dig deeper, browse job boards like Indeed or Glassdoor to compare salaries, job growth, and demand for specific trades. Local career counseling offices and trade-specific associations are also excellent resources. If possible, spend a day shadowing a professional in the trade you're considering. This hands-on experience can confirm whether it's the right fit for you.

Filling out trade school applications

Trade school applications are often simpler than college applications. Most schools don't require SAT/ACT scores or lengthy essays, but you may need a high school diploma or equivalent. Here's how to get started.

>> **Find accredited programs:** Use sites like CareerOneStop (www.careeronestop.org/) to locate trade schools recognized for quality education.

>> **Gather your documents:** These typically include transcripts, proof of identity, and letters of recommendation.

>> **Write a compelling statement (if required):** Some programs may ask for a short essay about your career goals (keep it clear and focused).

REMEMBER

Apply for financial aid! Many trade schools accept federal aid, so fill out the Free Application for Federal Student Aid (FAFSA) form. Additionally, look into scholarships specific to your trade.

Looking at trade school — the benefits

Trade schools come with plenty of advantages, starting with their shorter programs. Most programs take between six months and two years to complete, meaning you'll enter the workforce and start earning money faster. The cost is another big perk. While the average cost of a four-year college is over $132,000, trade schools average about $33,000, making them a far more affordable option.

TIP

Job security is also a significant benefit. Many skilled trades are recession-proof because people will always need electricians, plumbers, and healthcare workers. And the pay can be great, too. Careers like electrician and radiation therapist often start at over $50,000 per year, with room for growth as you gain experience.

Looking at trade school — the downsides

While trade schools have many benefits, they aren't without challenges. One drawback is their limited flexibility. Unlike a college degree that opens doors to various career paths, trade schools focus on one specific skill, which can make changing careers later more difficult.

Social experience is another consideration. Trade schools don't typically offer the same vibrant campus life or networking opportunities that traditional colleges provide. Additionally, while trade schools are generally more affordable than colleges, they can still be expensive upfront, and not all programs offer financial aid.

However, many trade schools include apprenticeships, allowing students to earn money while they learn, which can offset some costs.

There are some similarities between going to college and going to a trade school. Figure 11-1 illustrates how the options compare and contrast.

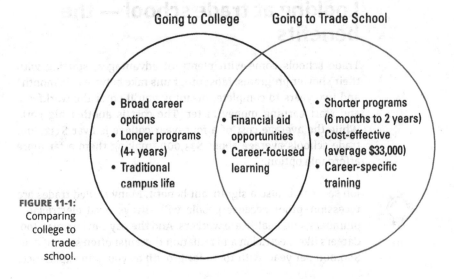

Going to College   Going to Trade School

- Broad career options
- Longer programs (4+ years)
- Traditional campus life

- Financial aid opportunities
- Career-focused learning

- Shorter programs (6 months to 2 years)
- Cost-effective (average $33,000)
- Career-specific training

FIGURE 11-1: Comparing college to trade school.

Choosing to Join the Military

Deciding to join the military is a big step and one that can open up unique opportunities for education, career growth, and personal development. It's a path that requires careful consideration, preparation, and plenty of research. The military has many options to join and serve your country:

>> ROTC (Reserves Officer Training Corps): a college program where students train to become commissioned officers in the military

>> The Reserve: part-time military service where you maintain a civilian job

>> Enlist: joining the military as an enlisted member, typically with a full-time active duty commitment

Whether you're interested in serving full-time or exploring options like ROTC or the reserves while attending college, this section will help you understand what to expect.

Taking the ASVAB

The Armed Services Vocational Aptitude Battery (ASVAB) is a critical first step for anyone considering the military. This test determines your eligibility for enlistment and helps identify which roles within the military are the best fit for your skills and interests.

To prepare, start by understanding the test structure, which includes sections on mathematics, vocabulary, mechanical comprehension, and more. Use free online practice tests, flashcards, and ASVAB prep books to strengthen your skills. You can find resources through the official ASVAB website and even at your local library.

TIP

Check out 2025/2026 ASVAB For Dummies, which includes practice tests, flashcards, and videos online.

TIP

Take multiple practice tests to get familiar with the format and identify areas where you need improvement. Scores matter, as higher scores can open up more job opportunities.

Researching the military's different branches

The U.S. military is made up of six branches:

>> Army

>> Navy

>> Air Force

>> Marine Corps

>> Coast Guard

>> Space Force

Each branch offers different roles, missions, and commitments. For instance, the Navy focuses on maritime operations, while the Air Force emphasizes aerial and space missions.

You also have options like the Reserves, joining ROTC in college, or attending a military academy (such as Westpoint), which can allow you to balance military service with civilian life or further education.

REMEMBER

Talk to a recruiter from each branch to get a clear understanding of what they offer. Make sure their answers align with your goals and values.

Preparing for boot camp

Boot camp, or basic training, is designed to prepare recruits physically and mentally for military life. It can be intense, but knowing what to expect can make it less intimidating.

Start preparing by building a fitness routine that includes running, strength training, and endurance exercises. Pay attention to guidelines provided by your chosen branch to ensure you're meeting their fitness standards.

TIP

Focus on teamwork and adaptability. Boot camp isn't just about individual performance; it's about learning to work as part of a team.

On the mental side, practice self-discipline and organization. Boot camp requires early mornings, strict schedules, and attention to detail. Good thing these are skills you'll rely on throughout your military career.

Joining military life — the benefits

Military service can provide a strong sense of purpose and community, which can be rewarding for those seeking structure and camaraderie.

Joining the military offers benefits that extend beyond a steady paycheck.

>> **Education opportunities:** The GI Bill can cover college tuition and living expenses after your service, and some branches offer tuition assistance while you serve.

>> **Skill development:** You'll gain valuable skills in areas like leadership, problem-solving, and technical expertise.

>> **Career pathways:** Many veterans find successful careers in civilian industries, thanks to the training and experience gained during service.

>> **Travel and adventure:** Serving in the military often comes with the opportunity to travel and experience new cultures.

Joining military life — the downsides

While the military offers many advantages, it's not without its challenges.

>> **Physical and emotional demands:** Military life can be physically and mentally exhausting, especially during deployments or combat situations.

>> **Time commitment:** Enlisting typically requires a multi-year commitment, which can delay other life goals like attending college or starting a civilian career.

>> **Separation from family and friends:** Long deployments can be tough on relationships and personal connections.

TIP

Speak with current or former service members to get a realistic view of what military life is like. Hearing firsthand experiences can help you decide if this path is right for you.

Going to AmeriCorps VISTA

AmeriCorps VISTA (Volunteers in Service to America) offers a unique opportunity to make a real difference in communities across the U.S. while gaining valuable skills for your future. It's ideal if you're passionate about service and want to address challenges like poverty, education, or community development. Unlike college or traditional career paths, joining AmeriCorps allows you to learn by doing and to directly impact people's lives.

AmeriCorps offers a range of projects, so whether you're interested in education, public health, environmental work, or another area, there's likely a program that aligns with your passions.

Getting started with AmeriCorps VISTA

AmeriCorps VISTA requires a one-year commitment, so be sure you're ready to dedicate that time to service. If AmeriCorps VISTA feels like a good fit for you, here are some next steps:

>> **Research opportunities:** Check out the official AmeriCorps website (www.americorps.gov/serve/americorps/americorps-vista) for available positions and programs.

>> **Prepare your application:** AmeriCorps applications often ask for essays about why you want to serve and how your skills align with their mission. Take the time to write thoughtful responses.

Focus on your passion for service and any experiences that show your dedication to helping others.

>> **Talk to alumni:** Reach out to former AmeriCorps members through social media or local networks. They can provide valuable insights into what to expect and how to prepare.

Joining AmeriCorps — the benefits

AmeriCorps alumni often report that the experience gave them clarity about their career goals and helped them build confidence in their abilities.

There are several upsides to choosing AmeriCorps VISTA as a post-high school or post-college option.

>> **Skill development:** You'll gain practical skills like project management, leadership, and problem-solving. These are valuable for future careers or college applications.

>> **Living allowance and education award:** While the stipend isn't large, it's enough to cover basic living expenses. Plus, after completing your service, you can receive an education award that you can use to pay for college or student loans.

Make a budget before starting your service to ensure the stipend lasts throughout the year.

>> **Networking opportunities:** You'll work alongside professionals and community leaders, building relationships that could open doors in the future.

>> **Making an impact:** AmeriCorps VISTA focuses on capacity building, as well as helping organizations grow and sustain their efforts. Your work can have a lasting effect on the community you serve.

Joining AmeriCorps — the downsides

While AmeriCorps has many benefits, it's important to be aware of the challenges.

>> **Low living allowance:** The stipend is designed to help you live modestly, but it may not cover unexpected expenses. This can be especially challenging if you're in a high-cost area.

>> **Emotional challenges:** The work you'll do can be emotionally demanding, especially if you're addressing tough issues like poverty or homelessness.

TIP

Take care of your mental health by setting boundaries and seeking support when needed. AmeriCorps offers resources to help its members.

>> **Commitment length:** A full-year commitment may feel overwhelming if you're not sure what you want to do in the long term.

REMEMBER

It's okay to take the time to decide if AmeriCorps fits your goals before applying.

IN THIS CHAPTER

» Deciding on whether to go to college

» Looking at what colleges require from you

» Taking the SAT or ACT

» Building a strong college application

» Completing applications that show your best self

Chapter **12**

Getting Into Your Dream College

G oing to college is a huge financial decision, not just for you but for all the people that love and support you as well. Preparing to get into your dream college is a big task that takes a lot of work and time. (We cover your options after high school in Chapter 11.)

Before we get into this chapter, you need to do a little daydreaming, researching, and reflecting.

Daydreaming. Imagine what job or career you would like to have in the future. Consider some of your favorite mentors, teachers, family members, television shows, and books. What jobs did the people you admired have? What did you like about their lifestyle? Imagine yourself doing the same job as them; what does your life look like? What college did they attend? What do they say about their college experience? Think about what college experience you want to have. What college fits the aesthetics you are looking to create for your life?

Researching. Research your dream job. Be sure to find out what degrees you need, how much the median salary is for new graduates, and what other expenses are required (such as licenses, insurance, and continuing education). You should also include the potential workplace hazards in your research to help you weigh the pros and cons. Research what industries the job is available in, as well as the different career tracks that are open in that industry. For example, if you want to be a medical doctor, the industry is healthcare; however, you can choose either a patient care track or a clinical research track (both tracks have very different requirements). Maybe you want to consider a career in the accounting field. You can be an accountant in the automotive industry or in the software tech industry. Research your top three colleges that you imagine attending. Review the entry requirements, potential majors and programs, notable alumni, location, school size, and cost of attendance.

Salary ranges by location, experience, education, and industry. The median salary is a better indicator than the average salary because outliers cannot skew the data.

Reflecting. After researching all the information you can think of, reflect on your dream career and your dream college. Does the college you dream of attending have the major or program you need to get to your dream career? Do you care more about going to your dream college or getting your dream career after graduation? Do you imagine yourself at a huge university or do you prefer to be in a smaller, family-like environment? If cost was not an issue, what school would meet all your needs and wants?

Deciding If College Might Be Right for You

College isn't the right choice for every person, but college might be right for you if. . .

>> You have a specific career path in mind that requires a degree (like being a teacher, nurse, engineer, or lawyer).

>> You're interested in taking advantage of internships or study-abroad programs that are often facilitated by universities.

>> You qualify for scholarships, financial aid, or other support that makes college more affordable for you.

>> You're excited about the idea of studying under experts, exploring new subjects, and developing specialized skills.

>> You've found colleges with programs or majors that align with your career goals and interests.

>> You've weighed the financial commitment and believe the potential opportunities after graduation make it worth the investment.

>> You value connecting with professors, classmates, and alumni who can support your journey and open doors for you.

If you can check off at least four of these, college might be the right move for you! Remember, your choice doesn't have to be perfect. It just needs to support your long-term dreams and goals.

Ticking Off the College Requirement Checklist

Once you have decided that college is the right fit for you, you must prepare in high school to get to that next college level. For this section, keep your number-one dream school in mind. All of the high school prep work you do will be designed to make sure you get a golden acceptance letter (with scholarships).

Taking the required courses

Think of high school courses as the foundation of your dream home; skip the essentials, and you're left with wobbly walls. Colleges love to see you challenge yourself with core classes: English, math, science, social studies, and a foreign language. Some competitive schools also require advanced classes like

Advanced Placement (AP), International Baccalaureate (IB), or honors courses.

TIP

Check the specific course requirements for your dream colleges early. This can keep you focused and ensures that when you are ready to apply for you dream school you meet the basic requirements. The more time you have to prepare the better you chances are of getting accepted.

Beyond the basics, sprinkle in electives that showcase your interests. If you want to study engineering, courses like physics or computer programming are like golden tickets. Dreaming of an art degree? Take advanced art classes or portfolio workshops. The classes you take in high school will give you the knowledge you need to get started on a high note in college.

Action Steps:

>> Meet with your guidance counselor to map out a four-year plan. (If you are starting later than your freshman year, that's okay! Create your plan with your counselor starting now.)

>> Research course requirements for colleges or programs you're eyeing.

>> Don't overload your schedule just to impress; it's better to do well in balanced courses than drown in stress.

Getting good grades

Good grades are like VIP passes to the college of your dreams. Yes, you're more than a GPA, but let's be real: a high GPA opens doors (and scholarships). Make academics a priority by staying organized and asking for help when needed. Study groups, tutoring, or even YouTube videos can be game changers.

Remember, colleges love to see growth. If you failed your freshman-year algebra test but came back swinging with As, that tells a story of resilience. Everyone cannot be number 1 in their class or a straight-A student, and you don't have to be to get into a great college.

If you are having trouble or feel like you need educational support, be sure to let a trusted adult (teacher, counselor, mentor, or parent) know. Learning differences and disabilities can make it harder for you to be a great student, but getting accommodations will help you succeed. Do not be afraid to speak up for yourself.

Action Steps:

>> Set up a study schedule and stick to it.

>> Use tools like planners or apps to keep assignments on track.

>> Don't be afraid to talk to teachers for extra help (they want you to succeed!).

Grades matter, but so does your mental health. Take breaks and recharge!

Participating in extracurricular activities

Extracurriculars are your chance to show colleges what makes you *you*. Whether it's playing on the soccer team, joining the debate club, or becoming the star of your school's *Hamilton* production, your activities reflect your passions.

Quality beats quantity here. It's better to be deeply involved in a few things than to spread yourself thin. If leadership opportunities pop up, consider becoming a part of your club's leadership team. Even better, start your own club or school initiative! Colleges love leaders who can collaborate and inspire.

Action Steps:

>> Explore clubs, sports, or creative outlets that match your interests.

>> Don't see something you love? Start your own club!

>> Aim for leadership roles or long-term commitment to show dedication.

REMEMBER

These activities should bring you joy. Don't do something just to look good on paper (it'll show).

Engaging in community service

Volunteering is a win-win: you help your community *and* your future. Colleges value applicants who give back because it shows compassion, responsibility, and initiative. Think beyond the bake sales and aim for meaningful work.

Love animals? Volunteer at a shelter. Passionate about social justice? Join local advocacy groups. The key is consistency; committing to one organization over time has a bigger impact than sporadic efforts.

Action Steps:

>> Look for volunteer opportunities through your school or local nonprofits.

>> Track your hours and experiences for scholarship and college applications.

>> Reflect on what you learned (colleges often ask about this in essays!).

Getting stellar recommendations

A glowing recommendation can make your application shine. But it's not just about picking someone with a fancy title, it's about choosing someone who *knows you well*. Teachers, coaches, and mentors who can highlight your strengths are your best bet.

Ask early and politely. Provide a list of your achievements, goals, and the deadline to help them craft a thoughtful letter. Remember, your teachers and mentors are on your side and want you to win; they are excited to help you get to the next level by writing a letter that will highlight all the best parts of you.

REQUESTING A LETTER OF RECOMMENDATION IN WRITING: TWO EXAMPLES

When it comes to applying to college, a strong letter of recommendation can make a lasting impression on admissions committees. Whether you're reaching out to a teacher, coach, employer, or mentor, how you ask can influence their ability to craft a meaningful and impactful letter. Use these examples as a guide to approach your potential recommenders confidently and professionally.

Formal Request to Someone You Don't Know Intimately

Subject: Request for a Letter of Recommendation

Dear [Recipient's Name],

I hope this message finds you well. My name is [Your Name], and I am currently [your position, e.g., "a senior at [High School Name]"]. I am reaching out to ask if you would be willing to write a letter of recommendation for my college application.

I greatly admire [specific quality or experience about the person, e.g., "your teaching approach in AP English, which helped me refine my writing skills"]. I believe your insights into my [specific strength or trait, e.g., "dedication to academic growth and creativity"] would provide a valuable perspective to the admissions committees.

I am applying to [name of colleges/programs], and the deadline for submitting the letter is [date]. If you agree, I would be happy to provide you with my resume, details of my achievements, and any other materials that may assist you in writing the letter.

Please let me know if you are available or if you have any questions. Thank you so much for considering my request — it would mean a great deal to me.

Best regards,

[Your Full Name]

(continued)

(continued)

[Your Contact Information]

_____

Informal Note to Someone You Know Intimately

Subject: Huge Favor

Hi [Recipient's Name],

I hope you're doing well! I'm working on my college applications, and I was wondering if you'd be willing to write me a letter of recommendation. Since you've seen [specific context, e.g., "how I handled leadership challenges in the debate team"], I think you'd be able to highlight some key aspects of my work ethic and character.

The deadline is [date], and I'd be happy to share more details about my applications or anything else that might help you write the letter. Let me know if this is something you can do — I'd really appreciate it!

Thanks so much,

[Your Name]

Action Steps:

>> Build relationships with teachers, counselors, and mentors now.

>> Request letters well before deadlines (at least a month ahead).

>> Follow up with a thank-you note to show your appreciation.

Working with your guidance counselor

Your guidance counselor is like your college prep GPS; they will guide you to the right steps you need to take to successfully get that acceptance letter from your dream school. They can help you pick the right courses, narrow down college choices, and understand financial aid options. They have quizzes, questionnaires, and worksheets to help you get clear on jobs and colleges, too. Don't be shy about asking for help at every stage of the process. (It's what they are paid to do!)

Action Steps:

>> Schedule regular check-ins to stay on track.

>> Come prepared with questions and goals.

>> Be open about your dreams and concerns; they're there to support you!

What to ask your counselor:

Freshman/sophomore year: Starting off strong

"What courses should I take to prepare for college and meet graduation requirements?"

"How can I get involved in extracurricular activities that align with my future goals?"

"Are there any summer programs, internships, or workshops you recommend?"

Junior year: Narrowing down options

"What colleges or programs match my academic interests and career goals?"

"Can you help me understand and prepare for standardized tests like the SAT or ACT?"

"What scholarships or financial aid options should I start researching now?"

Senior year: Polishing and finalizing

"Can you review my college applications and essays to ensure they're strong?"

"What should I know about FAFSA and other financial aid processes?"

"Can you write me a recommendation letter, and how can I support you in doing so?"

College-Readiness Programs

Outside of your in-school activities, college-readiness programs are a great way to give you an idea of what it will be like to transition into your smarter, cooler college version of yourself. There are many different types of programs (some are free, some are not). If your family cannot afford to pay for expensive college-readiness programs, that is perfectly fine; there are some amazing programs that don't cost a dime.

Dreams don't just happen; they're built, and sometimes they need a little extra help to come true. Meet our friends Taylor and Brianna, two high school sophomores with big plans to attend Hampton University, a prestigious HBCU known for its rich history and incredible alumni network.

Taylor and Brianna couldn't have been more different. Taylor was the top student in their class with glowing grades but was worried about the cost of college. Brianna, on the other hand, struggled academically after a rocky freshman year and didn't have the same resources as her peers. Despite their challenges, both girls were determined to make it to Hampton. The secret to their success? College-readiness programs.

Finding free programs

Brianna's journey started with a conversation with her guidance counselor (yes, that's the person you should *definitely* talk to). Her counselor told her about Upward Bound, a free program funded by the federal government. She applied and was accepted into a summer program that offered her the structure and support she needed: tutoring sessions, essay-writing workshops, and a chance to visit college campuses. Brianna isn't the only one who benefitted from Upward Bound. I (Mykail) attended the

Howard University Upward Bound Math and Science program in high school and still connect with the students years after graduating.

For students like Brianna, free programs are a lifeline. If you're looking for something similar, start by checking out the following:

>> TRIO programs like Upward Bound

>> Local community organizations that offer free college prep classes

>> Online resources like Khan Academy for SAT prep

TIP

Research free programs in your area or online. Many schools and community organizations partner with nonprofits to provide resources at no cost. Ask your counselor or teachers for recommendations; they often have connections to free services.

Paying for programs

Taylor, on the other hand, had more financial flexibility. Their parents signed her up for a paid summer college-readiness program through a nearby university. It wasn't cheap, but it offered a ton of perks: small-group SAT prep, one-on-one essay coaching, and even networking events with admissions officers.

Taylor took full advantage of the program, attending every session, and asking a million questions. By the time they applied to Hampton, their essays were practically award-winning, and her SAT score had jumped significantly.

Paid programs can be a worthwhile investment, but they're not for everyone. If you're considering this route, look for programs that offer the following:

>> A clear schedule of activities and deliverables

>> Access to experienced mentors and coaches

>> Scholarship or financial aid options

TIP

Research paid programs and evaluate their benefits versus costs. Look into programs like Pre-College Summer Institutes at major universities. If the cost is high, don't hesitate to ask about scholarships or fee waivers.

Following different paths to success

By the time senior year rolled around, both Taylor and Brianna were ready. They had discovered how to ace interviews, write standout essays, and navigate the college application process. Brianna's free program gave her the guidance she needed to stay on track and improve her grades. Taylor's paid program helped them polish her already-strong application.

The result? Both girls were accepted to Hampton University with scholarships. While their journeys looked different, their determination and hard work were the common threads.

Taylor and Brianna proved that regardless of your background or starting point, success is possible when you're willing to work for it. Your dream school is waiting for you. Whether you're joining a free program, investing in a paid one, or blazing your own trail, take that first step today. The future is yours to create, and trust us, you're going to crush it.

Taking Your Standardized Tests

Sometimes your dream school may require you to take a standardized test. The SAT and ACT are the most common college admissions tests that you need to be accepted. It is also important to do your best on these tests to qualify for scholarships and grants (helping to lower the cost of college).

Tests are just one part of your application, not the whole story. Many colleges now allow you to apply without a test score, so don't let it define you. College admissions committees care about who you are as a person, not just how well you filled in bubbles.

Preparing for your tests

Standardized tests might sound intimidating, but with the right preparation, you can crush them like a pro. First things first: Build your confidence! Think of the test as a marathon, not a sprint. The more practice you put in, the better you'll perform.

Simulate the test environment. Take timed practice tests to get used to the pacing and pressure (it's like warming up before the big game).

Here's a timeline to keep you on track.

>> **Sophomore year:** Familiarize yourself with the test format. Take a free online practice test from Khan Academy (for SAT prep) or ACT.org.

>> **Junior year:** Enroll in a test prep program if needed; paid options like Magoosh or free community workshops can work wonders. Create a study schedule and stick to it, focusing on areas where you need improvement.

>> **Senior year:** Retake the test if your first score isn't where you want it to be. Many students improve significantly on their second attempt, so don't stress if it doesn't go perfectly the first time.

Action Steps to prep:

>> Use tools like flashcards, apps (like Quizlet), and prep books from your local library.

>> Join study groups or partner up with friends to keep each other accountable.

>> Don't cram! Space out your studying and give yourself time to absorb the material.

If your score isn't as high as you hoped, it's okay! Many schools are now test-optional, meaning they don't require a test score to apply. Focus on making other parts of your application shine, like your essays, extracurriculars, and recommendations.

Affording the test fees

Standardized tests come with a price tag, but there are ways to lighten the load. If the $60-ish fee for the SAT or ACT feels like a stretch, check if you're eligible for a fee waiver. These waivers are available through your school counselor and cover not only the actual test, but often other related costs like score reports that are sent to colleges.

Beyond fee waivers, here are some tips for reducing costs:

>> Borrow prep books from your library instead of buying new ones.

>> Look for free online test prep resources like Khan Academy or ACT's free study guides.

>> Find community organizations or local nonprofits that offer free or discounted prep courses.

TIP

If your family's budget is tight and you qualify for a fee waiver, not only can you take the test for free, but you can also use free prep tools like those offered by Khan Academy. You could even join a local test prep class at no cost through a community program.

TIP

Consider test-related expenses like transportation. If the test center is far, plan ahead to carpool with friends or ask a family member for a ride. Every little bit of planning helps.

Filling Out Your College Applications

You've done the research, aced your tests, and gathered the grades. Now comes the big moment: applying to your dream school. This process might feel like a marathon, but it's really a series of manageable steps. Each application is an opportunity to tell your story. Who are you? What makes you tick? Why should the school pick *you* out of thousands of applicants?

Think of this as curating your greatest hits album. Every section — your essays, activities, recommendations, and transcripts — is another track that shows off your range. With some planning and focus, you can hit all the right notes.

Using the Common App

The Common Application, often called the Common App, is a lifesaver for students applying to multiple colleges. It lets you fill out one application and send it to many schools at once. However, don't mistake it for a one-size-fits-all deal. Many colleges still require supplemental essays and unique materials, so staying organized is crucial.

Here are four steps to using the Common App to apply to your dream school (and some of those back up schools on your list):

1. **Create an account early:** The application opens in August, but you can start browsing colleges on the platform sooner.

2. **Gather your documents:** Have your high school transcript, standardized test scores, and a list of extracurricular activities on hand.

3. **Craft your activity descriptions:** Use action-oriented language to showcase your achievements. Instead of "Helped with school play," write, "Organized and managed props for a cast of 20, ensuring smooth performance nights." You can always research a list of action-packed verbs to have handy when writing.

4. **Tackle the personal essay thoughtfully:** This is your big moment to shine. Take time to brainstorm, draft, and revise.

Applying to specific schools

While the Common App streamlines applications for many colleges, some schools prefer their own systems. These schools often have unique requirements, which might include longer essays, portfolios, or specific recommendations. Elite schools, such as Georgetown University, MIT, and Harvard, require potential students to apply directly. Some state-specific universities do not use the Common App, either (check their websites for more details).

Here's how to handle direct applications.

>> **Start with research:** Each school has its own portal. Bookmark important deadlines and requirements.

>> **Tailor your essays:** Use existing content when possible, but customize it for the school's specific prompts.

>> **Submit all required materials:** Some schools require unique documents like a resume or additional test scores.

Direct applications might feel like overkill, but they're an excellent opportunity to stand out by showing your dedication.

Preparing for college interviews

If your dream school offers interviews, consider it an opportunity to impress in person. Admissions interviews can feel intimidating, but they're more like friendly conversations. Think of them as a chance to give depth to your application.

Here are some tips to help you ace your college interview.

>> **Do your homework:** Know the school's mission, programs, and unique features. This shows genuine interest.

>> **Practice common questions:** These might include, "Why do you want to attend this school?" and "What's an academic challenge you've overcome?"

>> **Be yourself:** Don't recite a script. Highlight your passions and experiences with authenticity.

Dress neatly (business casual is safe), bring a resume, and send a thank-you note afterward. Even small gestures, like emailing a polite follow-up, can leave a lasting impression.

Writing a good college essay

The college essay is your golden ticket to stand out. Admissions officers sift through thousands of applications, so your essay needs to grab their attention and leave a lasting impression. No pressure, right?

TIP

The best essays aren't flashy. They're authentic. Write about something meaningful to you, not what you think they want to hear.

Here are some tips for a standout essay.

> » **Choose a topic that matters:** It doesn't have to be dramatic. A simple story about a lesson learned can be just as powerful.

> » **Show, don't tell:** Instead of saying, "I'm a leader," describe a moment where you led others to solve a problem.

> » **Proofread like your future depends on it:** Typos and grammar errors can distract from your message.

Want more essay tips? Flip to the "Part of Tens" section later in this book for detailed guidance. For now, remember that this is your chance to speak directly to the admissions team; let them hear *your* voice.

Paying for application fees

Applying to college isn't just about essays and transcripts; it also comes with a price tag. Application fees can range from $25 to $90 per school, which adds up quickly if you're applying to several colleges. The good news? You don't have to let fees stand in the way of your dream school.

Here's how to navigate application fees.

Fee waivers are your best friend

Many colleges offer fee waivers for students who meet specific financial criteria. If you qualify for free or reduced lunches, participate in programs like Upward Bound; if your family experiences financial hardship, you might also be eligible.

Here's how to get a waiver.

> » Check with your school guidance counselor. They can provide forms like the NACAC Fee Waiver.

>> If you're using the Common App, the platform allows you to request a waiver directly.

>> Some colleges accept their own fee waiver forms, so check their websites.

>> Fee waivers can cover multiple schools, so apply early and save!

Look for colleges with free applications

Some schools don't charge application fees at all. This is especially common for community colleges or colleges hosting application fee–free days. Research your options; you might be surprised at how many schools skip the fees altogether.

Reduce hidden costs

Beyond fees, you may run into other application-related expenses: printing resumes, mailing transcripts, or even traveling for interviews. Keep costs down by doing the following:

>> Use digital submissions whenever possible.

>> Ask your counselor about free resources for printing or mailing documents.

>> Apply during fee-free weeks, which some schools or states offer.

Plan your applications strategically

To avoid overspending, prioritize where you apply. Focus on a mix of dream, match, and safety schools (only if they truly interest you). There's no need to send applications to 20 schools "just in case."

Ask about scholarships for application costs

Some local organizations, high schools, or college-readiness programs offer small scholarships specifically to cover application fees. Support is out there! Don't be afraid to ask for it.

Chapter **13**

Securing the Bag (for College, That Is)

A thena will never forget the day she signed her life away to student loans. Okay, she is very dramatic, but she does remember the day she agreed to accept her first student loan and assume the responsibility to pay it back according to the terms and conditions provided. Athena didn't realize how easy it was to use student loans to help subsidize her lifestyle in college, and took a little too much out during her first year of college. But toward the end, she only accepted what she absolutely needed to cover her tuition and books, and that was it.

Many people talk about student loans because they have them. The Education Data Initiative estimates that the total student loan debt for the United States is $1.773 trillion as of January 2025. More than 42.7 million borrowers have federal loan debt, while the remaining borrowers have loans from other financial institutions like banks.

The average federal student loan balance is $38,375, while the total average balance (including private loan debt) may be as high as $41,520. It's common to have more than that depending on a variety of factors, such as the length of your program and where you attended school. Athena graduated from Arizona State University with $50,000 of student loan debt, while Mykail graduated from Hampton University with $75,000 of debt. We both are working hard to pay back the student loans that helped us go to school.

While taking out student loans made sense for us, it doesn't make sense for everyone. And while it made sense, that doesn't mean student loans haven't affected our finances when it comes to budgeting. That $400 or $500 payment every month could be doing a lot instead of paying back our loans, and that's money you can save if you know how to secure the bag for college. That's why it's important to know what your options are so that you can make the right choice for you.

This chapter looks at the various ways you can pay for your college education, and how you can reduce costs to avoid being strapped by huge debt once you graduate.

Different Types of Financial Aid

Financial aid is money that helps students pay for their college education. It can take various forms, including scholarships, student loans, grants, government programs, and work-study.

Scholarships

Scholarships are financial awards that help students pay for college or other educational programs. They are typically given out based on various criteria, such as academic achievement, athletic ability, artistic talent, or financial need. Unlike loans, scholarships do not have to be repaid, which makes them a great way to reduce the cost of education.

Many different types of scholarships are available. Some are offered by colleges and universities, while others come from private organizations, companies, or community groups. To apply for a scholarship, you'll usually need to fill out an application and also may need to submit essays, letters of recommendation, or transcripts.

Receiving a scholarship can not only help you pay for school, but also recognize your hard work and achievements. It's important to research and apply for scholarships early, as many have deadlines well before you start college.

Here is a list of resources for scholarships you can apply for:

>> CareerOneStop, sponsored by the U.S. Department of Labor (www.careeronestop.org/toolkit/training/find-scholarships.aspx)

>> Scholarships.com (www.scholarships.com/)

>> Fastweb (www.fastweb.com/)

>> Going Merry (https://goingmerry.com/)

>> Scholly Scholarships (www.sallie.com/scholarships/scholly)

>> RaiseMe (www.raise.me/)

Student loans

Student loans are a type of financial aid that has to be repaid, usually after you graduate or leave school. Private loans from banks and other lenders are one option, while federal student loans (which offer lower interest rates and more flexible repayment options) are another. While both types of student loans help students pay for college, they have some critical differences.

Private

Private lenders, such as banks or credit unions, offer student loans. The interest rates and terms can vary widely among lenders. Lenders look at your credit score and income and sometimes require a co-signer, especially if you're a first-time borrower with little to no credit history, when determining your rate.

With private loans, the interest rates can be fixed or variable and are often higher than federal rates, depending on the lender and your credit score. If you have a co-signer with good credit, that may help you get a better rate.

Private loans also have less flexible repayment options. Once you take out the loan, the terms the lender sets usually remain until it's paid off. Many people will refinance their student loans with a private lender in hopes of a lower payment and rate.

Public

The government provides federal (also known as *public*) student loans through the U.S. Department of Education, and applications are usually made through the FAFSA (Free Application for Federal Student Aid). Eligibility is determined based on financial need, and most students qualify. You don't need to have a credit history or a co-signer. However, there are limits on how much you can borrow each year, depending on your tuition and whether you're a dependent or independent student.

Public loans generally have fixed interest rates, which means the rate stays the same throughout the loan period. Since the government sets the rates, they can be lower, making them more affordable than a private loan.

Public student loans also offer more flexible repayment plans. For example, there are options for income-driven repayment based on how much money you make after graduation, and some loans may even be forgiven after a certain period if you meet specific criteria.

Here are the most common loans taken out by students.

>> **Direct subsidized loans:** These loans are made out to eligible undergraduate students who demonstrate financial need. These loans are lent under the premise that a student will use them for tuition and other expenses related to attending school.

>> **Direct unsubsidized loans:** These loans aren't based on financial need and are available to eligible undergraduate, graduate, and professional students to help with costs associated with attending school.

- » **Direct PLUS loans:** These loans are usually taken out by graduate or professional students with their parents (or guardians) to help pay for their education. Undergraduate students and their parents can also receive this type of loan, but it is less common, given that other financial aid options are specific to undergraduates. While these loans aren't based on eligibility, they are based on your credit history, requiring a credit check for both you and your parents (or guardians). If you or your co-signer have an adverse credit history, you need to meet additional requirements to qualify.

- » **Direct consolidation loans:** These loans allow you to combine all your eligible public loans into one loan with a single loan servicer. This is usually done when applying for income-based and other government programs to help pay your loans down affordably.

TIP

Find out if there are ways to put additional money toward your loan. Some student loan services will give you a discount if you sign up for automatic payment when it comes time to paying them back!

Grants

These are funds that you don't have to pay back. They are usually based on financial need, so if your family's income is low, you might qualify for more grant money.

- » **Federal Pell Grant:** This is one of the most desirable forms of financial aid available. Unlike loans, grants do not require repayment to the government, except in specific situations. While it may be more challenging to obtain a grant if the U.S. Department of Education assesses your Student Aid Index (SAI) as high, it is not entirely out of reach.

- » **Federal Supplemental Educational Opportunity Grant (SEOG):** If your college takes part in the federal SEOG program, it receives extra funding to assist students who show significant financial need. Similar to federal Pell

Grants, these funds do not need to be repaid if your school confirms your eligibility. However, unlike Pell Grants, the determination of eligibility is made by the financial aid office at your institution. It's important to note that these funds are limited; once they have all been distributed, the school will not have any federal SEOG funds available until the following year.

Government programs

You can also access government-based help to cover your college tuition. AmeriCorps is a federally funded program that engages communities through public, private, and government collaborations to serve members in specific communities. AmeriCorps volunteering opportunities include education, economic opportunity, disaster services, environmental stewardship, healthy futures, and veterans and military families.

Along with a living stipend, AmeriCorps also offers the Segal AmeriCorps Education Award, equal to the maximum amount for a Pell Grant for the fiscal year in which the term of national service is approved. As Pell Grant amounts change every year, so does the amount of the Segal AmeriCorps Education Award. The award amount varies based on the term of service completed.

Another option for a government program is to join the military. Each branch of the military offers scholarships to current members that help cover the costs of tuition and books. Additional programs for those looking to serve are the Coast Guard and Junior Reserve Officers' Training Corps (JROTC), which may already be offered at your high school campus. The GI Bill helps previous service members pay for college tuition as well as their families, if their parent has not used their benefits.

WARNING

The military is hard work. Many try to join only to find themselves hating it and, even worse, getting a dishonorable discharge from the military because they were unable to fulfill their commitment. Only look into the military if you genuinely want to serve your country.

Work-study

Work-study is a program that provides part-time jobs for college students to help them pay for their education. It's often part of financial aid packages, meaning that if you qualify for financial aid, you might also be eligible for work-study opportunities.

With work-study, you can work on or off campus in a job that aligns with your field of study or interests, which can also give you valuable work experience. The pay from these jobs typically helps cover school expenses, such as tuition, books, and living costs.

To participate, you generally need to fill out the Free Application for Federal Student Aid (FAFSA) to determine your eligibility. If you're accepted into the work-study program, your school will provide you with job options based on your skills and availability. Overall, it's a great way to earn money while going to school.

Internships

An internship is a temporary job or position that allows students or recent graduates to gain practical experience in a particular field or industry. It's often related to what you're studying in school or something you're interested in pursuing as a career. Internships can vary in length, usually lasting a few weeks to several months, and they can be paid or unpaid.

During an internship, you get the chance to work alongside professionals, find out about their daily tasks, and develop new skills. It's a great opportunity to see what working in that field is really like and to apply what you've learned in the classroom to real-world situations.

Additionally, internships can help you build your resume and make valuable connections in the industry, and may even lead to job offers after graduation. Overall, they're an excellent way to explore your career options and gain hands-on experience!

WHAT YOUR FINANCIAL AID COVERS

The financial aid you receive covers costs that you incur while attending school, as well as associated costs. Here are some examples.

- **Tuition:** This is how much you must pay your school to attend your classes. Some schools charge per credit hour, while others charge per class. While Athena paid per credit hour while attending community college, she only paid a flat fee at Arizona State University for any course load over three classes. This means she paid the same amount.

- **Fees:** Many colleges charge fees in addition to tuition. These fees can apply to registration, supplies needed for a science lab, library use, and access to certain student services such as tutoring, counseling, and career guidance.

- **Textbooks and other supplies:** Some classes may not require you to purchase a textbook and instead offer access to materials online. Others will require you to purchase one or sometimes several textbooks, depending on the level of the class and subject. In addition to buying textbooks, you'll also need to buy other necessities, like a computer, backpack, pens, paper, a planner, and any other office supplies you think you'll need. Athena recommends buying extra chargers when they are on sale if you frequently misplace yours, or if you need a backup when your charger goes out at 2 a.m. and that paper is due at 8 a.m.

- **Room and board:** After you sign up for classes, you'll need to figure out where you'll lay your head down at night. Financial aid can help cover your room and board if you stay on campus. It can also help you with living expenses off campus if that's what you decide to do, such as living in an apartment with roommates. We both used our financial aid for this very purpose. Be sure to include expenses, such as any items needed for your living arrangements, such as bedding, cleaning supplies, and other expenses like your cell phone.

- **Transportation:** You'll need to figure out how you get to and from class. Financial aid can help cover this expense by helping you get a parking pass, a bike to cruise across campus, or public transportation.

Always research your parking options if you're driving yourself to class. Parking passes can easily cost hundreds of dollars; sometimes, you may not need one if you can get creative. For example, Athena would park in the pay-by-hour section, and it only came out to less than $10 a week!

Only use what you need when it comes to financial aid and student loans. Borrowing more than what you need so you can spend frivolously takes away from your future you's income and opportunities.

Looking into the FAFSA

The most crucial form when it comes to securing the bag for college is the Free Application for Federal Student Aid (FAFSA). Your FAFSA determines how much you'll receive in terms of financial aid for your education. You'll want to qualify for as much as you can when it comes to financing your education, and one of the best ways to do that is to fill out your FAFSA.

This is how it works: You create a username at https://student aid.gov/ and use that name to fill out the FAFSA application online or send it by mail (online is the quickest and easiest way to do this, but the option to mail is available). After you've filled out your application (see the section, "Info needed to apply"), the U.S. Department of Education will review your information to decide how much financial aid you qualify for. This is based on how much money the U.S. Department of Education feels your family should contribute to your education.

This doesn't mean that your family will or even can. The cost of living is expensive for everyone and it seems to only go up, putting stress on everyone's budget. This can definitely feel unfair and in our opinion, it is. But we wanted to ensure that you knew this and didn't feel alone, thinking everyone's parents except yours are paying for their education, because that is simply not the case, and you won't know that until someone points it out.

After your application has been reviewed, your information will be sent to the colleges you listed as possible contenders on your application. Once your college's financial aid office has reviewed your information, they will send you what's known as a financial award letter. This is the amount of assistance you qualify for.

To be eligible, it is recommended that you

>> Have completed high school or an equivalent under state law.

>> Are enrolled as a regular student for a degree or program that is eligible for FAFSA funding.

>> Have a valid Social Security number along with proper citizenship and documentation.

>> Have provided consent and approval from your parents to have their tax information directly transferred into the FAFSA application.

>> Agree that you are not in default on financial aid repayment and you will only use the loan for educational purposes.

TIP

If you are part of a multicultural family, check out Immigrants Rising. While based in California, this organization provides resources that offer assistance to anyone receiving or eligible for DACA, as well as help to those who have your parents that might need additional assistance. For more info, go to https:// immigrantsrising.org/resources/.

Info needed to apply

You'll need to provide the following information, so make sure to gather it before completing your application.

>> A StudentAid.gov account. You use this account to fill out the information needed for your FAFSA application as well as to check on your application status. It's also a resource for other questions you may have.

>> Your Social Security number and your parents' Social Security numbers if you are a dependent student.

>> Contact information for both student and parents. This includes phone numbers, addresses, and email addresses.

>> College and career plans.

>> Current high school information.

>> College information where FAFSA results should be sent.

>> Any documentation that can help substantiate any student's unique personal circumstances, including but not limited to being in the foster care system, juvenile system, homeless, or an unaccompanied minor (if you need help getting such documentation, ask your trusted adult). For more info on finding a trusted adult, see Chapter 3.

>> Tax returns.

>> Current balances of cash savings and checking accounts.

>> Net worth of investments, businesses, and farms that are owned.

TIP

If you are eligible to file as an independent, you do not need your parents' information. Your eligibility depends on your own unique circumstances. Check out https://studentaid.gov/apply-for-aid/fafsa/filling-out/dependency for more details on how to apply as an independent and advice on your next steps.

TIP

If you are unsure of your college's code (the number the Department of Education uses to identify your school), check out https://studentaid.gov/fafsa-apply/colleges for an easy way to find that information.

With the information collected, you can then go to https://studentaid.gov/h/apply-for-aid/fafsa to fill out your application online. There is also a link to download a PDF version of the FAFSA form that you can mail instead.

TIP

Print the PDF form of the FAFSA and use it to collect all of your information in one place. You can then use this form to complete your application more easily and reference it as needed. Be sure to keep it in a safe place as it has all of your personal information on it!

For applicants in foster care or experiencing homelessness

If you are in foster care or experiencing homelessness, you may not have access to traditional FAFSA information. Because of this, the FAFSA includes amendments that allow you to indicate that you are either in foster care or homeless. It is *very important* to make sure that you understand what your dependency status is — you should be independent!

By marking that you are in foster care or homeless, you do not have to provide financial documentation from your parents. It is very *important* that you do not do this! If a higher education institution sees that you currently have access to any money (even if your parents are not supporting you), they will mark you as a dependent and you may lose these funding opportunities.

Once you answer "yes" to the general homelessness question on the FAFSA form, you are asked whether you have received a homeless youth determination. If you indicate that you have, the financial aid administrator at the college you plan to attend may request the determination to prove that you are "unaccompanied" and homeless or at risk of becoming homeless.

You can secure this information from the following people or organizations:

>> Your high school or school district homeless liaison

>> The director of an emergency shelter or transitional housing program funded by the U.S. Department of Housing and Urban Development

>> The director of a runaway or homeless youth program

>> Local school district personnel

>> State homeless education coordinators

>> The National Center for Homeless Education (NCHE)

>> Third parties such as private or publicly funded homeless shelters and service providers

>> Financial aid administrators from colleges other than the school to which you're presenting the documentation

>> Staff from college access programs such as TRIO (Talent Search or Upward Bound), GEAR UP (Gaining Early Awareness and Readiness for Undergraduate Programs), or JAG (Jobs for America's Graduates)

>> College or high school counselors

>> Mental health professionals, social workers, mentors, doctors, or clergy

If you need additional information, ask your trusted adult for more help. For more about finding a trusted adult, see Chapter 3.

Determining your FAFSA award

The amount of assistance you can expect is influenced by four main factors: the cost of attendance (COA), your Student Aid Index (SAI), your Expected Family Contribution (EFC), the EFC is now the SAI, my apoligies, this has been cut and your financial need. The COA represents the total expenses for attending school for a year, which includes not just tuition and fees, but also estimated costs for room and board, books, supplies, and transportation.

Once your COA is established, the institution will evaluate your SAI. The U.S. Department of Education determines the SAI when it reviews your household's yearly income — most likely from your parents — and your parents' financial resources to see if they can contribute to your educational costs. After the college subtracts your SAI from your COA, you will discover what you need financially, which represents the amount of federal financial aid you may qualify for.

Following up with your school

After you've received your financial award letter from your school, you will be able to reach out to their financial aid department to find out more information about their award process. You should get updates throughout the process, and if you do not, make sure you check in with the financial aid office to ensure your information is being processed correctly. If it is not, they can provide resources to help you move forward, as well as help you with the application if you are stuck and need assistance.

If you are taking out public loans, you will need to fill out a Mastery Promise Note, or MPN. The MPN is an agreement that states you understand any loans taken out for your education must not only be used for educational purposes, but also be paid back when the time comes.

Find out more about your MPN at https://studentaid.gov/mpn/.

If a school does not take the FAFSA, ask why. Schools that aren't accredited are often not eligible for financial aid, so do your research! Athena knows a lot of students who signed up for a school that was unaccredited, and not only was their certificate not recognized, but they were also deep in private student loan debt!

Discovering Ways to Cut Education Costs

Here are a few more ways to cut costs when paying for your education.

Finding out about CLEP and AP

CLEP (College-Level Examination Program) and AP (Advanced Placement) classes allow high school students to earn college credit before they even step foot on a college campus.

AP classes are rigorous courses offered in high schools that follow a college-level curriculum. If you take an AP class and do well on the end-of-year exam (the AP exam), you can earn college credit for that subject. For example, if you take AP Calculus and score high enough on the exam, many colleges will give you credit for introductory college calculus. AP classes can also help you stand out in college applications, showing that you're willing to take on challenging coursework.

CLEP allows students to take exams in various subjects to demonstrate their knowledge and potentially earn college credit. If you feel confident in what you've learned in high school or through self-study, you can register for a CLEP exam. If you pass, you can earn credits for that subject at many colleges, similar to AP classes. This is a great option if you want to skip introductory courses.

Both options can save you time and money in college by allowing you to complete some requirements before you even start. Plus, they give you a taste of college-level work while you're still in high school!

Considering community colleges

One way to automatically save on tuition is to look into attending a community college. Attending a community college can be an excellent choice for several reasons.

>> **Cost-effective:** Community colleges typically have much lower tuition rates compared to universities. This can help you save money and avoid taking on a lot of student debt.

>> **Flexible schedule:** Many community colleges offer flexible class schedules, including evening and weekend courses. This can make it easier to work part-time or manage other commitments while you study.

>> **Smaller class sizes:** Community college classes often have smaller student-to-teacher ratios. This means you can get more personalized attention from your instructors, which can be helpful if you need extra support.

>> **Explore academic interests:** If you're not completely sure about your major or career path, community colleges allow you to take a variety of courses. This can help you explore different fields before making a decision.

>> **Transfer opportunities:** Many community colleges have partnerships with four-year universities, making it easier to transfer your credits if you decide to pursue a bachelor's degree later on. This pathway can also make it possible to achieve a degree at a university while saving on the first two years of college.

>> **Skill development:** Community colleges often offer programs focusing on practical skills and training for specific careers. This means you can earn a degree or certificate in a year or two, which can lead directly to job opportunities.

>> **Local learning environment:** Attending a community college often means you can stay closer to home, making it easier to balance school with family and friends.

Overall, community college can provide a solid foundation for your education, help you save money, and give you the flexibility to grow and explore your interests.

TIP

To find a community college near you, visit www.dol.gov/ agencies/odep/program-areas/individuals/youth/ community-colleges.

Looking at state schools

In addition to community colleges, attending a local university can be another financially wise decision due to residency status.

If you have lived in the state where your school is located for a certain amount of time, you are considered a state resident. If you do not live in that state or will be living there for a short amount of time, you are most likely considered a non-state resident.

Most state schools offer lower tuition costs if you are a state resident as an incentive to stay home and attend school locally. Sometimes, out-of-state residents pay three times the amount that an in-state resident pays! Here are some other reasons why attending a state school might make more sense.

>> **Cost savings:** Staying local often means lower tuition fees than out-of-state or private universities. Additionally, you can save on housing costs by living at home or finding nearby accommodation. Not paying for room and board can save you thousands each semester.

>> **Community connections:** Being at a local university allows you to maintain connections with your community, friends, and family. This support system can help ease the transition to college life and make you less likely to drop out.

>> **Familiar environment:** You'll be in a setting you're familiar with, which can reduce stress and help you adapt more quickly. You'll likely know the area, public transportation, and places to hang out or study.

>> **Potential for networking:** Attending a local university can help you build a network of professionals in your area. Many local companies and organizations recruit from nearby institutions, which could lead to internships or job opportunities after graduation.

>> **Diverse programs:** Local universities often offer a wide variety of programs and majors, allowing you to explore different fields of study without having to travel far.

>> **Smaller class sizes:** Depending on the university, you might find smaller class sizes, which can give you more direct access to your professors and create a better learning environment.

>> **Extracurricular activities:** Local universities often have plenty of clubs, organizations, and events that can enhance your college experience, allowing you to meet new people and develop new interests without the pressures of moving far away.

>> **Support services:** Many local universities have resources to help students succeed, such as tutoring, career counseling, and mental health services. Being close to home can make it easier to access these resources.

Overall, attending a local university can provide a great balance of academic opportunities, personal connections, and cost savings, making it a smart choice for many students.

Looking into employer-paid tuition programs

An employer tuition reimbursement program is a benefit offered by some companies to help employees pay for their education.

If you're working for a company that has a tuition reimbursement program, they will cover part or all of your tuition costs for classes related to your job or field of work. This means that you can pursue a degree or take courses to enhance your skills without worrying as much about the financial burden.

Usually, there are some eligibility requirements. For example, you might need to work at the company for a certain period before you qualify, or the courses you take may need to be relevant to your job or career path. You may also need to pay for your classes upfront, and after you have met the requirements, you can then submit your expenses for reimbursement.

Some employers may require you to stay with the company for a certain amount of time after you receive reimbursement. This helps them ensure they're investing in employees who will stick around and apply what they've learned.

4

Making Money Like an Adult

Find out all about earning money and the different ways to get paid.

Understand how to read and make sense of your paycheck.

Explore the true costs of working, including expenses and taxes.

Discover how to protect your money from fraud and theft.

Grasp the importance of managing and paying your bills on time.

IN THIS CHAPTER

» Becoming a wage earner

» Creating a resume for different stages in your career

» Understanding the power of networking

» Handling interviews

» Getting a job offer

» Discussing the job offer

Chapter **14**

Earning Money at Work

E arning your own money can be so rewarding. As soon as you get that first paycheck, your mind runs a mile a minute about all the fun things you can buy with your money. Whether it's your favorite meal, an outfit to wear, or a new video game to play, it's only possible by going to work and earning a paycheck.

People enter the workforce at different ages. Many folks earn their first official paycheck from a part-time job between the ages of 16 and 19. Others wait until they are completely finished with their educational studies and start working around the age of 20. No matter when you decide to jump into the workforce, here are a few things you can learn to get and keep a job you love, which is the subject of this chapter.

Creating the Resume of a Rockstar

Your resume is the first impression you will make to a hiring manager. Take your resume seriously! The difference between getting a job you want and getting a rejection email lies with your resume. You need to highlight your experience and show that you are willing to learn new skills. Your resume will continue to evolve with you while you learn, grow, and gain more experience.

Let's meet Jackson, a high school sophomore who's ready to land his first part-time job at the local coffee shop. Jackson doesn't yet have much work experience, but he's eager to show off his skills and potential. Over the years, we follow Jackson as he goes from landing his first job to internships in college, and finally to his first full-time job after college graduation.

Landing your first part-time job with your resume

When Jackson first sets out to create a resume, he's nervous. He's never worked before, so what's there to write about? A lot, actually! For teenagers, resumes focus on transferable skills from school, volunteer work, and extracurricular activities. Employers hiring for part-time jobs are looking for enthusiasm, dependability, and a willingness to learn.

Here are the key sections of Jackson's resume:

Contact information

At the top of the page, Jackson lists his name, phone number, email, city, and state.

Objective statement

Jackson writes a short, one-sentence goal:

High school sophomore with strong organizational skills and a passion for customer service, seeking a part-time barista position to gain work experience and grow my communication skills.

Skills section

Even without work experience, Jackson highlights skills he's gained in school and life:

>> Excellent time management (balanced school and extra-curriculars).

>> Strong teamwork skills (member of the school soccer team).

>> Reliable and punctual (perfect attendance last semester).

Education

Jackson lists his high school, the city and state, and his expected graduation date.

Volunteer work and activities

This section includes the following.

Library Volunteer (10 hours per week, Summer 2023): Helped organize book displays and assisted visitors.

Soccer Team Member (Fall 2022 Present): Demonstrated teamwork and dedication.

TIP

Use action verbs like *organized*, *assisted*, or *demonstrated* to make accomplishments stand out.

Landing an internship with a college resume

Fast-forward to Jackson's junior year in college. He's studying marketing and ready to land an internship with a digital advertising firm. Now, Jackson has more experience to showcase, but his resume still needs to be focused and tailored to the job. He also removes his high school achievements, like his perfect attendance and the volunteer activities, as his college and work experience now carry more weight.

Key upgrades for Jackson's college resume include the following:

Professional summary

Instead of an objective, Jackson writes a summary of his experience:

Motivated marketing student with hands-on experience managing social media campaigns and organizing on-campus events. Skilled in content creation and analytics, seeking an internship to apply classroom knowledge in a real-world setting.

Relevant skills

Jackson updates his skills to include the following:

>> Social media management (Instagram and TikTok)

>> Basic graphic design (Canva)

>> Data analysis (Google Analytics coursework)

Experience section

Jackson adds part-time job and campus leadership experience.

>> Student Marketing Assistant, University Office of Admissions (10 hours per week): Designed flyers for campus tours and increased engagement on Instagram by 20 percent.

>> Event Coordinator, Marketing Club: Organized biweekly guest speaker events, managing logistics for 100-plus attendees.

Education

Jackson lists his degree program, university, and expected graduation date.

TIP

Quantify your achievements when possible. Numbers make your impact stand out, like "increased engagement by 20 percent" or "managed events for 100-plus attendees."

Landing your first full-time job with a college graduate resume

Now a fresh college graduate, Jackson is ready for his first full-time job as a junior marketing associate. This resume focuses on combining academic accomplishments, internship experience, and transferable skills from his part-time jobs. Jackson removes early college experiences, like club participation that isn't directly related to his desired career. Instead, he focuses on internships and work that showcases professional impact.

Key additions for Jackson's professional resume include the following:

Professional profile

Jackson highlights his career-ready skills:

Recent marketing graduate with 2-plus years of hands-on experience in digital advertising and event management. Proficient in content strategy, social media campaigns, and data analytics. Eager to bring creativity and strategy to a fast-paced marketing team.

Expanded experience section

Jackson combines his internships and student jobs.

>> Marketing Intern, XYZ Advertising Agency: Managed a content calendar for three client accounts, creating posts that increased audience engagement by 30 percent.

>> Student Marketing Assistant: Supported five university-wide events by designing materials and promoting them on social platforms.

Technical skills

Jackson includes advanced tools like the following:

>> Adobe Photoshop and Illustrator

>> Hootsuite (Social Media Management)

>> Google Analytics (Certified)

REMEMBER

Keep resumes to one page for most roles, especially as an entry-level candidate. Only include the most relevant experiences.

Networking

Your network is an important component to your success. Many times, it's not just about what you know, but also about who you know. They say your network is your net worth, so it's important to create a network of people who want to help you succeed. We like to think that there are three important types of connections that you should make as a young professional in the workforce: peers, mentors, and sponsors.

Your *peers* are people that have the same experience, or level, as you. They are the people who are interning with you or starting their entry-level job with you. This is often known as *networking across*, because you and your peers are at the same level of experience.

Your *mentors* are people who have more experience than you. They could be a few years your senior or much older than you. Mentors are great to have in your network to help you think through problems (big or small) and help you plan the next steps in your career.

Lastly, your *sponsors* are people who are more senior and have significant influence. They are folks that put you in positions to help you advance your career faster. Your sponsors are more active in sending you opportunities than your mentors. Your network needs to contain all types of people to truly work and help you reach the level of success your desire.

A strong network doesn't happen overnight, but by consistently investing in peer, mentor, and sponsor connections, you'll build a support system that helps you succeed. Your peers will walk alongside you, your mentors will guide you, and your sponsors will help you rise to the next level.

REMEMBER

Networking is about relationships, not transactions. Be genuine, curious, and helpful to those in your network, and it will naturally grow into a powerful resource for your success.

Networking across: Peer connections

Your peers are the people who are navigating the same path as you. These might be classmates, coworkers, or even friends from extracurricular activities. Building a strong peer network is about creating a group of people who understand your journey because they're on the same one.

Here are some ways you can build peer connections.

>> **Join clubs and organizations:** Whether it's a school group or a community activity, these spaces are natural places to meet peers who share your interests.

>> **Collaborate on projects:** If you're working on a group project at school or on a team at work, take the opportunity to bond and support each other.

>> **Stay in touch:** After internships or summer jobs, connect with your peers on platforms like LinkedIn, or follow up occasionally to maintain the relationship.

Networking with peers doesn't have to feel formal. Build friendships first; your network will grow naturally when you treat people with respect and kindness.

TIP

Learning from experience: Mentor connections

Mentors are people who have been in your shoes but have taken a few (or many) steps ahead. They're like a personal guide who can help you see your potential, avoid mistakes, and plan for the future. Mentors don't need to be intimidating — they could be a former teacher, a manager at your part-time job, or even a family friend who works in a field you're interested in.

Here are some ideas for how to find a mentor.

>> **Ask for advice:** Start by approaching someone you admire and ask for their perspective on a specific topic.

>> **Show genuine interest:** Let them know why you respect their work or experience. People love to share their expertise when they feel appreciated.

>> **Be a good mentee:** Come prepared with questions, be respectful of their time, and follow through on their advice.

Mentors aren't mind-readers. Be clear about what you need, whether it's career advice, feedback, or help in setting goals.

REMEMBER

Opening doors: Sponsor connections

Sponsors are the people who actively advocate for you. They're more senior than mentors and have the power to put you in places you might not have access to on your own. Sponsors speak up for you in meetings, recommend you for opportunities, and help you climb the ladder faster.

Here is how to build sponsor relationships.

» **Prove yourself first:** Sponsors look for individuals who consistently deliver great work. Focus on excelling in your current role or responsibilities.

» **Make your ambitions known:** Sponsors can't advocate for you if they don't know your goals. Share what you're aiming for, whether it's a leadership role or a specific project.

» **Show gratitude:** Always acknowledge their support. A simple "thank you" or a note of appreciation goes a long way in maintaining a sponsor relationship.

TIP

Sponsors are earned, not assigned. Focus on building a reputation for being reliable and talented, and the right sponsors will notice you.

Landing Your First Interview

Between having a rockstar resume and submitting a strong application, you will surely have landed your first interview. It's an exciting and anxiety-filled time! Preparing for your interview is critical to ensure that you show up feeling confident. When you feel confident and ready for the interview, you can let your personality shine, speak to your expertise, and land that job.

Discovering two types of interviews

The most common types of interviews are behavioral interviews and technical interviews. Depending on the type of job and industry, you can have multiple interviews that are a mix of behavioral and technical. The interview process can also include one-on-one conversations, panel rounds, case studies, tests, or portfolio reviews. Each part of the interview is meant to assess your different skills and find out more about your personality.

Behavioral interviews

Behavioral interviews focus on how you've handled situations in the past, giving the interviewer a sense of how you might perform in similar scenarios. These questions often start with phrases like, "Tell me about a time when . . ." or "Can you give an example of . . ." The goal is to evaluate your problem-solving abilities, communication skills, and how you work with others. Below is an example of a behavioral interview question and how to use the STAR method to answer:

Question: "Can you tell me about a time you worked with a team to overcome a challenge?"

Answer: Use the STAR method and structure your response using the following four steps.

1. Situation: Set the scene. Briefly describe the context of the challenge.

Example: "During my time as a team member on a school project, we faced a challenge with meeting the deadline due to conflicting schedules."

2. Task: Explain your responsibility in the situation.

Example: "As the team organizer, it was my responsibility to find a solution that worked for everyone."

3. Action: Share what you did to address the issue.

Example: "I created a shared calendar, organized shorter meetings, and assigned clear tasks to each team member."

4. Result: Highlight the outcome.

Example: "We completed the project on time and received an A for our efforts."

Be Specific. Avoid vague answers. Detail your actions and the results.

Stay Positive. Even if the story involves a challenge, focus on how you resolved it and what you learned.

Technical interviews

Technical interviews assess your knowledge and skills directly related to the job. These questions often test your ability to solve problems, think critically, or demonstrate expertise in a specific area. If the job involves technical tasks (such as coding, trouble-shooting, or creating designs), this type of interview is common. Below is an example of a technical interview question as well steps to answer:

Question: "How would you troubleshoot a computer that won't connect to Wi-Fi?"

Answer:

» **Clarify the problem:** Ask follow-up questions if necessary to fully understand the issue.

   Example: "Is the Wi-Fi network visible to the device? Have other devices connected successfully?"

» **Outline your thought process:** Walk the interviewer through each step logically.

   Example: "First, I would check if the device's Wi-Fi is turned on. Next, I'd ensure it's connected to the correct network. If that doesn't work, I'd restart the router and device to eliminate connection issues."

» **Explain solutions clearly:** Share your reasoning for each step and how it leads to solving the problem.

   Example: "Restarting the router and device often resolves temporary glitches. If the issue persists, I'd check the network settings for potential misconfigurations."

» **Highlight problem-solving skills:** Even if you don't reach the final solution, emphasize your logical approach and adaptability.

TIP

Practice responding to both types of questions with a friend, family member, or mentor. Rehearsing aloud helps you to feel more confident and to refine your answers.

Preparing for your interview

Interviews are a two-way street. Be ready to ask questions about the job, team, and company culture to show that you're invested in finding the right fit.

Preparing for an interview takes more than just showing up — it's your chance to make a strong first impression. By researching the company, practicing common questions, and planning your outfit, you'll feel more confident and ready to showcase your skills. Here's how to prepare effectively.

>> **Research the company:** Find out about the company's mission, values, and recent achievements. This helps you tailor your answers and show genuine interest in the job.

>> **Practice common questions:** Rehearse answers to both behavioral and technical questions. Ask a friend, teacher, or family member to do a mock interview with you.

>> **Plan your outfit:** Choose an outfit that's professional but comfortable. Look up the company's culture — business casual is a safe bet for most entry-level jobs.

>> **Bring essentials:** Bring printed copies of your resume, a notebook, and a pen. If it's a virtual interview, test your technology ahead of time.

REMEMBER

Within 24 hours after the interview, send a thank-you email. Thank the interviewer for their time, mention something specific that you enjoyed discussing, and reiterate your excitement about the job. A simple follow-up note shows professionalism and keeps you at the top of the interviewer's mind.

TIP

If you don't hear back right away, be patient. It's okay to follow up after a week to check the status of your application.

Reading Your Job Offer

Once you have hit a home run with your interviewing skills, the next step is to wait for a job offer. It is very important to thoroughly read your job offer before signing. A job offer has a few parts that you should pay close attention to. The job offer will outline your total compensation package, any additional benefits, and other important information (such as your start date).

Carefully read and understand your job offer, because you want to set yourself up for success and avoid surprises down the road. Each part of your offer, from pay to benefits, contributes to the full picture of your compensation and working conditions. Taking the time to review every detail ensures that you start your new job with confidence and clarity.

Understanding compensation pay

The compensation section of your job offer explains how and when you'll be paid. This is one of the most important areas to review because it determines your income and financial stability. Understanding the type of pay arrangement — whether salary, hourly, freelance, contract, or stipend — is crucial to knowing how your earnings will be calculated and distributed. Make sure you know whether there are additional terms like overtime pay or performance-based bonuses that could affect your overall compensation. Clarity here ensures that you can budget effectively and avoid surprises later.

Salary versus hourly wages

If you're paid a salary, you'll receive a set amount of money each year, divided into regular paychecks (usually biweekly or monthly). This means you'll earn a consistent amount, regardless of how many hours you work each week. Hourly pay, on the other hand, compensates you for each hour worked and often includes overtime pay for hours beyond a standard workweek. If the job is hourly, it's important to confirm whether there's a guarantee for minimum hours or if your schedule might vary. Consistency in income is often a key difference between salary and hourly jobs, so understanding this distinction can help you decide which option aligns best with your financial goals.

TIP

If the job is hourly, check whether there's a guaranteed minimum number of hours per week or a cap on how many you can work.

Per-project or freelance work

Per-project or freelance work means you're paid based on the completion of specific tasks rather than for a set schedule of hours. This type of pay is common for creative or gig-based jobs, where you may handle short-term assignments. While this arrangement can provide flexibility, it also means your income can vary widely from one project to the next. Be sure to clarify how and when you'll be paid for each project, as some employers may pay upon completion while others follow a specific billing cycle. Knowing these details helps you manage your cash flow and plan for periods of inconsistent income.

REMEMBER

Ask about payment timelines (weekly, monthly, or upon project completion) to plan your finances.

Contractor jobs

Contractor jobs are different from regular employee positions in several ways. As a contractor, you're often responsible for managing your own taxes, benefits, and work-related expenses. These jobs may offer higher pay rates to compensate for the lack of traditional benefits, but they also come with more financial responsibility on your part. Before accepting a contractor job, ensure you understand your obligations, such as setting aside money for taxes or securing your own health insurance. Verifying your employment classification — contractor versus employee — can help you avoid legal and financial misunderstandings.

Stipends

Stipends are fixed amounts of money provided for specific expenses, such as travel, meals, or equipment. Unlike a salary or hourly wage, stipends are typically supplementary and tied to specific needs. For example, an internship might provide a stipend to cover transportation costs or supplies. It's important to check whether stipends are taxable or reimbursable, as this can affect your overall income. Understanding the purpose and limitations of any stipends included in your offer ensures that you can take full advantage of them without unexpected financial implications.

Looking at paid time off

Paid time off (PTO) is a critical part of your compensation package, as it determines how much time you can take off work while still being paid. Understanding your employer's PTO policy helps you plan your vacations, personal days, and sick leave effectively. PTO policies can vary widely, so it's important to know whether your time off is accrual-based, unlimited, or includes dedicated sick leave.

Accrual-based paid time off

Accrual-based PTO means you earn time off incrementally as you work. For example, you might earn one vacation day for every month you work, or a set number of hours for each pay period. This system rewards long-term employment and allows you to save up time for larger trips or extended breaks. When reviewing your job offer, check whether unused PTO rolls over to the next year or if it expires at the end of the current year. Knowing how and when you can use your accrued time off will help you make the most of this benefit and avoid losing earned days.

TIP

If you plan to take a vacation early in your employment, ask whether you can borrow against future accruals or if you need to wait until the time is earned.

Unlimited paid time off

Unlimited PTO policies allow employees to take as much time off as they need, provided their work is completed and approved by their manager. While this system sounds appealing, it's important to understand the expectations. In some workplaces, employees might feel hesitant to take time off because there's no specific limit. When reviewing an unlimited PTO policy, ask about the company culture and how time off is typically used by employees. This will give you a sense of whether the policy is truly flexible or just a formality.

WARNING

Unlimited PTO tends to benefit the employer more than the employee in many cases. Be sure to ask questions about how the unlimited PTO is handled at the company.

Sick leave

Sick leave is a specific category of PTO meant for health-related absences. This includes taking time off when you're ill, attending medical appointments, or caring for a sick family member. Some employers combine sick leave with general PTO, while others provide a separate allocation for sick days. Understanding your sick leave policy is important for prioritizing your health and ensuring you don't lose pay when you're unable to work.

Find out if your employer requires a doctor's note for extended sick leave or if there's a cap on the number of consecutive sick days you can take.

Uncovering benefits

The benefits section outlines additional perks and protections that come with your job. These benefits can significantly enhance your total compensation package, so it's important to review this section carefully. Benefits often include insurance, retirement plans, discounts, tuition reimbursement, and even company stock. Understanding the full scope of your benefits helps you make the most of what your employer offers.

Insurance

Health, dental, and vision insurance are among the most common benefits. These plans help cover the cost of medical care for you and, in some cases, your dependents. Review who is covered, how much you'll need to contribute to premiums, and what your out-of-pocket costs might be. Knowing the details of your insurance benefits allows you to plan for healthcare expenses and avoid unexpected bills.

Retirement and other pre-taxed accounts

Many employers offer retirement savings plans, such as 401(k)s, as well as other pre-tax accounts like health savings accounts (HSAs) or commuter benefits. These options allow you to save money while reducing your taxable income. Check if your employer offers matching contributions to retirement accounts, as this is essentially free money toward your future. Taking full advantage of these benefits can significantly impact your long-term financial stability.

Tuition reimbursement

Tuition reimbursement is a benefit that helps cover the cost of furthering your education while you work. Employers often have specific criteria, such as maintaining a certain grade or staying with the company for a set period, to qualify for this benefit. Before signing your offer, ask about repayment requirements if you leave the job shortly after using this benefit. Understanding these terms ensures you can take advantage of educational opportunities without financial risk.

Company stock and equity

Some employers offer stock options or equity as part of your compensation. This means you own a small portion of the company and can benefit if its value increases. These benefits often come with a *vesting schedule*, which outlines when you fully own the stock or equity. Reviewing these terms helps you understand the long-term value of this benefit and how it fits into your financial goals.

Negotiating Your Offer: How to Ask for More

True story: I (Mykail) negotiated my first job offer after college. Thinking back to the audacity I had at 19 gives me the energy to encourage you to ask for more from every offer you are given. Negotiating is kind of weird when you think about it because it might feel like you are being greedy or ungrateful to your new potential employer. But you must always remember: working for a company should be an equally beneficial arrangement. Both you (the employee) and them (the employer) are seeking to gain something from each other. You are depending on them to compensate you for the work you produce for them. They are gaining your expertise to help them make money.

Negotiating might feel intimidating, but it's a skill worth building early in your career. Whether it's your first full-time position, an internship, or a part-time job, you should always consider negotiating your offer. Why? Because negotiating shows confidence, self-awareness, and a strong understanding of your worth. Employers often expect candidates to negotiate and might even respect you more for doing so. Remember, the worst they can say is no — and you'll never know what's possible unless you ask!

Clearing up negotiation myths

Let's talk about some common worries you might have about negotiating. First, there's the fear that negotiating might make the employer withdraw the job offer. It's natural to worry about this, especially when it's your first big opportunity. But here's the truth: employers almost never take back an offer because you asked for more. They expect candidates to negotiate, and in many cases, it shows them that you're confident and serious about your value. As long as you're polite and professional, negotiating won't hurt your chances.

Another misconception is that entry-level roles aren't negotiable. You might think that because you're new to the workforce, you have to accept whatever is offered. Not true! Even in entry-level positions, there's often room to negotiate things like starting pay, PTO, or flexible schedules. It's all about knowing your worth and being willing to ask for what you need. The key is to focus on areas that matter most to you and approach the conversation with confidence.

Finally, let's address the fear of messing up the negotiation. Maybe you're worried about saying the wrong thing or being turned down. That's okay — negotiating is a skill, and it gets better with practice. Even if you don't get everything you ask for, the experience of negotiating is valuable. It helps you discover how to advocate for yourself, and that's a skill you'll use throughout your career. Remember, it's not about being perfect; it's about showing up, being prepared, and giving it your best shot.

Negotiating all the perks

Negotiating isn't just about salary (though that's important!). Here are a few key areas you can bring to the table.

- **Salary or hourly pay:** Research the market rate for your role and location. Tools like Fishbowl or PayScale can help you determine a reasonable range.

- **Paid time off:** If the offer includes limited PTO, you can ask for more vacation or personal days.

- **Benefits:** These include health insurance, retirement contributions, or additional perks like tuition reimbursement or professional development budgets.

- **Flexibility:** Requesting remote work options, a compressed workweek, or flexible hours can also be part of your negotiation.

- **Relocation assistance or stipends:** If the job requires a move, you can ask for help covering moving costs.

REMEMBER

Always prioritize what's most important to you. If the salary isn't negotiable, focus on other areas like benefits or work-life balance.

Preparing for negotiating

You can either negotiate live (phone or in-person) or via email depending on the company. Our favorite way to negotiate is via email. It's an easy way to prepare and explain all your requests without the added pressure of having to talk to the recruiter live. We provide examples of how to do both.

Preparing for a negotiation is the same no matter how you plan on executing it. Keep in mind that it is important that you understand three key things: what the company wants from you, what your skills can provide to the company, and how the market is valuing your skills at the time.

NEGOTIATION CHECKLIST

Here are some steps and considerations to make when preparing for or navigating a negotiation.

Before the negotiation:

Research the market rate for your position and location.

Identify your priorities and decide what's most important to you.

Practice your pitch and be ready to explain your reasoning.

During the negotiation:

Be polite and professional in your tone.

Start by expressing gratitude for the offer.

Clearly state what you're asking for and why.

After the negotiation:

Send a thank-you email to show professionalism, even if your request wasn't fully met.

Review the updated offer carefully before accepting.

Before you negotiate, preparation is key. Here's how to get ready.

>> **Know your value:** Research the market value for your role based on industry, location, and your experience. Use salary calculators or talk to professionals in similar positions to get accurate numbers.

>> **Identify your priorities:** What matters most to you? A higher salary? More PTO? Flexibility? Create a list of your must-haves and nice-to-haves to guide your negotiation.

>> **Understand the offer:** Read your job offer thoroughly to understand what's already included. Highlight areas where there's room for improvement.

>> **Practice your pitch:** Practice how you'll ask for what you want. Use a confident, respectful tone, and focus on what you bring to the table.

NEGOTIATING VIA EMAIL

Here's an example of how to negotiate via email.

Subject: Follow-Up on Job Offer for [Position Name]

Dear [Hiring Manager's Name],

Thank you for offering me the [Position Name] job. I'm excited about the opportunity to join [Company Name] and contribute to [specific team/project]. After reviewing the offer, I'd like to discuss the compensation package.

Based on my research and the market rate for this role, I was hoping we could adjust the salary to [$specific amount] to better reflect the value I bring to the team. Additionally, I'd like to discuss [specific benefit, such as paid time off or professional development opportunities].

I'm enthusiastic about joining the team and am confident we can find a package that works for both of us. Please let me know a convenient time to discuss this further.

Thank you again for this opportunity. I look forward to your response.

Best regards,

[Your Name]

Handling negotiation outcomes

How you respond will naturally depend on how the negotiation concludes. Here are some tips for responding to various scenarios.

When they make the offer

"Thank you so much for this offer! I'm really excited about the opportunity to work with [Company Name]. I've had a chance to review the offer, and I'd like to discuss [specific aspect, such as salary or paid time off]. Based on my expertise and knowledge, I believe [specific amount or benefit] better aligns with the market value for this job and the skills I bring to the team. Is there flexibility to adjust this?"

If they push back

"I completely understand. I'd love to work with you to find a solution that works for both of us. If increasing the salary isn't possible, could we explore [alternative benefit, like paid time off or a signing bonus]?"

Closing the conversation

"Thank you for taking the time to discuss this with me. I'm really excited about the opportunity and appreciate your flexibility. I look forward to finalizing the details and starting date with [Company Name]."

Chapter **15**

Reading Your Paycheck

Your paycheck is special because it is money you earn in exchange for your great work. But it's super crucial for you to understand how to read your paycheck. It's so much more than just the hours you work multiplied by your pay per hour. (That's quick math for you to get a rough estimate.)

However, the government requires some dollars from your paycheck to help your local, state, and federal government stay funded. It's important to understand all parts of your paycheck, and it can even help you catch some errors in your payment, too.

Understanding Your Gross Pay versus Net Pay

There are two types of pay you will see when you review your paystubs for each pay period from your job: the gross pay and the net pay. If these two were siblings, you could think of gross pay as the cooler, smarter, older sibling that everybody knows but never sees. Net pay, on the other hand, would be like the pesky, annoying, younger sibling that you can always count on to show up to all the family cookouts and take extra plates to go. That's because once all your required taxes and optional benefits have been subtracted from your gross pay, your net pay is what you are left with to pay bills and spend how you see fit.

For the math, if you had a job that paid you $10 per hour and you worked 15 hours per week, your gross pay would be $150 per week or $600 per month. After taxes, your net pay would be about $138 per week or $552 per month, depending on the city and state you live in. If you had a full-time salary of $60,000 per year, your monthly gross pay would be $2,500 bi-weekly or $5,000 monthly. After taxes and company benefits, your net pay could range anywhere from $1,500 to $1,930 bi-weekly or $3,000 to $3,860 monthly, depending on your city and state. This might seem like a lot of money disappearing from your paycheck, but let us explain where that money is going and what deductions are required versus what deductions are optional.

Finding out your base salary

After you secure a new job, you are provided with an offer letter. In this offer letter, your new employer will outline the following: your start date, your base salary, your total compensation, and your position title. Your *base salary* is defined as the fixed minimum amount you as the employee will be paid as set by your employer during the hiring process. Your base salary does not include any bonuses or benefits in the calculations.

Understanding pre-tax benefits

When you read your paycheck, you'll see a section of benefits that are deducted from your gross pay *before* taxes are calculated. These benefits are considered *pre-tax deductions*. Typical pre-tax deductions include, but are not limited to, health insurance, group-term life insurance, and retirement plans. These deductions are usually optional, meaning you are not required to have them.

REMEMBER

Some benefits of having pre-tax deductions include reducing your tax burden and ultimately keeping more money in your pocket.

Understanding post-tax benefits

Post-tax benefits are deducted from your pay *after* pre-tax benefits and taxes are paid. These deductions will vary, but some examples of post-tax deductions are Roth 401k contributions, pension contributions, union dues, charitable contributions, and other optional benefits offered through your employer. Depending on your employer, deductions such as union dues may be required; however, many post-tax deductions are optional.

TIP

Every year as an employee, you have the opportunity to change your pre- and post-tax deductions. This period is called *open-enrollment*; during this time, you have the option to change your contribution to optional deductions and benefits your company offers. Once this enrollment period ends, you will be locked into those contributions until the next open enrollment period begins.

Discovering your total compensation

If your base salary is the minimum you will earn, then think of your *total compensation* as your maximum income. Your total compensation includes your base salary, any bonuses that will be earned, stock options, medical benefits, retirement, and other benefits.

For most people, your base salary will make up most of your total compensation. All other benefits make up the rest.

Making Mandatory Paycheck Deductions

While some deductions and benefits are optional, there are some mandatory deductions that everyone must pay. The mandatory deductions are for people who have income reported through an employer that provides employees with W-2 forms. These deductions are used for an array of public services that other American citizens take advantage of.

Paying Social Security and FICA

Social Security and FICA taxes are amounts taken out of your paycheck to help fund programs that benefit people in need, including you in the future. These programs are designed to provide financial support for people who are retired or disabled, or in some cases, for families if a parent passes away.

Social Security is like a big savings plan that helps people after they stop working (usually when they get older and retire) or if they can no longer work because of a disability. By paying into Social Security, you're building up credits, and when you're older or if you need help, you can collect money to support yourself. The amount you eventually get depends on how much you earned and paid into the system over your working years.

FICA stands for the Federal Insurance Contributions Act. It's the law that requires both you and your employer to pay a portion of your income toward Social Security and another program called Medicare. Medicare helps pay for medical expenses when people are older or disabled. So, when you see FICA taxes on your paycheck, that's money being contributed to both Social Security and Medicare.

Here's how it works: A small percentage of your paycheck goes to Social Security and Medicare. Your employer also pays an equal amount. This money doesn't just disappear; it helps support people today, like your grandparents who may be retired or those unable to work due to health issues. One day, when you need it, the system will help you, too.

REMEMBER

While it might seem annoying to have money taken out of your paycheck now, think of it like an insurance plan. You're helping others today, and when it's your turn, the system will help you. It's all about making sure that when you're older or in need, you won't have to worry about not having enough money to live on or pay for medical care. So, FICA and Social Security taxes are there to support you and others throughout life.

Paying taxes

City, state, and federal (and sometimes county) taxes are amounts taken out of your paycheck to help pay for services and programs that benefit the area you live in. Both taxes fund things that make your city and state run smoothly, like schools, roads, public safety, parks, and other services you use regularly.

City taxes (sometimes called local or municipal taxes) are used to take care of things closer to home, within your city or town. This includes maintaining public transportation, keeping parks clean, paying for local police and fire departments, and funding local schools. If your city has a special project, like building a new community center or fixing roads, city taxes help cover the costs.

State taxes are collected by the state government to fund bigger projects and services that impact the whole state. These might include highways, state universities, healthcare programs, and state law enforcement. Not every state has income tax; some states, like Florida and Texas don't collect this tax at all. But if your state does have income tax, the money helps keep your state functioning and supports things like education, transportation, and public health.

Federal taxes are amounts taken out of your paycheck to help fund the operations of the U.S. government and provide essential services to the country. These taxes support a wide range of programs, including national defense, public education, healthcare (like Medicaid and Medicare), Social Security, and infrastructure projects like roads and bridges. Federal taxes also fund government agencies that ensure public safety, regulate industries, and provide assistance during emergencies or natural disasters.

These taxes are usually a percentage of your income. The exact amount varies depending on where you live. When you see these deductions on your paycheck, it means the government is taking out your share of the costs needed to provide services and improve your community.

Though it might be frustrating to have these amounts deducted from your pay, city and state taxes help make sure that your community is safe, well-maintained, and full of services that you and others rely on. Without these taxes, many things you might take for granted — like public libraries, streetlights, snow removal, or even trash pickup — wouldn't happen.

City and state taxes are your contribution to your community. You're helping to pay for the services and resources you use every day, and this money ensures your community stays a place where people can live, work, and enjoy life.

REMEMBER

City and state taxes are your contribution to your community. You're helping to pay for the services and resources you use every day, and this money ensures your community stays a place where people can live, work, and enjoy life.

Paying union dues

Union dues are payments taken out of your paycheck if you're a member of a labor union. A *union* is an organization that represents workers in your job or industry and works to protect your rights, improve working conditions, and negotiate better pay, benefits, and job security.

The money from union dues helps the union cover its operating costs and fund the services it provides to its members. These services include negotiating with your employer on your behalf (called *collective bargaining*), ensuring fair treatment in the workplace, and offering legal support if there's a dispute between you and your employer. The union also works to make sure that everyone is being paid fairly and that safety regulations are being followed at work.

Think of union dues as a membership fee. Just like you'd pay to be part of a club or group, union dues are your contribution to help keep the union running and effective. In return, the union fights to protect your interests at work. They often negotiate contracts that include things like better wages, health benefits, vacation time, and workplace safety rules.

TIP

Paying union dues can also give you access to training and professional development opportunities, job security resources, and sometimes even special discounts or benefits that are available to union members.

Making Optional Paycheck Deductions

In the previous section, we mention making mandatory paycheck deductions. However, it is also important to discuss optional paycheck deductions. Optional means you have the ability to choose how much of your check is dedicated to a benefit (some can be opted out altogether). Some of your optional deductions are pre-tax, while others are post-tax. What these deductions are depends on your company and your preferences.

Paying for health insurance

Health insurance is extremely important for you to feel happy and secure, because health is wealth. Any U.S. employer with at least 50 employees is required to provide healthcare coverage to their full-time employees. However, if you are a part-time or contract worker, you may not be eligible to enroll in these benefits. If you are under the age of 26 in the U.S., you can use your parent's health insurance. If you are not covered by your parent's health insurance before the age of 26 you will have to get your own coverage.

REMEMBER

Healthcare insurance, vision insurance, and dental insurance are different types of coverage that have separate costs. (For more information, check out Chapter 21.)

Health insurance premiums

Health insurance premiums are the amount of money you pay, often directly out of your paycheck, to maintain your healthcare insurance coverage. These payments ensure that you have financial protection if you need medical care, like doctor visits, hospital stays, or prescription medications.

You pay the monthly premium with pre-tax paycheck dollars, and this keeps your healthcare insurance active. Even if you don't use medical services that month, the premium ensures that if you do need care later on, you won't have to pay the full cost out of pocket. Your employer may help cover part of the premium, meaning they pay a portion and you pay the rest.

While premiums don't cover everything (you may still have to pay for things like copays or deductibles), they help lower the overall cost of your healthcare. The price of your healthcare premium will depend on what insurance company your employer uses, the different plans offered, and how much coverage you need.

Health savings account

A health savings account (HSA) is a special savings account that lets you set aside money, tax-free, to pay for qualified medical expenses. You can use the money in your HSA to cover things like doctor visits, prescriptions, medical equipment, and even dental or vision care.

To qualify for an HSA, you need to be enrolled in a high deductible health plan (HDHP), which means you have to pay more out of pocket before your insurance kicks in. The money you contribute to your HSA is pre-tax.

One big benefit of an HSA is that the money in the account rolls over each year — you don't lose it if you don't spend it by the end of the year. Plus, the account belongs to you, even if you change jobs. HSAs offer a smart way to save for future medical expenses while also getting a tax break.

Flexible savings account

A flexible savings account (FSA) is a special account that lets you save money, tax-free, to pay for eligible medical expenses. Just like an HSA, you can use an FSA to cover things like copays, prescriptions, medical supplies, and even some dental and vision costs. The money you put into an FSA is also pre-tax paycheck dollars.

You decide how much to contribute at the start of your new job or during the open enrollment period (discussed in the section, "Understanding post-tax benefits"). The downside is that FSAs have a "use-it-or-lose-it" rule, meaning you have to spend the money by the end of the plan year, or you may lose it. Some plans offer a grace period or let you roll over a small amount to the next year, but this varies.

FSAs are useful for covering predictable healthcare costs, like regular doctor visits or prescriptions, but you need to plan your contributions carefully to avoid losing unspent funds.

Employer retirement benefits

The cool thing about a full-time job is that the company can help you save for your future retirement plans. They let you set aside a portion of your paycheck to save for retirement, and in some cases, your employer might even throw in extra money to help you out. The great thing about these benefits is that they help you build a financial cushion for when you stop working someday.

However, because the money is taken directly from your paycheck, it means you'll see a slightly smaller take-home pay each time. But the benefit is worth it, because you're setting yourself up for long-term financial stability. Starting early and contributing regularly can make a huge difference by the time you retire!

401(k), 403(b), Thrift Savings Plan

There are three common employer-related retirement accounts: 401(k), 403(b), and the Thrift Savings Plan (TSP). Each of these plans helps you save for retirement, and they're available through different types of jobs, with some key differences.

1. **401(k):** The most well-known retirement plan, a 401(k) is offered by most private-sector employers (like companies or businesses). You contribute a portion of your paycheck before taxes, which lowers your taxable income. Many employers offer a matching contribution, meaning they'll add to your savings if you contribute. (This is like free money for retirement!) The money grows tax-deferred until you withdraw it when you retire. You can also choose where to invest your 401(k), like in stocks or bonds.

2. **403(b):** This plan is similar to a 401(k), but it's offered by public schools, nonprofit organizations, and certain government departments. Just like a 401(k), you contribute pre-tax money from your paycheck, and it grows tax-deferred. Some employers may offer a match, but it's less

common than with a 401(k). One difference is that 403(b) plans sometimes have fewer investment options, but they can still be a great way to save.

3. **Thrift Savings Plan (TSP):** A TSP is a retirement plan for federal employees and members of the military. It's similar to a 401(k) in that you contribute pre-tax money from your paycheck, and it grows tax-deferred. A TSP also offers matching contributions for federal employees, but not for military personnel. One unique feature of a TSP is that it offers very low fees compared to other retirement plans, making it a great value for participants.

Here are some comparisons of the three plans:

>> **All three plans allow you to save for retirement with pre-tax money,** meaning your contributions reduce your taxable income today.

>> **The main difference among the plans lies in who can access each one.** A 401(k) is for private-sector employees, a 403(b) is for public schools and nonprofit organizations, and a TSP is for federal employees and military members.

>> **Investment options vary.** The 401(k) plans typically have the most options, while the TSPs have fewer options with lower fees.

No matter which plan you have access to, taking advantage of employer–sponsored retirement benefits can help you build a strong financial future.

Pensions

A *pension* is a retirement plan that some employers offer, where they promise to pay you a certain amount of money regularly after you retire. Unlike a 401(k), where you have to save your own money, a pension is mostly funded by your employer, though sometimes you may also contribute a small amount.

Here's how it works: While you're working, your employer sets aside money for your pension, and once you retire, you'll start getting regular payments based on factors like how long you worked there and how much you earned. It's like getting a pay-check, even though you're no longer working!

Pensions are common in government jobs or older companies, but less common in today's private sector jobs. A big benefit of getting a pension is that they are predictable because you know how much money you'll receive in retirement. However, since pensions are managed by your employer, you don't control the investment like you would with a 401(k).

Other company benefits you can pay for

The different benefits your company can offer are limitless. Each company has unique offerings to make employees want to work for them. These benefits are the company's investment in you and all of their employees.

Here are five optional company benefits that you can choose to pay for from your paycheck. These aren't as common as health or retirement benefits, but they can still be super useful depending on your needs.

1. **Life insurance:** Some companies offer life insurance, where a portion of your paycheck can go toward coverage that provides money to your family if something happens to you. It's not fun to think about, but it's a way to make sure your loved ones are taken care of. This is usually paid with post-tax dollars.

2. **Disability insurance:** This insurance helps replace part of your income if you get injured or are too sick to work for a long time. It's like a financial backup plan for you when things don't go as expected. Disability insurance is often paid with post-tax dollars.

3. **Tuition reimbursement:** Some companies help pay for your college or extra training. If you're going to school while working, this benefit could cover part of your tuition or fees, which means less student loan debt! This is typically reimbursed with post-tax dollars, but the benefit itself may have tax advantages.

4. **Commuter benefits:** If you take public transportation to work or pay for parking, some employers let you use part of your paycheck to cover these costs before taxes, which can save you money. This means you use pre-tax dollars to pay for things like bus passes or parking fees.

5. **Gym memberships or wellness programs:** Some companies offer discounted gym memberships or wellness programs to keep you healthy. It's a great way to invest in your physical and mental well-being without paying the full price. This is usually paid with post-tax dollars.

These benefits help you get more out of your paycheck by covering useful stuff that you might pay for anyway. Depending on the benefit, using pre-tax dollars can help you save even more money by lowering

Chapter **16**

The Real Cost of Work

Athena will always remember her first job. She started her career in youth development while in high school and oversaw various locations at an after-school program. Athena loved working as much as she could, partly because she liked to stay busy, but also because she loved to go shopping.

While Athena was filing taxes for the first time, she discovered she owed the state of Arizona a few hundred dollars. As it turned out, she hadn't determined the right amount of money to be deducted on her behalf by her employer for taxes. Learning the hard way would mean that Athena overpaid her taxes for years until she figured out the right balance.

Athena also found out that the saying, "It takes money to make money," might actually be, umm, true. She hadn't accounted for expenses such as getting to and from work in a small town that had no public transportation, and paying for extra uniforms so she wouldn't have to rewash the same one all the time.

In this chapter, we'll share typical expenses that people have to pay when they are working. While we might not cover all of them, these are definitely the ones you should keep an eye out for (and also plan for). Knowing how much it costs to go to work every day can help you pick out the right job for you and your finances.

TIP

To find out more about the rules regarding your age, how many hours you can work, and other questions, check out YouthRules at www.dol.gov/agencies/whd/youthrules.

Looking at What Taxes Cover

Taxes are essentially the money that individuals and businesses pay to the government to help pay for services around their community. This money is collected to fund various public services that everyone can benefit from, like schools, policing, emergency services, and public transportation. Taxes also help cover expenses like the roads we drive on, parks, and hospitals. Without these services, we wouldn't be very safe.

Discovering types of deducted taxes

You fund several different types of taxes through your paycheck. The most common one is income tax. *Income tax* is a tax on the money you earn. The most common way to pay your income tax is to have your employer take money directly from your paycheck and send it to the Internal Revenue Service (IRS) on your behalf.

You pay two different types of income tax. Federal income tax is paid to the IRS, as we previously mentioned. This tax funds federal services like the military and other national programs. Then there is state income tax, which funds services that are local. Not all states have a state income tax.

Two other programs that are funded through your paycheck by taxes are Social Security and Medicaid. Social Security is a government program in the United States that provides financial support to people when they retire, become disabled, or in the event of a family member's death. It's designed to help ensure that people have some income when they can't work.

Medicaid is another government program in the United States that helps provide health coverage to people with a low income. Medicaid helps families and individuals cover costs like doctor visits, hospitals, and medicine. Medicaid plays a crucial role in making healthcare accessible for people who might not otherwise be able to afford it.

Filing your taxes

Once you start earning money, you'll need to file a tax return every year. A tax return is a form filed with the IRS that verifies how much money you have earned for the year. Once you have verified your income, the IRS will help you determine if you paid enough in taxes. Depending on a variety of factors, you may owe (like Athena did!), or you may get money back from overpaying your taxes.

Getting familiar with taxes now can help you a lot in the future when you start working. One of the worst things someone can do is to owe the government tax money. If you don't keep up on your taxes, the IRS can take money from your paycheck, even if it's from money owed years ago. This is called *wage garnishment*. That's why it's best to pay your taxes on time, every time, so you don't have to worry about it later.

Understanding Job-Related Expenses

Job-related expenses are costs that you might incur while working or looking for a job. These expenses are often necessary to do your job effectively or to get a new job. While some of these costs are an occasional purchase, others are everyday expenses. It's important to understand how much you'll be spending on job-related costs when it comes to deciding which job will work for you.

Uniforms

If your job requires you to wear a specific uniform or to dress in a certain way, the cost of those clothes can be considered a job-related expense.

A work uniform is a specific set of clothing that employees are required to wear while they are at work. The main purpose of a uniform is to create a sense of identity and professionalism among workers, but it can also help customers easily identify who works for a particular company.

For example, if you think about a restaurant, you might notice that waiters and waitresses wear matching shirts or aprons. In a hospital, nurses and doctors often wear scrubs. Some companies even have uniforms that include specific colors, logos, or styles to represent their brand.

Uniforms can vary widely, depending on the job. For instance, police officers wear uniforms that help them stand out and look professional, while healthcare workers, like nurses and doctors, wear scrubs for hygiene and comfort.

Wearing a uniform can also be practical. It may be designed to be comfortable or functional for the job, and it helps protect your personal clothes from getting dirty or damaged. For some jobs, like in construction or manufacturing, uniforms can include safety gear to keep you safe.

Some companies will provide you with part of a uniform such as a shirt, but you'll still be responsible for the remaining part of your outfit. On the other hand, some companies don't offer you a uniform at all and instead, provide a dress code, which may mean you need to buy additional clothing to complete an entire outfit.

TIP

Uniforms can add up, which is why it's important to find deals when you can. Check out thrift stores and overstock stores, like Marshalls and TJ Maxx, to find good quality at a decent price. You can also check out local uniform warehouse stores to find everyday basics for a fraction of the price you'd find elsewhere.

Don't get too crazy with clothes. Unless you're an influencer, you don't need to have a different look every time someone sees you. Several good tops and bottoms are all you really need. When President Barack Obama served in office, he would only wear the same gray suits repeatedly and no one even noticed!

Supplies and equipment

If you buy anything for your job — like tools, computers, or even pens and notebooks — those costs are related to your work. It's more common to buy your own supplies and work equipment when you're self-employed, which we talk about later in this chapter.

Like when you were in school, it's a good idea to ask what supplies you will need for a job. A lot of companies will cover supplies for you, but some jobs, like construction or mechanical work, may ask you to bring your own tools. You may also need a vehicle to drive around if your job requires it. When Athena was a case manager, she'd sometimes drive 60 miles in one day seeing clients!

Transportation

Transportation to work refers to the different ways you get from your home to your job. It's important because it's a part of your daily routine, especially if you want to earn money while gaining work experience. Some jobs may even require you to use your vehicle to perform job duties.

Driving to work, paying for gas, or using public transportation, all have costs that can add up. If you have to travel for work to different locations, those expenses also count.

If you have a car and a driver's license, you can drive yourself to work. This gives you flexibility, but you also need to consider gas prices, parking costs, and maintenance for your vehicle. Some offices require you to purchase a parking pass or pay for parking the days you are there.

Another common way of getting to work is public transportation. This includes buses, trains, or subways. Sometimes this can even include a ferry! Many cities have public transit systems that are economical and can take you to your workplace. It's a great option if you don't have a car. But some cities may lack accessible public transportation, which can make it a bit tricker to get to your job. Mykail prefers the subway when she is going into the office in Washington, D.C.

If your workplace is close to where you live, you can also consider biking or walking to work. It's free, healthy, and maybe the simplest or fastest way to get somewhere!

TIP

Try carpooling. *Carpooling* is when you share a ride with other people who work or live near you. It can save money on gas and is also a way to spend time with friends or meet new people. You can also carpool with friends as a way to save time and money!

REMEMBER

The way you choose to get to work can affect your schedule, how much time you spend commuting, and your overall job experience. It's always a good idea to consider your options and pick what works best for you!

Food

When it comes to food expenses related to a job, there are a few key points to consider. Some jobs provide a set allowance for meals, called a *meal allowance*, especially if you're traveling or working long hours. This means you may get a certain amount of money each day to buy lunch or dinner, which can help cover costs.

Many workplaces host events or meetings where food is provided. This could mean snacks during meetings or lunches during conferences, which can help you save money since you're not paying for those meals out of pocket. Some companies offer food as a perk in the office, like free coffee, snacks, or even full meals. This can be a great way to reduce your daily food expenses. (As someone who's obsessed with coffee, Athena can easily spend $40-plus at Starbucks!)

If your job requires you to travel, you might be able to claim back the cost of meals. You should keep receipts and know the company's policy on what's reimbursable. Ultimately, it's important to budget for food expenses, especially if your job doesn't cover meals. Keeping track of how much you spend on lunches or coffee breaks can help you manage your finances better.

TIP

Learn to plan meals. Planning your meals for the week is a great way to save money. One easy way to plan meals is to make one meal large enough for five people and divide it up into five separate Tupperware containers. Then, you have lunch for every day of the week. We often do this for breakfast and dinner, too, if we know we are going to be busy. You can also pack snacks like granola bars, fruit cups, jerky, and other items that don't need to be refrigerated so you're always ready.

Certifications and further training

What does an electrician, lawyer, and an accountant all have in common? They all need to pass a test to get a special certification to get a job. Passing your certification exams prove to future employers and clients that you did all the hard work to be the best professional. Even with a degree or diploma, your chosen career path may require you to be a life long learner. Yes, even when you are done with school you will still take a class or two in order to help you keep up with the latest trends in your industry. These are courses are called "Continuing Education" courses.

Professional tests

If you take classes, attend workshops, or get certifications to improve your skills for your job, those fees are considered job-related expenses.

Further training refers to additional education or skill development after you've completed a basic level of education, like high school. It's often aimed at improving or adding to the skills you already have. This can make you more competitive in the job market or prepare you for specific career paths that you want to follow.

This can include various forms of education like college degrees, vocational training (like learning a trade), workshops, online courses, or certifications in specific fields. Many jobs require further training to move up the career ladder, and so you may need to meet professional standards and requirements related to that position.

Further training emphasizes the idea that learning doesn't stop after high school. People continue to take courses and attend workshops throughout their lives to keep up with changes in their fields or to explore new interests. Engaging in further training can also connect you with professionals and peers in your field, which can help you to network and sometimes get an even better job!

Take advantage of free training, certificates, and programs!

There are hundreds of free certificates and free further education courses online. If you are looking to sharpen your skills in the job market, check out the following.

>> **Google:** One of the world's biggest online search engines also provides quite a few certifications as well. Some of the certificate topics include digital marketing and e-commerce, cybersecurity, data analytics, IT support, project management, and user experience (UX) design. Check out https://grow.google/enroll-certificates/ for more information.

>> **Harvard:** Known as one of the most prestigious universities in the world, Harvard offers a free computer science certificate program known as CS50x (Introduction to Computer Science) that introduces you to computer programming and software engineering. Courses include various software languages for all different fields. Visit https://pll.harvard.edu/course/cs50-introduction-computer-science to find out more.

>> **LinkedIn Learning:** LinkedIn is more than just a networking site. Along with keeping up with professional contacts, it also offers free courses and programs in various areas to help keep your resume fresh. Over 80 certificate programs await from partners like Microsoft, Adobe, Docker, Hootsuite,

Atlassian, and the OpenEDG Python Institute. Visit www.
linkedin.com/learning/browse/certifications
for more info.

>> **freeCodeCamp:** freeCodeCamp is a non-profit organization
that offers over 11,000 tutorials for free along with computer
programing certifications in JavaScript and Python, just to
name a few. Check out www.freecodecamp.org/ to find
out more.

In summary, further training is about continuing your education
and skill development to prepare for a career, improve your
skills, or change your career path altogether.

License

Certain jobs require a license because they involve specialized
skills, knowledge, and responsibilities that could impact public
safety or well-being. For example, professionals like doctors,
lawyers, and electricians deal with critical tasks that, if done
incorrectly, could harm people or lead to significant problems.
While some employers cover the license fee for their employees,
others do not, which means it's something you may have to
cover on your own.

Licensing ensures that these professionals have met specific
educational standards and passed examinations to confirm their
knowledge and skills. This process helps protect the public by
ensuring that only qualified individuals can practice in these
fields.

Additionally, having a license often means that there are regulations and ethical standards that these professionals must adhere
to, which promotes accountability. For instance, licensed professionals can face consequences, like losing their license or fac-
ing legal action, if they don't follow the rules. Overall, licensing
helps maintain a level of trust between the public and those in
certain professions.

TIP

Look into tuition reimbursement with your employer. Some
well-known companies that offer tuition reimbursement are
Chipotle, Verizon, McDonald's, and Lowe's.

Job searching

Job searching is the process of looking for employment opportunities that match your skills, interests, and career goals. It usually involves several steps that require spending money on your part, but not always. Networking can be done free or online through a platform like LinkedIn. LinkedIn offers a membership that comes with more perks to help you connect with recruiters and employers you may be interested in.

A *resume* is a document that outlines your education, work experience, and skills. A cover letter accompanying the resume is a way to introduce yourself to potential employers and explain why you're a good fit for the job. You can create both of these documents for free online, but they may require you to print copies for an extra fee. You may also spend money on professional clothing if you don't have anything appropriate to wear to an interview.

Job searching can take time and effort, but it's a valuable process that helps you find a job that's right for you and starts you off on your career path.

Costs of being self-employed

If you're becoming your own boss, there are several items you might need to purchase to set up your business and ensure smooth operations. Here's a list to consider:

» **Office equipment**

- Desktop computer or laptop
- Printer and scanner
- Telephone or VoIP system
- Office furniture (desk, chair, filing cabinets)

» **Software**

- Productivity software (Microsoft Office, Google Workspace)
- Accounting software (QuickBooks, FreshBooks)

- Project management tools (Trello, Asana)
- Graphic design software (Adobe Creative Suite, Canva)

>> Office supplies

- Notebooks, pens, and stationery
- Printer paper and ink
- Business cards
- Post-it notes and organizers

>> Technology accessories

- External hard drive or cloud storage
- Keyboard and mouse
- Webcam and microphone (for video conferencing)
- Surge protectors and chargers

>> Home office setup

- Chair and desk
- Desk lamp
- Decor and organization items

>> Marketing materials

- Website domain and hosting
- Marketing collateral (brochures, flyers)
- Social media advertising
- Online tools for email marketing (Mailchimp)

>> Legal and financial needs

- Business licenses and permits
- Insurance (liability, health)
- Consultation fees for accountants or legal advice
- Subscription to a business management service

>> Personal development

- Books or online courses related to business skills
- Networking membership fees or event tickets
- Coaching or mentorship programs

>> Miscellaneous

- Business registration fees
- Safety and health items (first aid kit, fire extinguisher)
- Transportation (if you need to travel for meetings)

This list can vary, depending on the type of business you're planning to run. You can adjust it based on your specific needs and goals!

Chapter **17**

Protecting Your Money Online

We live in a world full of technology, and banking has gone mostly digital. A surprising fact is that financial institutions are 300 times more likely to face a cybersecurity attack than any other type of business. Even if you don't see them, hackers and digital thieves are out there.

You might think that you don't have enough money in your bank account for a scammer to want to steal from you. However, money isn't the only thing these grifters are after. Your banking information is valuable information to steal. Once your sensitive data is in the hands of cybercriminals, they can use it to open accounts, falsify loans and checks, make unauthorized purchases in your name, and commit other financial crimes using your name and information.

This chapter will discuss why cybersecurity is so important for protecting your money, and introduce tools that can help protect you. It will also tell you how to look out for common scams.

Taking Your Personal Finance Cybersecurity Seriously

Your financial cybersecurity is super important, especially as you start managing your own money. Think about it like this: Would you give your name, address, and Social Security number to a stranger on the street? Probably not. A cybercriminal is even worse than a random stranger on the street because they have malicious intentions: Your bank account, credit card info, and personal details are valuable to hackers.

WARNING

Cybercriminals are always looking for weak spots, and sometimes we make it easy for them without realizing it. For example, using weak passwords, not updating devices, or clicking on suspicious links can all lead to your financial information being exposed.

Taking your financial cybersecurity seriously is like locking the door to your money. It's a simple way to keep your hard-earned cash safe from scammers who are always looking for ways to break in.

Concealing your email address

When it comes to your financial security, the email address you use for banking is just as important as a password. Hackers and scammers often target email accounts to gain access to sensitive information, so it's crucial to keep your banking email private and separate from the one you use for things like social media.

WARNING

If you're using the same email for both your public social media accounts and private banking, you're putting your financial information at risk. Think about it: Social media accounts are often public and can easily be hacked or used to gather info about you. Once hackers know your email, they can try to break into your banking or financial accounts.

To stay safe, create a separate email address just for banking and other important financial activities. This way, even if your social media gets hacked, your money stays protected. For an extra layer of security, consider signing up for a free encrypted email service like ProtonMail. Encryption keeps your emails private and safe from prying eyes, making it even harder for hackers to access your financial info.

Separating your email for banking and opting for encrypted services helps protect your money and personal info from online threats. It's a simple move that keeps you one step ahead of hackers.

Creating strong passwords

Having strong passwords for your financial accounts is very important. Passwords are the locks on the door to your money and personal info. Weak or simple passwords are easy for hackers to crack, which means they can break into your accounts, steal your money, or even commit identity theft.

Hackers use programs that can guess passwords by trying millions of combinations quickly. If your password is something simple like "password123" or your birthday, it's much easier for them to figure out. A strong password, though, makes it way harder for hackers to break in.

So, how do you create a strong password? Here are some tips:

>> Use at least 12 characters with a mix of uppercase and lowercase letters, numbers, and special symbols (like !, @, #).

>> Avoid using common words or anything personal like your name or birthdate.

>> Try a passphrase: Combine random words like "Giraffe$Skateboard3Sunshine!"

To keep your passwords safe and easy to manage, use a password manager. These tools store all your passwords securely and can even generate new, strong passwords for you. You can find free password managers that aren't connected to Apple or Google, like Bitwarden or LastPass, which offer great security features. They help you stay organized and make it easy to update your passwords regularly (something you should do often).

Getting cybersecurity tools you need

The good news about cybersecurity is that you don't have to do all the heavy lifting alone. Protecting your financial data is in the best interest of the bank and other helpful third-party services. Different tools are designed to help protect your identity and financial information. Some tools are free, and some are not, but what's important is finding the best tools for your finances.

Authentication app

If your password is like a lock, then two-factor authentication (2FA) is like adding an extra deadbolt to your door on your online accounts. We love 2FA because it means that even if someone gets your password, they still need a second way to prove it's really you before they can access your account. The first factor is your password, and the second factor could be a code sent to your phone or email, or from an app. This extra step makes it way harder for hackers to break in.

Having said that, using text or email codes for 2FA isn't as secure as it seems (although these methods are better than nothing). Hackers can still steal these codes through SIM swapping (where they take control of your phone number) or by hacking your email. That's why using an authenticator app is a better option.

Authenticator apps, like Duo Security or Authy, generate unique codes that refresh every 30 seconds. The codes aren't sent over the internet or through your phone carrier, so they're much harder for hackers to get. Plus, these apps work even if you don't have cell service or access to your email.

Password manager

A *password manager* is a tool that stores and organizes all your passwords in one secure place. Instead of trying to remember all your different passwords or writing them down (which isn't safe), a password manager saves them for you and even helps you create strong, unique passwords for each of your accounts. You only have to remember one master password to access all your other passwords.

Why is this helpful? Well, strong passwords are important for protecting your financial accounts and other sensitive information. Let's be real, you can't (and won't) remember a bunch of complex, secure passwords. A password manager saves you the trouble by storing all your passwords securely, so you don't have to worry about forgetting them or using the same weak password everywhere.

Now, you might think, "Why not just use Google or Apple's password managers?" While they are convenient, third-party managers like Bitwarden or LastPass are generally considered more secure. Third-party managers aren't tied to your devices or specific accounts (like your Google or Apple ID), which means if your Google or Apple account gets hacked, your passwords won't be exposed, too. Plus, third-party options offer extra features like multi-device syncing, better encryption, and more control over your security.

Encrypted email address

An *encrypted email provider* is a service that keeps your emails private by scrambling (encrypting) the contents, so only the person you're sending the email to can read it. This makes it much harder for hackers or anyone else to intercept and read your messages, especially if they contain sensitive information like your banking details or personal info.

Why should you use one? Well, most regular email providers (like Gmail or Yahoo) don't fully protect your emails. If someone hacks into your account or your emails are intercepted, they could easily read them. With encrypted email providers like ProtonMail or Tuta, your emails stay protected, giving you better privacy and security.

If you're sending or receiving important info (like financial or personal data), using an encrypted email provider adds an extra layer of protection to make sure only the right people can access it. It's especially helpful for keeping your financial information safe from hackers, ensuring your privacy, and giving you control over your digital communications.

Avoiding Online Scams

Scammers are getting really good at tricking people into giving up their money and sensitive data. It's their job to outsmart you. But we want to prepare you for some potential scams that you might face online. Being able to stop online scams means you are less likely to be impacted by identity theft or bank account fraud. Online scammers love to target younger people because they think it is easy to trick them out of their money.

Dodging online phishing

If you have ever gotten a weird text about some random purchase with a link, you have experienced an online phishing scam. Online phishing scams occur when scammers try to trick you into giving them personal information like passwords, bank account details, or credit card numbers.

WARNING

These scams often involve fake emails, texts, or websites that are designed to look like they're from a trusted company or person, such as your bank or a popular website. The scammers want you to click on a link or provide sensitive information, which they can then use to steal your identity, access your accounts, or commit fraud.

Here are five things to watch out for to detect if you're being sent a phishing message.

1. **Suspicious sender:** Check the sender's email address. Phishing emails often come from strange or slightly misspelled versions of real company emails.

2. **Urgency or threats:** Be cautious if the message says something urgent, like "Act now!" or threatens you with account suspension or financial loss.

3. **Spelling and grammar mistakes:** Many phishing messages have obvious spelling, grammar, or formatting errors that legitimate companies would not make.

4. **Unfamiliar links:** Hover over any links before clicking to see where they actually lead. If the URL looks strange or doesn't match the company's website, it's probably a phishing attempt.

5. **Asking for personal information:** Legitimate companies will never ask for sensitive information like passwords, Social Security numbers, or account details via email or text.

TIP

It's important to double-check by visiting the official website directly or contacting the company to verify the message. Staying alert helps you protect yourself and your personal information from scammers.

Evading sale of nonexistent goods or services scams

Those random ads on social media that are selling your favorite expensive items for $2.99 are what we call a sale of nonexistent goods or services scam. A *sale of nonexistent goods or services scam* occurs when someone tricks you into paying for something that doesn't actually exist. Scammers set up fake online stores or ads, promising great deals on popular items like electronics, clothes, or concert tickets. They might make the website or ad look real, but after you send them money, you never get what you paid for because it doesn't exist.

For example, you might see an ad on social media for a super cheap PlayStation 5. The website looks legit, so you pay for it, but then it never arrives, and the seller disappears. In this type of scam, the product or service was never real in the first place, and the scammer's goal is just to take your money.

Here are three things to help you detect a sale of nonexistent goods or services scam.

1. **Unbelievably low prices:** If a deal seems too good to be true, like an expensive item being sold for way less than usual, it's often a scam. Scammers lure people in with crazy discounts on popular items.

2. **Lack of reviews or sketchy website:** Check for customer reviews and feedback about the seller or website. If the site has little to no reviews or looks unprofessional (bad design, spelling mistakes, no contact info), it's a red flag.

3. **No secure payment options:** If the website doesn't offer secure payment options (like credit cards or PayPal) and asks for wire transfers, gift cards, or other sketchy payment methods, it's likely a scam. Always look for the "https" and lock symbol in the web address for security.

Detecting debt collection scams

While debt collectors are real, a *debt collection scam* occurs when someone pretends to be a debt collector to trick you into paying money for a debt you don't actually owe. These scammers often call, email, or send messages claiming you owe them money and may even threaten legal action or arrest if you don't pay up immediately. Their goal is to scare you into giving them your money or personal information.

REMEMBER

To avoid debt collection scams, never panic when you receive a suspicious debt collection message. Always verify the debt by asking for written proof of what you owe. Legitimate debt collectors are required by law to provide this. Never give out personal or financial information, like your Social Security number or bank details, without confirming that the collector is real.

Here are three things to help you detect a debt collection scam.

1. **No written proof:** Real debt collectors must send you a written notice with details about the debt within five days of contacting you. If they refuse to provide this or say it's not necessary, it's a red flag.

2. **Pressure and threats:** Scammers often use aggressive tactics like threatening legal action, jail time, or even violence if you don't pay immediately. Real debt collectors don't do this.

3. **Requests for unusual payments:** If they ask for payment via wire transfers, gift cards, or prepaid debit cards, it's almost certainly a scam. Legit collectors don't ask for payment in these forms.

Not falling for romance scams

If you have ever heard of the Tinder Swindler, then you have absolutely heard of romance scams. A *romance scam* occurs when someone pretends to be interested in a romantic relationship to gain your trust and then take your money or personal information.

Scammers usually target people through dating apps, social media, or online chat platforms, building a relationship over time. Once they think you trust them, they start asking for money, gifts, or personal info, often with made-up stories about needing help for a personal emergency or travel costs.

WARNING

To avoid romance scams, be cautious if someone you meet online seems too perfect or moves the relationship forward very quickly. Never send money or share sensitive personal details, like your Social Security number or passwords, with someone you've only met online. It's always a good idea to video chat with someone to verify they are who they say they are before trusting them too much.

Here are three things to help detect a romance scam.

1. **Avoiding in-person meetings:** Scammers will often make excuses about why they can't meet in person or video chat. If someone always has an excuse to avoid face-to-face interaction, it's a warning sign.

2. **Sudden requests for money:** If someone you've been talking to online suddenly asks for money, especially for emergencies like medical bills or travel, be skeptical. Real love doesn't come with sudden financial requests.

3. **Inconsistent stories:** Scammers might slip up and give conflicting details about their life, location, or background. If their story changes or doesn't add up, it's a red flag.

Bypassing government scams

The IRS will never call or email you to pay them money . . . like ever. If a scammer is posing as the IRS or any other government entity asking for money and information, this is known as a *government scam*. A government scam occurs when someone pretends to be a government official or agency to trick you into giving them money or personal information.

Scammers often claim you owe taxes, need to pay fines, or have to verify your identity for a government program. They might call, email, or send letters that look official, trying to create a sense of urgency to make you act quickly and without thinking.

To avoid government scams, always be skeptical of unexpected calls or messages claiming to be from the government. Remember, legitimate government agencies will never ask for personal information or payment over the phone or through email. If you're unsure, hang up and call the official government agency using a trusted number you find online.

Here are three things to help you detect a government scam.

1. **Urgent threats:** Scammers often use scare tactics, like threatening arrest, legal action, or fines, if you don't pay immediately. The government doesn't make threats like this.

2. **Contacting you out of the blue:** If you receive an unexpected call, text, or email from someone claiming to be a government official, especially if they ask for money or personal details, it's likely a scam. Real government contact is usually through mail and official channels.

3. **Unusual payment methods:** If someone claims to be from the government and asks for payment via wire transfers, gift cards, or cryptocurrency, it's a scam. Government agencies typically only accept payments through official channels.

Looking out for employment scams

Scammers will always seek to take advantage of their target's vulnerabilities, and nobody is more vulnerable than a job seeker looking for a stable income. An *employment scam* occurs when someone pretends to offer you a job to steal your money or personal information.

Scammers often advertise fake job openings on big-name job boards (like LinkedIn or Indeed) or send unsolicited job offers via email or social media. They might promise high salaries for little work, ask you to pay for training or equipment upfront, or request sensitive information like your Social Security number before you even start working.

To avoid employment scams, be cautious of job offers that seem too good to be true. Always research the company to make sure it's legitimate. Look for reviews and see if the company has a professional website and contact information. If a potential employer asks for money upfront for training, equipment, or background checks, that's a major red flag.

Here are three things to help you detect an employment scam.

1. **Too good to be true:** If a job offers an unusually high salary for minimal work or requires little to no experience, it's likely a scam. Real job offers usually have realistic expectations.

2. **Lack of company information:** If the employer can't provide clear information about the company, like a website or physical address, be cautious. Legitimate companies should be transparent about who they are.

3. **Unprofessional communication:** If the job offer comes through unprofessional channels, like personal email accounts or social media DMs, or if there are lots of spelling and grammar mistakes, it's a warning sign. Real companies typically communicate through official channels and take the time to present themselves professionally.

Taking Steps After You've Been Scammed

If you have ever been a victim of an online cyberattack, do not feel embarrassed that you missed the signs. In fact, nearly two million people were scammed online in 2022 alone. Another feeling you might have after being scammed is violated.

I know when I, Mykail, was scammed by a fake customer service agent, I felt icky and violated. How could someone steal my hard-earned money? Why didn't I see the signs? After about two weeks and several calls and reports, I got my $400 back. But that didn't stop me from feeling violated. After getting scammed once, I decided never again.

Let's talk about what you should do after you have fallen victim to an online scam attack to prevent it from happening again.

Contacting the authorities

If an online scammer ever steals your money, it's extremely important to take action right away by contacting the right authorities. First, you should report the scam to your local police. They can help create a record of what happened, and if needed, they can guide you on what steps to take next. To find your local police department's number, just look it up online or call the non-emergency line, which you can easily find on your city or county's website.

Next, you'll want to report the scam to the Federal Trade Commission (FTC). The FTC is the agency in charge of dealing with fraud and scams across the U.S. You can visit their official website (ftc.gov) to report what happened, and this helps them to track down scammers and prevent them from targeting more people.

Finally, contact your bank's fraud department to let them know what happened. This is key because your bank might be able to reverse the transaction or protect your account from further charges. Most banks have a fraud hotline, and you can find this number on your bank's website or on the back of your debit or credit card.

REMEMBER

You should contact these authorities as soon as you realize you've been scammed. Acting quickly increases your chances of getting your money back and helps prevent more people from falling for the same scam.

Recovering lost funds

Getting your money back after a scam has occurred could be easy or difficult, depending on a few factors: how the money was accessed, how much money was stolen, the account (either credit or checking) the fraud impacted, and policies (from your bank or government). Sometimes you might not be able to recover all or even some of the funds; this is why it is important to be extremely vigilant and cautious about exposing your sensitive financial information.

Let's first look at the difference between fraudulent activity on your credit card account and on your checking account (accessed through a debit card). With a credit card, you're protected by something called a *zero-fault policy*. This means if someone steals your card or information and makes charges, you won't be responsible for paying them back, as long as you report it quickly. Credit card companies often handle fraud more swiftly, and it doesn't affect your actual cash, just your credit limit.

With a debit card, the money is taken directly from your bank account. It can take longer to get your stolen money back, and you could be out that money during the investigation. Plus, if you don't report the fraud within a certain time frame, you could be responsible for part of the loss. In both cases, acting fast is key, but credit cards usually offer better protection when it comes to fraud.

REMEMBER

Routinely checking your banking statements is very important in identifying fraudulent activity. At least once a month, you should review your statements to ensure all transactions are accurate and made by you.

If someone steals your money, here's what you need to do to try to get it back:

1. **Contact your bank or credit card company immediately.** Explain what happened and report the fraudulent transaction. For debit cards, you need to reach out to your bank's fraud department. If the fraud happened with a credit card, call your credit card company.

2. **Request a chargeback.** This is when your bank or credit card company reverses the fraudulent charge. They usually start an investigation and might ask you to fill out some paperwork or provide evidence.

3. **Freeze your account or cancel your card.** To prevent any further charges, ask your bank or credit card company to freeze the account or issue you a new card with a new number.

4. **Monitor your account.** Keep an eye on your bank or credit card account for any additional suspicious charges, and report them right away if you see anything else weird.

TIP

Turning on banking notifications is a great way to have constant contact with your bank. You can turn settings on to be notified when any transactions happen with your accounts.

In some cases, if your personal information was exposed in a data breach or if a bank was caught doing unethical business, you might be able to join a civil lawsuit to get money. These lawsuits happen when companies or banks mishandle your data or engage in shady practices that harm customers.

After the lawsuit, there may be a settlement where the company or bank agrees to pay money to everyone impacted. If you're part of the lawsuit, you'll usually get a notification (by mail or email) explaining how to file a claim. Payouts can sometimes take months or even years, but it's worth keeping up with because you could be compensated for damages, whether it's stolen data or unfair fees from a bank. Keep an eye on news about breaches you're involved in, and always protect your data moving forward.

Changing your information

If a hacker has weaseled their way into your accounts through your email or password, it is a good idea to change your information to avoid getting hacked again, or if you have multiple accounts to secure the others. Hackers know that oftentimes, people use the same passwords and emails for multiple accounts (another reason why it is important to have strong, unique passwords).

After an attack, it's best to change your email address and password associated with the impacted account and any other financial accounts that use that email address. This is why we strongly suggest you also use a secure password manager like LastPass or 1Password. These secure password managers have features to prompt users to change their passwords every 3 to 6 months to keep their financial data safe. Use the tips in the previous sections to strengthen your security and make the switch after a cyberattack.

IN THIS CHAPTER

» **Living independently**

» **Choosing who to live with and where**

» **Covering expenses**

» **Paying bills and securing resources**

» **Finding resources to protect yourself**

Chapter **18**

Bills, Bills, Bills

B ack before Beyoncé was *Beyoncé,* she was the lead singer of a successful girls' group called Destiny's Child. While they had a lot of bops, one that particularly stands out to this day is titled "Bills, Bills, Bills." The song is technically about a girl fighting with her boyfriend and hinting that because she can pay her own bills, he needs to go somewhere else with his nonsense.

Paying bills is something you may have to start doing before you are 18 years old, for a variety of reasons. For instance, Athena remembers paying her own cellphone bill when she was in high school. She also remembers paying for bus passes to get to work. (Work expenses are covered in more depth in Chapter 16.) But since a lot of cellphone providers won't issue you your own account without a cosigner until you're at least 18, you have time to get ready.

Even if you're already paying bills, this chapter is still packed with tips on how to stay organized, live independently, and take care of your own individual housing needs so that you can feel confident in your ability to be the independent young adult you want to be, whenever the time comes.

Becoming More Independent

We have led pretty independent lives since graduating high school. In some instances, we were independent in high school, too. It was important to both of us to seek higher education, and that involved both of us having to figure out a lot of stuff on our own.

Finding transportation and figuring out how to pay for various things (even food) helped both of us realize how important it was to be able to do things on our own. Whether you decide to strike out on your own, grab some roommates, or just take on more responsibility at home with your family, there are a few perks you get when doing so.

>> **Learning to be self-reliant:** When you live on your own, you find out how to become self-reliant. Living independently comes with a lot of responsibilities, such as paying your own bills, shopping for household items, and making sure that you have a clean and organized space to relax in. No one reminds you to do these things; you have to remember to do them.

>> **Developing life skills:** Paying bills, keeping your place clean, doing laundry, and making household decisions are all life skills that you develop when living alone. Mykail learned how important her location to amenities like the grocery store was when it came to where she lived, while Athena learned how to pay her own utility bills in a way that worked for her and her ADHD. When you are on your own, you figure out how to fix things, cook, and keep yourself on schedule!

>> **Getting privacy and space:** Living on your own or with just roommates instead of close friends and family can give you that space you may need when spending time by yourself relaxing or even sleeping in!

>> **Learning who you are without anyone telling you otherwise:** We like to think that you are always learning about yourself throughout your life. A growth mindset is important in all areas of your life, especially your finances. Living on your own allows you to do just that. When living on your own, you can figure out what foods you like and when you like to eat.

Do you like clutter, or do you prefer a more minimalist approach? Are certain things, like streaming services, less important so you have money to spend somewhere else? This is the time to answer these questions.

Choosing to Live with Roommates or Alone

Deciding whether to live with roommates or on your own can be tricky. Both options have advantages and disadvantages. We've done both, and we can honestly say there was a time and place for each kind of arrangement, when we were getting established and finding out who we were. Let's talk about both scenarios and which one might work better for you.

Renting with roommates

A roommate is someone who shares a living space with you. Sometimes it's sharing a room like you might do in college, or living in an expensive place like New York City. It might also be sharing an apartment or house where you both have your own room but share the common living areas like the living room and kitchen. Here are some of the pros and cons of having a roommate.

PROS

>> **Sharing expenses:** Splitting rent and utility bills can significantly lower your living expenses, which can help you live in a better area. Sharing expenses can also help you work toward your financial goals since you'll need less money to live on.

>> **Sharing chores:** Household tasks can be divided up, making it easier to manage the upkeep of your living space.

>> **Having built-in company:** A roommate can provide companionship, reducing feelings of loneliness and creating a sense of community at home. This can come

in handy if your family lives far away or if you are building a new, healthy community for a fresh start.

>> **Experiencing different perspectives:** Living with others can expose you to different lifestyles, ideas, and new ways of doing things. This can help inspire you when you are working on yourself.

CONS

>> **Having to rely on someone to cover their expenses:** While it's nice to have someone to split expenses with, it can also be nerve wracking. If a roommate fails to pay their share of the rent or bills, you might have to cover them on your own. This can lead to strained finances as well as strained relationships. There can also be big consequences for paying your bills late!

>> **Having different cleaning styles:** Having an additional person in your space will create additional messes to clean up. A roommate should be timely with cleaning up after themselves and taking care of shared spaces. If you find yourself having a different opinion on what's clean, this might cause tension between you and your roommate. Usually, you can find a medium ground; however, sometimes you can't.

>> **Dealing with noise and unwanted people in your living space:** Both of us eventually chose to live on our own after having roommates. Athena started to attend class full-time, which required control over her environment for studying. Mykail also needed control over her own environment to record her videos for The Boujie Budgeter. Having roommates may mean that you have to put up with additional noise and possibly undesirable people around, like loud movie nights or someone's girlfriend.

Ultimately, living with roommates can be a fun experience if you find people you get along with and who have similar ideas to you. It's important to always practice clear communication and respect each other's boundaries, too.

TIP

Ask your landlord about amenities. Amenities are additional items that an apartment complex or housing development might offer to add value to living there. Amenities can include a pool, spa, or gym; a clubhouse where you can host large gatherings; an office center with access to a printer and the internet; a park, walking trails, and an area for your pets; and even free coffee and snacks! You'd be surprised at what comes with your living space for you to take advantage of.

Living on your own

If sharing a place with a roommate isn't for you, you can look into finding your own place. Here are some pros and cons of living on your own.

PROS

>> **Controlling your environment:** When you live by yourself, you can decorate, organize, and maintain your home exactly how you want to. Gone are the days where you had to ask someone if they liked the color of your pillows or to tell them those towels are for decoration.

>> **Prioritizing your schedule:** When you live alone, you don't need to consider anyone else's opinions, schedules, or needs when it comes to making a personal decision. That means there is no one to judge if you wake up at 4 a.m. to catch up on reality TV before class or work starts. You can also decide your routine around what time works best for you!

>> **Having privacy:** Gone are the days when your roommate's significant other randomly catches you dancing around with your cat in your pajamas while you make breakfast. Or, you know, just randoms waiting for your roommate to get home, where you don't want to leave them alone since they're strangers and you live there.

>> **Deciding which living expenses to incur:** Having the ability to choose what you will and won't pay for is financially empowering. For example, you can decide whether to use minimal electricity to save on your bill or to splurge on extra heating in the winter for added comfort.

CONS

>> **You are responsible for everything:** From paying the rent on time to making sure the house is clean, you're the one who is in charge of it all. When you start off on your own for the first time, being responsible for everything, especially financially responsible, can seem overwhelming.

>> **You might have to make sacrifices:** Because you have to cover everything, you might have to make some sacrifices in order to afford it and make it work. This might mean living in a less desirable area, living in a place that isn't as nice, or making due with fewer items around your home.

>> **You may deal with safety concerns:** It can be scary living by yourself, especially when you're young. It's important to live somewhere you feel comfortable, especially where you can come and go at all hours.

TIP

If you are moving into an apartment, ask the leasing office if they offer security. Most apartment complexes offer complimentary security after hours to help residents feel safer and prevent crime. On nights Athena knew she would be arriving home late, she would ask security to meet her at her car and walk her up to her door to ensure her safety.

Choosing a Location

When it comes to moving out on your own for the first time, you also need to think about location. Here are some questions to ask yourself when it comes to picking a spot to live:

>> **Is the area safe?** Previously in this chapter, we discussed how living on your own may come with additional safety concerns, so always check the crime rate of the area you are considering.

TECHNICAL STUFF

Check out the website SpotCrime at https://spotcrime. com/ to see what crimes are committed in your area using an interactive map. You can also google "Neighborhood + crime rate" to see what pops up.

>> **Do you like the area?** Liking the area where you live is important. While you might not always like the area you start off in, eventually you *do* want to live in an area or neighborhood that you like and that will help you live the lifestyle you want. For example, Mykail likes to be able to walk to restaurants, while Athena prefers to be close to her doctors in case she gets sick. Both of these scenarios would require a different type of neighborhood.

REMEMBER

Don't base where you live on your job! When Athena was looking for her first apartment, she was considering one that was close to the school where she was teaching. Her friend, who was a fellow teacher, sat her down and told her to pick a neighborhood she liked instead. Your job can be gone tomorrow, and then what? You're stuck in a place you'd rather not be. (Athena took the advice, and it was a good thing because a year and a half later, she was promoted and moved from that location!)

>> **Is it affordable?** We aren't gonna lie. Some areas are super expensive, sometimes for no reason. It may be a sign of how cool it is to live in that location, or just that property prices have always been high there. If an area isn't somewhere you really want to live, don't pay more than you have to.

Paying Utility Bills

As an adult, in addition to paying for your housing, you'll also be paying utility bills. Utility bills are the charges you pay for services that help keep your home running. These services include things like electricity, water, gas, and sometimes internet access or garbage collection.

Every month, you receive a bill for the services provided that tells you how much of each service you used and what you owe based upon that usage. Paying these bills on time is important because they keep your home comfortable and functional for everyday use.

Looking at fixed versus variable bills

Utility bills come in two different types: fixed and variable. Just like your expenses, it means something similar. Utilities that are fixed will be the same rate every month. Usually, utilities that are fixed include services like the internet, cable, trash, cellphone, and sewer.

Utilities that aren't the same amount of money every month are called a variable utility bill. These are the types of utilities where you pay based on how much of that service you use for that time. Electricity, water, and gas are all utilities that can vary from month to month in terms of pricing.

Negotiating bills

One way to keep your living expenses low is to find out how to negotiate bills. Negotiating bills is when you call your service provider to see if you can get a better deal than what you are already paying for your current service.

Sometimes you can find a cheap rate elsewhere, but it's a hassle to switch over, so asking first can save not only money but time. Here's a checklist of tips to negotiate:

>> **Understand the bills you want to negotiate.** Make sure you know how much you usually pay and what services you're getting.

>> **Check online for what other people pay for the same service.** This can help you figure out if you're paying too much. You can also ask your friends and family what they pay if you feel comfortable doing so.

>> **Be prepared.** Write down the main points you would like to discuss about why you should get a lower rate. For example, maybe you found a better deal with another company, or you've been a loyal customer for a long time and think you should be rewarded.

When you feel ready, call the customer service number or visit the office. Be polite and explain that you want to discuss your bill. Remember, you're not being rude; you're just asking for help!

Once you're talking to a representative, ask if there are any discounts or ways to lower your bill. You can say something like, "I've heard there are discounts for long-term customers. Can you help me find one?"

Always be nice during the conversation, even if things don't go your way at first. If they say no, ask if they can offer you any special deals or lower prices. Sometimes, they can offer reductions, especially if you mention other companies that have better rates. For every no, there is always a yes somewhere; you just have to find it.

TIP

Be ready to end the conversation if needed. If they can't help you, it's okay to say thank you and hang up the phone. Sometimes, just showing you're willing to leave can make them offer you a better deal!

TIP

If you get a better deal, ask for confirmation in writing, like an email. Keep track of your bills to see the changes. And if you didn't end up with a lower rate at this time, that doesn't mean you can't try again later on to see if you can.

Securing Resources

Part of living on your own for the first time is about securing items you need, also known as resources. Some of these items you'll buy rarely, and others you'll buy frequently. Let's take a look at what they are.

Cleaning supplies

One thing you're now fully responsible for when living on your own is making sure your place is clean! Disorganization can lead to cluttered minds along with trash everywhere and dishes in the sink. When you first move in, take time to go to your local dollar store or major retailer to stock up on the following items you might need:

- Sponges
- Dish soap
- Scrubbing brushes
- Disinfectant wipes
- Disinfectant spray
- Multipurpose cleaning spray
- Degreaser
- Bleach or bleaching alternative like vinegar and baking soda
- Bleach powder
- Microfiber cloth
- Dusting cloth

- Paper products such as paper towels and toilet paper
- Trash can
- Trash bags
- Broom
- Mop
- Vacuum
- Toilet cleaner
- Pair of rubber gloves
- Scent freshener
- Laundry detergent
- Fabric softener

TIP

Look on Amazon for a portable washer if you don't have one. They can be purchased for around $50. This, along with any drying rack or surface, can save you time and money from lugging around your laundry to the nearest laundromat!

Household items

Here is a list of items that you most likely need to run your household successfully.

- A toolbox (can be a small set with just the essentials for around $20)
- A set of pots and pans (you can buy these individually as you go)

- Dish towels and a drying rack
- Plates, cups, and glasses
- Measuring cups, kitchen utensils, and cutting boards

- » Trash can for the bathroom
- » Pillows
- » Blankets
- » Sheets
- » Bath towels
- » Shower curtain if there isn't one

- » Bath mat
- » Door mat
- » Laundry hamper
- » Organizing bins to hold smaller items

TIP

Check out Ikea, Amazon, Target, Walmart, and thrift stores for household items. For free finds, join "buy nothing" groups in your area on Facebook or NextDoor. Many stores have frequent sales along with already lower prices to help you get items as you need them.

Furniture

Last but not least, you'll most likely need to buy some furniture. The amount of furniture you need will be based on items you bring from your home and what your living situation may be. For instance, you'll most likely need fewer items if you're moving in with a roommate who's already established than if you're moving in by yourself.

- » Table
- » Dining chairs
- » Couch
- » Desk chair
- » Desk
- » Coffee table
- » Comfy chair

- » Bed
- » Dresser
- » TV
- » Nightstand
- » Bookcase
- » TV stand

TIP

Buy items as you go! If you don't need an item, don't force yourself to buy it. Athena lived without a TV for years before being given an old one by her dad, and she never ended up buying a dining room table or chairs since her apartment was small.

REMEMBER

Always check out second-hand stores for quality furniture at lower prices or places like Facebook Marketplace. If you are meeting up with someone, make sure you bring a friend along and meet in a public place for safety!

Protecting Yourself

It's important to protect yourself and your home once you are living on your own. It takes so much money and time to become established, and you will want to keep your things safe. Here are a few ways to do that.

Getting renter's insurance

Renter's insurance is an insurance policy that protects you while you are renting a home or apartment. It typically covers personal property against risks like theft, fire, and some types of water damage, such as flooding. Renter's insurance can also protect you by helping you cover legal costs if someone is injured in your rental unit or if you accidentally damage someone else's property.

Accessing local resources for help

Part of protecting yourself is knowing how to find resources when it comes to emergencies and financially hard times. One of the quickest ways you can find nearby resources is by entering your ZIP Code and "community resource center" in a search engine to find out the nearest location that can offer guidance and support. You can also use 211.org online or dial 211 on your phone to find out about more services that are nearby. Here are a few more resources to check out.

>> **Find Help:** This national database can help you find numerous services such as rental assistance, food-banks, and low-cost healthcare based upon your area. (www.findhelp.org/)

>> **Everyone On:** This organization helps you find low-cost or free internet for those who need additional financial assistance. (www.everyoneon.org/)

>> **The Trevor Project:** This is a nonprofit suicide prevention and crisis intervention organization for LGBTQ+ young people that offers help 24/7, 365 days a year. (www.thetrevorproject.org/)

>> **National Safe Place:** This hotline helps connect youth in crisis with emergency services in their area. (www.nationalsafeplace.org/txt-4-help)

>> **National Alliance on Mental Illness:** This directory offers numerous resources for mental health treatment and assistance with accommodations. (www.nami.org/wp-content/uploads/2023/11/NAMI-Teen-and-Young-Adult-HelpLine-Resource-Directory.pdf)

>> **U.S. Department of Housing and Urban Development:** Also known as HUD, this government department helps provide rental assistance with vouchers and one-time relief with partnering organizations. (www.hud.gov/)

>> **Community Action Partnership:** Much like 211 and Find Help, this organization helps match you to community resources in your area to help with various needs. (https://communityactionpartnership.com/find-a-cap/)

5

Preparing for the Big Things

IN THIS PART . . .

Discover how to make major purchases the smart way.

Find out about investing to secure your financial future.

Understand how insurance protects you and your assets.

Chapter **19**

Buying Your Dream Car and Other Big Purchases

L ife is full of big purchases — whether it's a new phone, a car, or even your first apartment one day. And while those things might seem far off, finding out how to save smartly now can make a huge difference later.

By planning ahead and saving the right way, you can avoid unnecessary fees, dodge high-interest payments, and make sure you're getting exactly what you want. Plus, taking your time to research and save means you won't end up regretting a rushed decision. In this chapter, we'll break down how to set savings goals, stay on track, and make big purchases the smart way.

By saving adequately, you can avoid extra fees and additional interest when it's not needed. You can also take time to research and plan so that you aren't stuck with something you don't want later on.

This chapter will guide you in getting ready to meet big financial goals.

Buying Your First Car

Buying your first car can be scary, but it can also be a lot of fun. Yup, we said fun. Your first car purchase is a huge accomplishment and deserves to be celebrated and enjoyed! While someone may hesitate to say car shopping is fun (we know, we know), we can say that it's way more enjoyable when you do research and know that you scored a good deal.

The first thing you'll want to figure out is how you'll be purchasing your car. Cars can be really expensive, depending on how new the vehicle is, as well as its make and model. While buying a used car can be a cheaper route to go, it's not uncommon for a used car to be five figures even after it's been out for some time or has additional mileage on it. Since cars are a large purchase, it's important to know your options when it comes to buying one. You have two main options when purchasing a car: financing or buying with cash.

Financing

When looking at financing a car — whether new or used — you have several options to explore. The following explains the various ways that you can secure financing.

Purchasing with a loan

If you have little (or no) money saved up to buy a car, you would most likely be looking to purchase a car with an auto loan. An auto loan is a loan given to you by a financial institution to purchase a vehicle. Like other loans, it is then paid back over time with interest and financing fees. Most auto loans are paid back over 5 to 7 years, but the terms and conditions of your loan are based on various factors such as your credit score, how much the car is worth, and how much you can reasonably afford to pay back every month.

TIP

Check your credit score. Your credit score plays a vital role in the auto loan process. Financial institutions use it to determine your creditworthiness and the interest rate you'll receive plus how much they will lend you. If your score is low, you might consider improving it before trying to get a loan, or saving up more money for a down payment. See Chapter 5 for more on credit.

The more money you are able to put toward a down payment on a car, the more money you might be able to borrow from a bank. You'll also need to finance less, saving you money over time.

WARNING

Only buy what you can afford. If you are unable to make payments, your financial institution may take the vehicle back, costing you more to get it back from them. If you aren't able to afford to get it back, they may officially take possession of the vehicle and sell it to someone else. Athena had this happen to her, which left her with a hit on her credit report that took years to fix.

Leasing

Leasing a car is like renting a home, but for a vehicle. When you lease a car, you're essentially borrowing it for a set period, usually a few years, and you make monthly payments for the time you have it.

Instead of paying the full price of the car, you pay a portion of the cost based on its expected depreciation during the lease period. This often results in lower monthly payments compared to buying a car. A lease will usually last anywhere between 2 and 4 years, and then once the lease is over, you return the car to the dealership.

Since you are giving the car back, you must keep the car in good condition if you don't want to be stuck paying an additional amount of money or worse, being forced to purchase the vehicle. That's why it's important to follow the terms and conditions of any lease you sign.

Most leases have a mileage limit, which is usually around 10,000 to 15,000 miles per year. You're also in charge of handling all oil changes and any other maintenance issues the leased vehicle may have.

Leasing can be a good option if you like driving a new car every few years and prefer lower monthly payments, but it's important to consider the restrictions and costs involved. It's also important to remember that you could be spending more money over time.

Purchasing with cash

Another way to purchase a car is to buy it outright with cash. Buying a car with cash can be easier than financing in more ways than one. For example, you don't have to worry about taking out an auto loan from a bank like you would if you were to finance a car. You also don't have to abide by mileage limits like you would when leasing, although it never hurts to take good care of your vehicle once you have it!

Buying a car with cash is a straightforward process that can save you from dealing with loans and interest payments. After determining how much money you are willing to spend on a car, aim to have that much in savings. Once you have calculated the amount of money you need to purchase the car with cash you will need to create a budget to help work towards your car buying goal.

You can then research cars to see what type of vehicle would most suit your needs. For example, if you drive a lot for work, you might want to look at what types of vehicles get good gas mileage. It's great to get a car that does it all, but you also need to make sure you are realistic with your wants while covering your needs. You'll also want to consider if you need to get a used car to fit within your budget.

Since you're paying with cash, you'll need to provide cash, a cashier's check, or a bank transfer. Make sure that you receive a receipt of the transaction from the bank.

TIP

If you're interested in buying a car, be prepared to negotiate. Research the car's market value and use that information to discuss the price with the seller. Make sure to be respectful but firm, and walk away if you are serious.

Once you find a vehicle within your price range, be sure to look at the vehicle history by researching the VIN (vehicle identification number) online using CARFAX. A quick CARFAX search can tell you all about the car you are looking to buy: registration information, how many previous owners your car has had, accidents, structural damage, airbag deployment, service and repair information, and what your car was actually used for. This can save you time and headaches by ensuring you're not buying a lemon!

Locating where to buy a vehicle

There are three different places where you can buy a vehicle.

Car dealership

Car dealerships are the most common place to purchase a vehicle. They have a variety of pre-owned (used) and new vehicles for customers to choose from. Most dealerships have a certain brand they specialize in, such as Ford or Chevrolet, which is typically their dealership name, and they usually have used cars for a reasonable price.

Buying a used car from a dealership can be a safer bet than purchasing it a different way because dealerships must inspect their cars and make sure they are safe for you to drive before they can sell them to you. They might also be in better shape than buying a used car from somewhere else and could be a better price, too.

Private sale

Another common way to buy a vehicle is directly from another person. This is known as a private sale as you are transferring ownership directly from buyer to seller with no middleman. Most cars purchased this way are used, and you can often get a better deal than going to a dealership. However, there is less regulation when purchasing a car this way. It's up to you to do your own due diligence when researching a car to make sure it is safe. You can find cars from private sellers through online marketplaces such as Autotrader, Facebook Marketplace, and a general online search engine.

Auction

An auto auction is another place where you can buy a vehicle for a reasonably good deal. As with other types of auctions, potential customers are given a number and can offer a price, known as a *bid*, for a car they want. Sometimes someone will offer more money than you. If this happens, it's up to you to decide if you want to offer more money than them. The person with the highest bid wins the car. A car auction can be a way to find a decent car for a lower price due to circumstances beyond their original owner's control.

Considering associated costs

In addition to the amount of money your new vehicle is worth, you're not done when it comes to paying for it. Here are a few other costs you need to consider when buying a car.

Insurance

Auto insurance is an important part of owning a vehicle. Insurance protects your investment, aka your car. If you are in an accident or something else happens to your car, damaging it, your car insurance company will help you cover the costs of fixing your vehicle. In addition to fixing any damage to your vehicle or another vehicle, depending on the type of coverage you select, auto insurance can also help you cover additional expenses, such as medical expenses or lost wages if the accident requires you to take time off from work.

TIP

Consider taking a safe driving class. Younger drivers are usually charged more for car insurance because of a lack of experience on the open road due to their age. A safe driving class can help your insurance company feel more confident in your driving ability, which, in turn, may mean a lower rate.

TIP

Compare car insurance quotes after you get them from insurance providers. Always ask if you qualify for a discount such as for being a student, living at home, and being a good driver. Some insurance providers also offer discounts if you sign up for automatic online bill pay! The main thing is to ask.

Maintenance

Cars need to be well taken care of so they don't break down. This means taking your car to a mechanic regularly for oil changes and engine inspections to fix any potential issues before they get any worse. This also includes items such as tires for your car, windshield wipers, fluid for your car's radiator, and transmission.

WARNING

In addition to cars needing annual upkeep, your car may need repairs that can be expensive. Transmissions wear out and need replacing. Always try to keep this in mind when trying to figure out how much you need for an emergency fund.

Fuel and registration

In order to keep your car on the road, in addition to regular maintenance and car insurance, you'll need money for gas and registration. Depending on the vehicle and how often you drive, gas could cost anywhere between $150 and $300 a month on top of your insurance and car payment, if you have one. It's also important to keep your car's registration renewed every year with the Department of Motor Vehicles (DMV). This will depend on how old your car is and where you live.

Taking a Dream Vacation

Once you turn 18, life opens up opportunities you may not have had access to when you were younger. One opportunity you may want to take advantage of is . . . traveling!

Traveling is great for many reasons, which is why so many people make a point to do it. Traveling to new places helps you explore cultures you may have always wondered about, including new-to-you places and food. It can also help you spend time with loved ones and to find out more about yourself. It's a great way to relax and become inspired, which is something we both love it for.

But traveling can also be expensive. Plane tickets, taxis, food, and experiences can all add up if you're not careful. That's why it's important to find out how to travel on a budget so that your money can go even further for you to make the most of it.

Opening a separate savings account

One way to hit any financial goal, including when it comes to traveling and exploration, is to open a separate savings account. You can put money aside this way to help keep you from spending it. You can fund your account as often (or as little) as you like while working on other financial goals you may have.

TIP

Just like with other goals, you can save money you get from windfalls or put aside money from your paycheck or side hustle. One thing Athena loves to do is to dedicate one side hustle to fund one goal. This way, she can keep better track of how much she is earning, and it motivates her to save more money.

Traveling off season

Another way to save money when traveling is to travel off season. Hawaii is a great example. People think of warm, tropical places when they are stuck in a cold and dreary winter climate. So, Hawaii is a very popular tourist destination from November to March and is less popular in the summer when people aren't stuck somewhere cold. When travel is busy to an area, this is known as *peak season*. When travel is slow, it's called *off season*.

When you travel off season, you have a better chance of scoring deals. Since business is slower during this time, you may find hotels and airlines offering discounts to help drum up some business. You may also find that restaurants and local attractions are running specials to draw you in. Some places to travel off season around the world are listed here.

>> **Europe:** This includes countries like the United Kingdom, Italy, France, Germany, Spain, and Greece. The off season, winter, is from November to March, with the exception of holidays: Christmas, New Year's, and sometimes Easter.

- >> **Asia:** Because Asia is a huge continent, seasons vary depending on which part you travel to.

  - **Central Asia:** Off season is from November to March. Some countries include Afghanistan, Pakistan, India, Nepal, and Bangladesh. It's chilly!

  - **East Asia:** Off season is from November to March. Countries include China, Japan, Taiwan, and both North and South Korea.

  - **South Asia:** In this part of Asia, the off season is from May to September, due to hot weather. Countries here include Thailand, Malaysia, and the Philippines.

  - **West Asia and the Middle East:** Off season is from May to September due to hot weather. Countries include Israel, Iran, Egypt, Saudi Arabia, and India.

- >> **Australia and New Zealand:** Cold weather puts these countries off season from April to June.

- >> **The Caribbean:** Off season is from August to November, which is hurricane season, and this can make traveling here riskier. Countries include Cuba, The Bahamas, Dominican Republic, Jamaica, and Haiti.

- >> **Central America:** Off season (the rainy season) is from June to August, Countries include Belize, Panama, Mexico, Costa Rica, and Guatemala.

- >> **South America:** Off season is from June to August. Countries include Argentina, Brazil, Peru, Ecuador, and Columbia.

- >> **Africa:** This is a huge continent, and so the seasons vary depending on which part you travel to.

  - **North Africa:** Off season is from June to August. Countries include Morocco, Algeria, Tunisia, and Libya.

  - **East Africa:** Off season travel for this part of Africa is from April to June and then again from October to December, due to rain. Countries in East Africa include Kenya, Uganda, Ethiopia, and Somalia.

  - **West Africa:** The best time to travel here is from July to September, but it can vary. Countries include Cameroon, Guinea, Ghana, Nigeria, and Sierra Leone.

- **South Africa:** With the exception of holidays, it's best to travel off season from November to April. Countries include South Africa, Zimbabwe, Botswana, and Zambia.

REMEMBER

Wherever you go, don't forget to share your location with a loved one so that at least one person knows where you are at all times. If you are using a ride share, opt to share your location there as well. When we travel, both our family members and friends know where we are in case we get lost!

WARNING

Meeting new people while traveling is always fun, but never go anywhere *alone with them or to an unknown place.* Safety first when traveling anywhere!

Using discount websites

Another tip to traveling on the cheap is to check out discount websites. A lot of hotels and airlines can't always fill their rooms and seats with guests. So instead of not filling them at all, they offer them at a sometimes steep discount so that they can at least make some profit, even if it's small. That's where these websites come in.

Websites like Expedia and Hotels.com help hotels fill empty rooms for a lower-than-average price. These websites also allow you to compare various hotels in one area, along with reviews, so that you can make the best choice for where you want to stay within a budget you feel comfortable with.

You can also grab a lower-priced airline ticket through similar websites. Google Flights allows you to set a destination up with a price alert and will then let you know if any tickets pop up for that rate. Google Flights also allows you to compare flights with other airlines and tells you if they offer better prices.

TIP

Another website you can check out for lower flight fare is called Skiplagged. This website lets you know what flights have layovers that happen to be at the destination you'd like to visit. So instead of continuing on somewhere else, you can visit your destination for a lower price.

TIP

Once you're at your travel destination, check out Groupon for discounted passes for popular attractions. We've both been able to take advantage of discounted tickets for day cruises, tours, and food festivals this way. Groupon is also great for concert tickets and other events in your local area! (Go to www.groupon.com/.)

Getting a Jump Start on a Home

Home ownership can be attainable at any age if you are strategic enough, but it can be expensive. We both know people who bought their first homes out of high school, and we know people who bought homes well into their eighties. There is no timeline of when someone can or can't buy a home despite what people might say. It's all about financial preparation, and even if you don't plan on purchasing a home right away, you can always start saving toward your financial goals at any age. Here's how to get a jump on home ownership.

Having a savings plan

The amount you need to purchase a home relies on many factors. Because it's hard to know how much you may need, it's okay to just start saving a small amount of money every week, even if it's only $10. If you can only afford $5 here and there, that's okay, too.

Every little bit adds up, and there is no amount that is too small when it comes to achieving your financial dreams, including owning a house. You can also set aside money from any additional windfalls you might get, such as from a birthday gift or a refund for something you returned to the store.

Researching home-buying assistance programs

One possible way to achieve your dream of owning a home is to see if you qualify for any home-buying assistance programs.

There are home-buying assistance programs on both the federal and local level.

The Federal Housing Administration (FHA) sponsors the FHA loan program. This program offers assistance to first-time homebuyers who qualify, as well as senior citizens and those who choose to buy a manufactured or mobile home.

It works like this: In order to offer you a better rate as well as a lower down payment and closing costs, the FHA will insure the loan you receive from a lender. Since the loan is insured, a lender feels more comfortable offering you a loan even if you don't have a huge down payment to offer or you have a less-than-stellar credit score. These types of loans can especially help a first-time buyer who doesn't have a lot of money put away to cover closing costs and other fees associated with buying a home.

You can also access local information, including state assistance programs, affordable housing, and utility assistance, by going to www.hud.gov/topics/rental_assistance/local. Along with state programs, you can also check out programs that may be offered in the city or county where you reside.

Getting clear on what house you want

First, think about what kind of home you'd like to live in. Different types of homes have their own pros and cons, especially at different stages in your life. Your finances and future goals will also impact your homebuying decision.

Single-family

A single-family house is a type of home that is designed to be occupied by one family. Unlike apartments or townhouses, which might have multiple families living in close proximity, a single-family house stands alone on its own section of land. It usually has separate entrances (this all depends on the home construction), and the family living there has full control over the interior and exterior of the property. This is what most people think of when they picture buying a home.

These houses typically include several rooms for different purposes, like bedrooms, a kitchen, and living areas. They can vary in size and style, from small casitas to huge mansions, and they usually have a front and backyard.

Condo

Short for condominium, condos are similar to apartments, but instead of renting one, you own it. Multiple condos owned by different people can all be in one or several buildings. Like apartments, most condos come with common areas like pools, BBQs, and gyms, which are all paid for and maintained by everyone who lives there.

Living in a condo can be a good option for those who want to own property but may not want the responsibility of a single-family house, especially when it comes to maintenance and yard work. Condos can vary in size and style, just like houses, and they often come with a range of amenities. Sometimes it's easier on one person to operate their home if it's smaller, and may also be cheaper than a single-family home.

Duplex

A duplex is a type of residential building that consists of two separate living units, usually side by side or stacked on top of each other. Each unit has its own entrance, kitchen, bathroom, and living spaces, which means that two families or groups can live in the same building while still having their own private space.

Think of a duplex like a house that has been divided into two. It might look like a single-family home from the outside, but inside, it's designed to accommodate two households. It's great for families who want to live close to each other but still maintain some independence. Both families in the duplex take turns taking care of the yard and other things that may pop up, like maintenance.

Examining the condition of a home

Another factor in how much a home will cost is what condition the home is in when you buy it.

New buy

A new buy, often called a new construction home, is a house that has just been built and hasn't been lived in before. Like a new car, new buys mean you are the first owner or, in this case, the first person who gets to enjoy the home!

Typically with a new buy, you get to choose a lot of the design. This can mean you pick out not only the house, but also the layout, finishes, and sometimes even the appliances. A new buy home is something built from scratch and designed by you!

Many new home communities (where new buy homes often are) include amenities for residents, like parks, pools, or clubhouses, which can make the cost of a new buy feel truly worth it.

Fixer-upper

A fixer-upper home is a house that needs some work or renovations before you can live in it. Sometimes you can live in a fixer-upper home, but it might not be what you would prefer to live in at first. Homes that need repairs, have outdated features, and look run down, are all considered fixer-uppers. Sometimes they just need new appliances and paint, but other times they might need new plumbing or even a new roof!

People often buy fixer-upper homes because they can be less expensive than new buy or turnkey homes. That's because they need work and upgrades that the original seller can't afford or doesn't want to take care of. A lot of people buy fixer-upper homes to save money but don't realize how expensive the repairs really are or, worst-case scenario, or they can't live in it until it is renovated.

WARNING

Try to only take on a fixer-upper home if you feel confident that you can handle the work it needs, whether it's done by you or you pay for a professional to come in and do the work for you.

REMEMBER

A home doesn't always need to be updated right away or all at once. It's common for homeowners to actually do it room by room over several years so that they don't run out of money all at once. This also allows you to save up and find the best deal, which can make your money go even further.

Turnkey

A turnkey home is a house that is move-in ready. This means it's fully finished and does not need any repairs or extensive renovations. When you buy a turnkey home, everything is in good condition, and you can start living there right away without worrying about fixing things up. It might not look the way you want it to, but you can still move in without worrying about anything and make the place your own over time.

TECHNICAL STUFF

Check out the website Zillow at www.zillow.com/. You can find houses for sale with pictures, their purchase history, and what other homes are selling for in that same area.

WARNING

Do not buy a house without a home inspection from someone who isn't affiliated with your real estate agent or mortgage company. An outsider can provide an opinion that isn't based on whether or not you buy the home in question. An inspection can let you know ahead of time if there is something seriously wrong with the home so that you aren't blindsided later on.

Discovering additional expenses

Just like cars, houses have additional expenses you need to keep in mind when buying one. It's important to account for these things because they can drive the price of home ownership way up!

Maintenance

As homes get older, they require touch-ups and repairs. While a new buy might not need anything right away, eventually it will need new appliances and paint, just like any other house. A fixer-upper home may require maintenance sooner than a turnkey home or new buy home, and it might be more costly because of the condition you are buying it in.

There are also different issues your home can have over time, such as needing new plumbing or electrical work. While you can have a general idea of what work your home may need, sometimes stuff happens out of nowhere and can cost as much as a new car to fix!

TIP

For minor upgrades around the house, check out stores like Home Depot or Lowes. Along with finding materials for a lower price, they also offer classes with qualified instructors to help you learn how to do projects around the house. A fresh coat of paint and new hardware throughout the home can do wonders!

Homeowner Association fees

Homeowner Association (HOA) fees are most common in new buy home communities. They may also be in other neighborhoods if the neighborhoods were designed to be that way. HOA fees, which can be quite expensive, are paid for by the people who live in that neighborhood for upkeep of the common areas, like landscaping. These fees can also be used to maintain amenities such as a pool or park that everyone can use. HOAs are also common for people who own condos. Older homes in older neighborhoods typically do not have HOAs.

WARNING

HOAs can be great to help your neighborhood feel like a home but they can also be expensive. You may also be subjected to rules and additional expenses that you may find don't suit you. Athena has a friend who was forced to repaint her house because her friend's HOA wanted to update the color of the neighborhood.

Property taxes

Property taxes are a way for local governments to collect money to support funding for various services in the community, such as schools, roads, parks, and emergency services. Based on how much your home is worth, the local government will send you a tax bill for how much they think you should pay to live there.

It's hard to know how much you will be paying in property taxes because they go up and down every year, depending on a variety of reasons, such as the condition of your house or neighborhood.

They can also fluctuate based on how many people live in your area and what services the city or county feels are needed.

WARNING

We have heard of small increases and then we have also heard of someone's property taxes going up $500 every month for an entire year! That's an additional $6,000 a year someone wasn't originally planning on paying.

TIP

Property taxes are public record so that you can research what the taxes are in that area to get a good idea of how much to add to your budget to cover them.

Insurance

Homeowner's insurance is a type of insurance policy that protects you when you own a home. Think of it like a safety net for your house and everything inside it. If something bad happens, like a fire or a storm, or if someone gets hurt on your property, homeowner's insurance can help cover the costs. Homeowner's insurance is usually required when taking out a mortgage for a home, and even if it's not, it's always a good idea to have it, just like it is for your car and your health. You may never use it, but it's always a good idea for it to be there!

REMEMBER

Just like any other type of insurance, make sure you compare quotes to help you get the best price.

Being open-minded

Keep in mind while on your home-buying journey, that you should stay open to a home you may not have considered before. A famous quote Athena once heard was that your mind must remain open to possibilities. Although this philosophy encourages personal growth and a positive mindset, which is important in general, it can also be applied to looking for somewhere to live.

For example, you might see a house with a lot of overgrowth and in need of landscaping, but it might be a way for you to plant the garden of your dreams. Maybe your house doesn't come with a pool, but you can try out an inflatable one. Maybe the space you're looking at is smaller than you had hoped for, but you can get creative with storage solutions, or living minimally. Mykail recently experienced this and got creative with an extra bedroom, turning it into her own content creator studio and closet. Not only does she have somewhere to film new content and write this very book, but she also has enough room for her shoe collection!

Keeping your mind open to possibilities means that you'll be able to spot opportunities when others may not.

Athena took an unused carport and made it into her own at-home spa for less than $700. She purchased an inflatable hot tub, some string lights, and plants at the grocery store for a relaxing feel. In addition, she found patio accents from Ikea and grabbed a wicker chair off of Facebook Marketplace. A Bluetooth speaker from the Target dollar section and voila, she was in business!

Chapter **20**

Investing for the Future

H ave you ever thought about what you want your life to look like 5, 10, or even 20 years from now? It's a difficult exercise, but take a moment to daydream. Do you imagine traveling, owning a cool car, maybe starting your own business, or just feeling financially free to make choices without worrying about money? Here's the thing: those dreams don't just happen out of nowhere, and to make them a reality, you need money (sometimes a lot of it). The way to make your money dreams into reality is by making smart moves early on, and one of the best ways to make future-you proud is by investing.

Investing might sound a little intimidating (or maybe even boring), but it's actually a tool to help you turn today's money into tomorrow's freedom. There are so many ways to become an investor (stock market, real estate, and other businesses), but we will focus on stock market investing. This chapter will break down the basics, making stock market investing feel way less mysterious and way more doable. This is just the start of your investing journey, and there will be so much more time to grow your $100 into a solid fortune for you to buy all the things that make you smile.

In this chapter, you'll find out how to get started with smart, practical steps: choosing a safe place to start investing your money, building an investment mix that works for you, and even planning ahead for retirement (yes, even if it feels far off!). Creating a solid foundation now will allow you to grow your money over time and build the future you want, no matter what that looks like. So, let's dive in and start making those dreams a reality, one smart investment at a time.

Getting money to start investing

Investing can feel like something only adults with big bank accounts do, but the truth is, you can start small, even with just a few dollars. Thanks to technology and creative ways to save, getting money to begin investing is easier than ever. Let's explore some ways you can tap into your resources and start building your investing journey, no matter your budget.

Asking trusted adults to get involved

Sometimes, the best way to start is by having a conversation with the adults in your life. Whether it's a parent, guardian, or trusted family member, they may be willing to support your investing goals. Start by explaining why you want to invest and how you plan to use the money. For example:

Are you saving for your future education or a big goal like starting a business?

Do you want to learn how to grow your money responsibly?

If they're on board, they might gift you money to start or match the funds you've saved.

Be specific when asking. Instead of saying, "Can I have some money to invest?" try, "I've saved $50 and want to start investing. Would you consider matching that amount to help me reach my goal?"

Respect their decision if they say no. Not everyone has the ability to contribute, and that's okay — you have other options.

Rounding up your allowance and other money

If you already receive an allowance, consider setting aside a small portion specifically for investing. Even $5 or $10 a week adds up over time and can get you started with platforms that allow fractional shares or micro-investing. Using money you are already getting in a different way is an excellent way to get started small.

Some robo-advisors offer features like round-ups, which automatically invest your spare change from everyday purchases. For example, if you spend $4.50 on a snack, the app rounds it up to $5 and invests the extra $0.50. Small amounts like this can grow surprisingly fast.

Putting your gifts to work

Special occasions like birthdays, holidays, or graduations are great opportunities to boost your investing fund. Instead of asking for items, consider requesting cash gifts that you can use to invest. There are even apps like Stockpile, that allow you to receive stocks from friends and family as gifts.

During the gift giving events you can also decide to put a portion of your received funds into your investment account. Hypothetically, if you got $200 in gifts for your birthday you can put $50 in your investment account and spend the other $150 on a new jacket you've been eyeing.

Let your family know how you'll use the money. For example, you could say, "I'm saving up to invest in my first stock or fund. Any amount helps me reach that goal!"

Avoid pressuring friends or family to give money. A simple request is enough, what they give should be up to them.

Using the money you earn from work to invest

If you have a part-time job or take on gigs, like babysitting, pet sitting, or mowing lawns, investing a portion of your earnings can be a great way to grow your money. Start by saving a small, consistent percentage — like 10 percent of every paycheck or payment — and depositing it into your investment account.

Treat investing like paying yourself first. Set the money aside as soon as you get paid, so you're not tempted to spend it elsewhere.

If you're not earning a steady income, consider creative gig options. For example:

Selling handmade items online.

Tutoring younger students in a subject you're good at.

Offering tech help to adults (like setting up phones or helping with apps).

Starting small, thinking big

The best part about investing today is that you don't need to start with thousands of dollars. Many apps and platforms let you begin with as little as $5 or invest in fractional shares, so you can own a piece of your favorite company without breaking the bank. Remember, what matters isn't how much you start with, but that you start at all.

The investing habits you build now will multiply over time. A small amount invested consistently can grow into something significant — and by starting early, you're giving your money the gift of time to grow.

REMEMBER

The goal isn't to get rich overnight but to create a steady foundation for your financial future. Starting small is still starting, and that's what counts.

Choosing a Brokerage That Fits

First thing first: You need to get the right accounts to access the stock market. Your checking and savings accounts will not enable you to buy and sell stocks in the stock market. You (or a trusted adult) will have to open a brokerage account to gain access to the stock market. All this stock market and brokerage talk makes us think of our friend Sophie.

Sophie was a high school junior who always had big dreams. She loved reading stories about young entrepreneurs and hearing about how they'd built companies from the ground up. One day, after watching a video about a young woman who'd started investing at 18 and was already growing her wealth, Sophie decided it was time to get serious about investing. She'd heard the stock market was a good place to start, and while she didn't know much about it, she knew she needed a brokerage account to start making moves.

She started with a little research on "brokerage accounts" and found out there were two main types she could go with: self-directed brokerages and robo-advisors. *Self-directed brokerages* seemed perfect for people who wanted to research and choose each investment themselves, while *robo-advisors* used technology to suggest investments based on personal goals and risk preferences. The idea of a robo-advisor sounded interesting; a little guidance wouldn't hurt. But Sophie was also intrigued by the control that a self-directed brokerage would give her.

The next step was figuring out where to open her account. Sophie knew she didn't want to rush it; she wanted to pick a company that fit her needs. So, she listed a few top options: big names like Fidelity, Vanguard, and E*TRADE, and newer, more app-based ones like Ellevest, Acorns, and Betterment. Each had its own set of perks: Some offered low fees, others had tons of educational resources, and some even gave free stocks just for signing up. She weighed the pros and cons of each, taking her time to consider what would work best for her. After all, this was her first step into investing, and she wanted to make sure she was setting herself up for success.

As she continued her research, Sophie felt a new kind of confidence building. Finding out about these different tools made the whole idea of investing feel less intimidating. She couldn't wait to open her first brokerage account and take her first real steps into the world of investing.

TIP

The moral here? Don't rush the process. Take your time to understand your options, weigh the pros and cons, and choose what feels right for you. A little research now can lead to a lot of confidence (and growth) down the road.

Using a self-directed brokerage for investing

When you think of stock market investing, you probably get images of crazy men ringing bells and scrambling on the trading floor of the New York Stock Exchange. To be honest, that's what I thought stock market investing was at first, too. In the 21st century, you now get to cut out the middleman and trade stocks without the madness and from the comfort of your own home (or on the go with your smartphone).

A self-directed brokerage account is a type of investment account where you're in charge. It's a lot like having your own door into the stock market, where you decide exactly what to buy and sell. In the past, investing in stocks meant going through brokers who'd handle all the trades, but with a self-directed account, you have access to the same markets from your phone or computer. You choose which stocks, funds, or other assets to buy, and you control how long to hold onto them.

Think of it this way: If you're interested in companies you know and like — say, a popular sneaker brand or a streaming platform you use — you can invest in them directly through your self-directed account. This means you're building a portfolio that reflects your choices and interests, not what a preset plan suggests. It's a great way to learn the ropes of investing because every decision is your own, from researching companies to deciding when to buy or sell.

To open a self-directed brokerage account, start by researching reputable online brokers that offer low fees and an easy-to-use platform. Look for reviews to see what others say about their features, and compare their account options. Once you pick a broker, head to their website or app and create an account, which usually involves filling out a form, verifying your identity, and linking your bank account.

Using a robo-advisor for investing

The latest and greatest update to stock market investing is robo-investors (or robo-advisors). Using a robo-investor, or robo-advisor, is like having a digital "investment assistant" for your brokerage account. Instead of you choosing every stock or bond yourself, a robo-advisor does the hard work of selecting investments based on your goals. When you open a robo-investor account, you'll typically start by answering a few questions about things like your age, how much risk you're comfortable with, and what you want to achieve (saving for college, building wealth over time, and so on). Based on your answers, the robo-advisor creates an investment plan, then manages it automatically.

One of the best parts? Robo-investors are low-cost, making it easy to start investing on any budget. Many robo-advisors have small or even zero minimums, which means you don't need thousands of dollars to get started. For a small fee, they'll buy and sell investments for you, keeping your portfolio balanced without you needing to know every market detail.

Imagine this: You want to invest but don't feel quite confident about picking the right mix of stocks and bonds. With a robo-advisor, you can still invest without having to learn everything about the market. The robo-advisor will buy and sell investments for you to keep your portfolio balanced, so you're not over-invested in one area. It's hands-off, so you can check your account anytime, but you don't have to make daily decisions.

To open a robo-investor account, choose a brokerage with robo-advisor options and fill out their questionnaire to set up your profile. You'll link your bank account and deposit money, and from there, the robo-advisor will take over. It's a straightforward, low-maintenance way to start investing, especially if you're busy or just want a bit of help getting started!

Researching the best brokerage

Once you have decided if you want to go with a self-directed or robo-advisor brokerage account, you have to do some research to pick the right company for your new stock portfolio. This part can feel a little overwhelming because there are so many different companies to choose from. To help make this task a little easier, start by asking yourself the following questions to create criteria to compare potential brokerage companies against.

Here are some questions to guide your research into finding the right brokerage company:

>> **What are my investment goals?** Think about whether you're saving for something specific or building long-term wealth. This can help you decide if you need a brokerage with lots of investment options or something more basic.

>> **How much money do I want to start with?** Different brokerages have different minimums for opening accounts. Knowing your starting budget can help narrow down your choices.

>> **What are the fees, and am I comfortable with them?** Look into trading fees, account maintenance fees, or fees for extra features. These can add up over time, so consider what you're willing to pay.

>> **How much control and guidance do I want?** If you like a hands-on approach, a self-directed brokerage might be best. If you prefer more support, look for a brokerage with advisory services.

TIP

Some self-directed brokerages have the option to use a robo-advisor or talk to an in-house advisor (sometimes free or for a small fee).

>> **What kind of educational resources or tools do they offer?** If you're new to investing, look for a brokerage that offers learning resources, research tools, or even live webinars to help you learn as you go.

>> **What are the company values, and how do they support communities I care about?** Some brokerages have initiatives that support financial literacy, sustainability, or other causes. Research how the company gives back to see if it aligns with what matters to you.

>> **How does the company make money?** It's good to know if the brokerage makes money mainly from trading fees, selling order flows, or other charges. This transparency can help you understand any hidden costs.

Next, you want to think about some features that align with your values, goals, and money habits. Every brokerage has different features and customer services that can help you in your stock market investing journey. Reviewing these features and comparing what different brokerages offer can help you find a platform that best matches your goals, preferences, and investing style.

Here's a list of features to consider when researching brokerage companies. Thinking about what's important to you can help you find a brokerage that fits your needs:

>> **Customer service options.** Look for 24/7 support, live chat, or phone support. Good customer service can be especially helpful when you're just starting out.

>> **Availability of fractional shares.** Some brokerages let you buy partial shares, which is great if you want to invest in pricey stocks without a big upfront investment.

>> **Round-ups and automatic investing.** Some brokerages let you "round up" purchases to the nearest dollar and invest the spare change or set up automatic transfers into your investment account.

>> **High-yield cash accounts.** A high-yield cash account alongside your brokerage account can help you earn interest on uninvested money.

>> **Mobile app and website usability.** Make sure the platform is user-friendly, especially if you plan to manage your investments on a smartphone.

>> **Commission-free trades.** Many brokerages offer commission-free trades, meaning you won't pay a fee for each trade, which can save you money in the long run.

>> **Research and educational resources.** Some brokerages offer tools, reports, or even courses that can help you find out more about investing and make informed choices.

>> **Account minimums and fees.** Check for minimum opening deposits and any recurring fees, as these can vary widely between brokerages. Many fee-free options are also available.

>> **Tax-advantaged accounts (such as Roth IRA and Traditional IRA).** If you're thinking about long-term, tax-advantaged investing, see if the brokerage offers these retirement account options.

>> **Dividend reinvestment programs (DRIPs).** A DRIP lets you reinvest dividends automatically, so your earnings can grow without you needing to reinvest manually.

>> **Alerts and notifications.** Notifications can help you stay on top of account activity, stock price changes, or any other updates you set up for peace of mind.

>> **Advanced trading tools.** For more experienced investors, some brokerages offer tools like options trading, advanced charting, and more.

After you have done thorough research, you can narrow your choices down to your top three companies. Remember to look at online reviews from various websites to see what real customers are saying about the company on social media and online forums. This should give you enough information to make a sound decision and choose the right brokerage for your investments. Don't worry about "choosing wrong" — nothing is set in stone; if you decide later on you don't like the brokerage you chose, you can move your money to another company.

REMEMBER

Don't get trapped in "analysis paralysis." Use these questions to narrow down your company selection and pick the company that most closely matches your requirements.

Here's a list of brokerage companies to start your search.

>> **Acorns:** Perfect for beginners; rounds up purchases and invests spare change.

>> **Alinea:** A blend of financial planning tools and robo-advisory services.

>> **Betterment:** Known for automated portfolio management and goal-based planning.

>> **Charles Schwab:** Known for its no-commission trades and extensive educational resources.

>> **E*TRADE:** Ideal for beginners and advanced users, with easy-to-use tools.

>> **Ellevest:** Focused on women investors, with personalized investment portfolios.

>> **Fidelity Investments:** Offers a wide range of investment options and user-friendly tools.

>> **M1 Finance:** Allows users to create custom portfolios with automatic rebalancing.

>> **Merrill Edge:** Combines banking and investment tools for Bank of America customers.

>> **Public:** A commission-free trading app focused on building community and education for investors.

>> **Stash:** Combines investing and banking features, with beginner-friendly guidance.

>> **TD Ameritrade:** Popular for its intuitive platform and access to educational webinars.

>> **Vanguard:** A great choice for low-cost index funds and long-term investing.

>> **Wealthfront:** Offers tax-efficient investing and easy-to-use tools.

Opening your first brokerage account

Alright, you've done the research and learned about different types of brokerages; now it's time to actually open an account. This step can feel big, but it's also the start of a journey into investing for your future self. Even if you're not quite old enough to open a brokerage account on your own just yet (you generally need to be 18), there are still ways to get started.

If you're under 18, you can still invest! You'll just need a custodial account. With a *custodial account*, a trusted adult can open the account with you and help you manage it until you reach the age of majority, which is typically 18 or 21, depending on your state. Once you're old enough, the account and any investments are yours. You'll still be able to find out how everything works, research investments, and even help decide which assets to buy.

If you're 18 or older, you can open a brokerage account on your own. Here's how to do it yourself:

1. **Choose your brokerage type.** Based on your research, decide between a self-directed brokerage (for a hands-on approach) or a robo-investing platform (for a more hands-off option). Remember that robo-investors can be a good choice if you want low-cost help getting started on any budget.

2. **Apply online.** Go to the brokerage's website or app and start the application process. Most platforms have a straightforward online application where you'll enter basic information, such as your name, address, Social Security number, and employment status. This is for identity verification and is required for all brokerage accounts.

3. **Choose an account type.** You'll be asked to choose your account type. Options might include an individual taxable account or a retirement account (like a Roth IRA if you're thinking long-term). For general investing purposes, a taxable account is often the way to go for beginners.

4. **Deposit funds.** You'll need to make an initial deposit to start investing. Some accounts require a minimum, while others let you start with any amount. You can usually transfer money directly from your bank account.

5. **Start investing.** Once your account is set up and funded, you're ready to start investing. Whether you're choosing stocks, ETFs, or something else, take your time to make thoughtful choices based on what you've found out.

REMEMBER

Building your portfolio is a gradual process. Start small, learn as you go, and keep your financial goals in mind. This account is your first step toward building wealth. Take it at your own pace!

Unlocking the Investment Strategy of Winners

Your investment strategy is critical to your success as a new investor. You can do research on your own to create a portfolio of stock market assets or you can get help from a financial professional (real person or robo-advisor). This section is important because it truly is the backbone of your financial growth in the stock market.

Think of your brokerage like a backpack with all the things you need to be a straight-A student. All the assets inside of your brokerage make up the parts of your success portfolio; they act as the different supplies you need to buy in order to be a successful student in school.

This section is all about building a smart, lasting strategy that'll put you on a path to grow your wealth and reach your financial goals. Investing isn't about getting rich overnight; it's about learning, planning, and staying consistent. In the next few pages, we'll break down what you need to know to create a winning strategy — one that fits you.

Finding an investment professional

We highly recommend that you consider talking to a financial professional before starting your stock market investing journey. They can take a look at your total financial profile (this includes your budget, income, expenses, and goals) and provide you with helpful advice to get started. They can help you build your portfolio, make future projections, and give you peace of mind. If you are opting for a robo-advisor to create a completely hands-off stock market investing experience, you can skip this chapter. But if you are still curious about knowing how investing works, this section will be very helpful.

TIP

Consider talking to a flat-fee fiduciary financial advisor if you prefer to talk to a real person. These are advisors that are working in your best interest, and you pay them a fixed rate for their helpful advice.

To find a trustworthy flat-fee fiduciary financial advisor (someone who charges only a set fee and is required to act in your best interest), start by looking in the right places. Sites like XY Planning Network, Fee-Only Network, and the National Association of Personal Financial Advisors (NAPFA) list advisors who work for flat fees and commit to fiduciary standards. You could also ask family members or teachers if they know someone reputable. Just remember: A fiduciary advisor is legally obligated to make decisions in your best interest, so they're there to help you succeed, not sell you products for a commission.

Once you've found a few options, it's time to check if they're a good match. Look for someone who has experience with young investors and can explain things in a way you understand. Some advisors specialize in helping beginners get started, while others may focus on different strategies. Make sure you're comfortable talking with them, as a good advisor will take the time to answer all your questions and help you feel confident about your decisions.

When you're ready for your first meeting, do a bit of prep work. Think about your goals, like saving for college or building wealth over time. Bring a list of questions about what you want to find out. Here are some questions to get you started:

>> "How can I start investing in the stock market with the budget I have?"

>> "What's a good balance between risky and safe investments for someone my age?"

>> "Can you help me set up an account and understand any fees?"

>> "How can I track my investments over time?"

>> "What are some strategies you'd recommend for growing my investment portfolio?"

With the right advisor, you'll feel supported and confident in your investing journey. They'll help you build a solid foundation, answer any questions, and offer strategies to meet your financial goals.

Practicing your skills with an investing simulator

Getting into the stock market can seem intimidating, but starting with a stock market simulator can make it way less scary, and way more fun. Imagine it like playing Monopoly, but instead of competing for Boardwalk and Park Place, you're "investing" in real companies like Apple or Nike. The best part? Just like Monopoly money, you're not using real cash, so there's zero risk of losing your hard-earned dollars. You get to make buying and selling decisions in a virtual setup, which helps you learn about stocks, price changes, and market trends without any pressure.

And it's not just solo learning; you can make it a game with friends, or even ask a teacher to make it a class competition. Picture you and your friends starting out with the same amount of virtual money, then competing to see who can grow their "portfolio" the most by the end of the month. It's a perfect way to practice, experiment, and get comfortable with investing, all while having a blast. You'll be learning skills that'll be incredibly useful down the road, but for now, it's all about testing out strategies and seeing what works in a totally safe, low-stakes way. And who knows? You might end up becoming the "top investor" in your friend group. Investing won't give you nightmares when you know your best friend is learning about the stock market right beside you.

Here are some great stock market simulators for beginners, both free and paid, that can help you get a feel for investing:

>> Investopedia Stock Market Simulator (free)

>> HowTheMarketWorks (free with optional upgrades)

>> Wall Street Survivor (free with premium options)

>> MarketWatch Virtual Stock Exchange (free)

>> TD Ameritrade's paperMoney (paid-for full version)

>> StockTrak (paid)

Creating a winning portfolio

Now that you have chosen your brokerage, it's time to understand all the different assets you can fill your portfolio with. Remember, your brokerage is your backpack and your assets are all the different supplies you put in your backpack to make sure you can become an honor roll student. When you are filling your backpack, it is important to buy different types of supplies. It wouldn't make sense to have a backpack filled with scissors and nothing else. There is no way you can be a successful student without pens, paper, and notebooks; a backpack filled with scissors just won't cut it (pun intended). When you buy different types of assets for your portfolio, it is called *diversification*, and when investing, diversity is key. Let's look at a few different types of assets you can buy with the money in your brokerage account.

Before you start investing, we need to explain that there is a risk of losing money you put into the assets in your portfolio, and that is totally normal. There is no such thing as a risk-free investment; all the assets you research will have an investment chart that looks like a spiky graph — there are no straight lines in investing. When building your portfolio, you need to reflect on how much risk you are comfortable with (this is also a conversation you can have with your financial advisor).

When researching new assets to add to your stock market portfolio, it's important to ask yourself a few key questions to make sure the investment aligns with your goals, risk tolerance, and strategy. Here are some questions to guide you:

>> **What is my investment goal for this asset?** Is this investment meant for short-term gains, or are you planning to hold it for the long run? Understanding your goal will help you decide if the asset fits your portfolio.

>> **How does this asset fit with the rest of my portfolio?** Are you diversifying, or are you adding something similar to what you already have? A good portfolio should be balanced with a mix of different assets.

>> **What is the risk level of this asset?** Is this asset high-risk, low-risk, or somewhere in between? Make sure you're comfortable with the potential for both gains and losses.

>> **What do I know about this company or asset?** Have you done your research? For stocks, do you believe in the company's potential to grow? For bonds, do you trust the issuer to pay it back? The more you know, the better decision you can make.

>> **Does this asset have the potential for steady growth or income?** Is this asset likely to appreciate over time (stocks, index funds) or provide regular income (bonds, dividends)?

>> **How does this asset align with my values or interests?** Do you believe in the company or sector you're investing in? If you're passionate about something, like clean energy or technology, you might want to look into assets in that area.

>> **What is the cost to invest in this asset?** Are there fees or commissions that could eat into your returns? For example, some mutual funds and ETFs charge management fees, so make sure you understand the costs.

>> **What is the track record of this asset?** Has the company or fund performed well over time? Look at past performance (though not a guarantee of future results) and analyze how it has handled market ups and downs.

>> **What is the liquidity of this asset?** How easy will it be to buy or sell this asset? Some investments, like real estate or certain bonds, may be harder to sell quickly than stocks or ETFs.

Individual stocks

When you buy an individual stock, you're buying a small piece of a company; it's kinda like becoming a mini-owner. If you believe in a company, like Apple or Nike, you can buy its stock and potentially make money if the company grows. But remember, individual stocks can be risky since the performance of each stock depends on that company alone. Think of it as putting all your eggs in one basket: If that basket drops, so do your eggs. Investing in individual stocks can be exciting, but it's important to balance them with other types of assets.

Fractional shares

Fractional shares let you buy less than a full share of stock. If a single share of Tesla costs hundreds of dollars, but you only want to spend $10, you can buy a fraction of that share. This is a great way to start small and diversify with limited cash. It's like buying individual colored markers instead of buying a huge 12 pack (sometimes you just need one or two to get the job done). Fractional shares make expensive stocks more accessible, especially for new investors.

Mutual funds

A mutual fund is a collection of different stocks, bonds, or other assets that are all bundled together. Instead of researching each stock yourself, you invest in a fund that's managed by professionals who do the work for you. It's like buying a pre-packed school supply kit instead of picking out each item one by one. Mutual funds can offer diversity in one package, making them less risky than single stocks. But keep in mind, they often come with fees for that management.

Index funds and ETFs

Index funds and ETFs (exchange-traded funds) are like mutual funds but with a twist: They're designed to match the performance of a specific market index, like the S&P 500. If you believe the overall market will grow, these funds let you invest in a bunch of companies all at once. It's like getting access to all the top students' notes for class, and then just using those stellar notes to help you study and ace every assignment. They tend to be low-cost, and ETFs can even be traded throughout the day, like stocks.

REITs

REITs (real estate investment trusts) are a way to invest in real estate without actually buying property. When you buy a REIT, you're buying into a fund that owns income-generating real estate, like apartment buildings, shopping centers, or office spaces. It's like owning a piece of an apartment complex without having to be the landlord. REITs can be a way to add diversity to your portfolio, especially if you're interested in real estate, and they often pay regular dividends.

Bonds

Bonds are like loans you give to companies or governments. When you buy a bond, you're essentially lending your money in exchange for a promise to pay you back with interest after a set period. Bonds are typically less risky than stocks, but the trade-off is that they usually don't grow as fast. They can provide steady income over time, making them a good choice if you're looking for something more stable in your portfolio.

Growing Money for Your 60s

Alright, we know retirement might not sound like the most exciting thing when you're still in your teens, but hear us out. The sooner you start thinking about it, the better off you'll be in the long run. The earlier you start saving for retirement, the more time your money has to grow, so even if you can't imagine yourself being 60 just yet, trust us, future-you will thank you. Plus, putting money away for retirement now can benefit you even before you hit retirement age. There are two main ways you can start saving for your 60s and beyond: employer-sponsored plans and individual retirement accounts (IRAs).

Investing in employer-sponsored plans

If you get a job that offers a retirement plan (like a 401k), this is one of the easiest ways to start saving. Your employer might match your contributions, which means they're giving you free money to save for retirement. That's basically like a bonus for being responsible! The best part? The money is taken out of your paycheck automatically, so you don't even have to think about it. The earlier you start, the more that money can grow.

Exploring Individual Retirement Accounts

An IRA is like a personal savings account for retirement, but with some special tax benefits. There are two main types: Traditional IRAs (where your contributions might be tax-deductible now) and Roth IRAs (where you pay taxes now but your withdrawals are tax-free when you retire). The cool thing about IRAs is that you can open one on your own, and you get to choose where to invest your money. Even if your job doesn't offer a retirement plan, you can still start building your nest egg with an IRA. If your company does offer a retirement plan, you can still get your own IRA for double the retirement investment fun. The earlier you start, the more your money can grow, and it doesn't take much to get started.

TIP

Just because your money is in a retirement account does not mean you can't use it before 65. There are special reasons why the bank can approve you to get money from your account without penalties or fees (such as when buying your first house).

Chapter **21**

Protecting Yourself with Insurance

I f you can get insurance for your smartphone in case it breaks, you can get insurance for your money, health, and other parts of your life in case things don't go as planned. (Just a word of advice: Life rarely goes exactly as planned.)

Insurance is a fancy way of saying you are paying people to help you recover funds or cover expenses if something happens to you or your valuable possessions. Some companies also offer different types of insurance to their employees, many for free and others for a reduced price. There are many different types of insurance. We won't discuss every type of insurance, but we do want to chat about the most common types, why they are useful, how to get a policy, and how much they might cost you.

In this chapter, we'll cover the basics of insurance and why it's so crucial to be properly protected by insurance. We'll look at the various coverage you can arrange, and get you up to speed with insurance terminology.

Understanding Health Insurance

Your health is important. If this isn't a shocker, it costs money to pay for doctors' visits, prescription medicine, hospital stays, and other medical care. Health insurance is important to help you pay for all the medical expenses that might pop up. Instead of covering the full cost of doctor visits, hospital stays, medications, or other health treatments on your own, your health insurance plan steps in to pay a big part of the bill. You still pay some costs, like copayments or deductibles, but insurance makes healthcare much more affordable.

WARNING

Health insurance is vital because medical bills can get really expensive, especially for unexpected things like accidents or serious illnesses. By paying for health insurance every month, you're protecting yourself from big, unexpected medical costs.

Many teenagers are covered through their parents' insurance (you can stay on your parents' insurance until the age of 26), but as you get older and start working, you'll need to sign up for your own plan. Having health insurance gives you peace of mind that you'll get the care you need without worrying about huge bills.

Now that you understand why health insurance is so important, let's look at some useful insurance vocabulary and concepts.

Comparing premiums and deductibles

When it comes to health insurance, two terms you'll hear a lot are premiums and deductibles, and understanding them can make a big difference in how you manage your healthcare costs.

Premiums are the amount of money you pay every month just to have health insurance. Think of it like a membership fee that you pay regularly . . . even if you don't need to visit the doctor. Whether or not you actually use your health insurance, you still have to pay the premium to keep your coverage active.

Deductibles, on the other hand, are the amount of money you have to pay for your medical care before your insurance starts covering the costs. For example, if your deductible is $1,000, you'll have to pay that much out of pocket for your medical expenses before your insurance kicks in to cover the rest.

Now, here's how they're different: Premiums are paid every month no matter what, while deductibles only come into play when you actually need healthcare.

Let's say you have a monthly premium of $100 and a $500 deductible. You pay $100 each month to keep your insurance, and if you get sick and have to go to the doctor, you'll pay for those visits out of pocket until you've spent $500. After that, your insurance will start paying a portion of your medical bills.

Premiums keep your insurance active, while deductibles determine how much you pay before insurance helps cover the costs.

Choosing between HMOs and PPOs

Choosing your health insurance plan can get kinda confusing. Hopefully, this section will bring you some clarity. You'll likely come across two types of plans: HMO and PPO. They sound similar, but they work in different ways.

An *HMO* (*Health Maintenance Organization*) plan is usually more affordable but has more rules. With an HMO, you have to pick a primary care doctor, and that doctor is your go-to for almost everything. If you need to see a specialist, like a dermatologist or a physical therapist, your primary care doctor has to give you a referral first. Also, HMO plans usually only cover doctors or hospitals that are in their network. So, if you go to a doctor outside of the HMO network, you might have to pay the full cost yourself.

A *PPO* (*Preferred Provider Organization*) plan gives you more flexibility. You don't need a referral to see a specialist, and you can visit doctors both in and out of the PPO network (although staying in the network will cost you less). PPO plans usually have higher premiums and deductibles compared to HMOs, but they offer more freedom in choosing where you get care.

Here's an example: If you have an HMO plan and want to see an eye doctor, you first need to visit your primary care doctor to get a referral, and you need to make sure the eye doctor is in the HMO's network. With a PPO plan, you can book an appointment with the eye doctor directly, and while it's cheaper if the doctor is in-network, you can still see someone out-of-network if you want, though it'll cost more.

Finding vision insurance

Here's the thing: Healthcare insurance does not include vision, nor does it include dental insurance. We hate to be the bearers of such confusing news, but it's true. Even though your vision and dental health are important, they require their own insurance coverage that is not included in healthcare insurance.

Vision insurance helps cover the cost of eye care, like eye exams, glasses, and contact lenses. It's usually optional, meaning you don't have to get it if you don't want to. Some people choose to pay for vision care out of pocket or to use money from their HSA or FSA (see Chapter 15 to find out more about HSAs and FSAs) instead of having separate vision insurance.

To help you decide if you should opt into vision insurance or pay for vision care yourself, here are four questions to ask yourself:

1. **How often do I need new glasses or contacts?** If you need them every year, vision insurance might save you money.

2. **Do I already have an eye condition?** If you have vision issues, like needing regular check-ups or treatments, insurance could help cover ongoing costs.

3. **How much am I paying for eye care each year?** Compare that cost to how much vision insurance would cost you. If you don't spend much on eye care, insurance might not be worth it.

4. **Do I have an HSA or FSA?** If you do, you can use those funds to pay for eye care without needing separate

insurance. You'd be using pre-tax dollars, which can save you money.

Using dental insurance

Although dental insurance is not included in healthcare coverage, it is still important and necessary to make sure you have a well-rounded, healthy lifestyle. Take it from someone like me (Mykail), who spent over $15,000 on fixing years of bad dental hygiene.

Dental insurance helps cover the cost of dental care, like cleanings, fillings, and sometimes braces or other procedures. Again, it's totally optional; you don't have to sign up for it if you don't want (or need) it. Some people choose to pay for dental care out of pocket or to use funds from their HSA or FSA (see Chapter 15 to find out more about HSAs and FSAs) instead of having separate dental insurance.

There are different options for dental care: you can get insurance through an employer, buy an individual plan, or just pay for visits as you go without insurance.

If you're unsure whether you should get dental insurance or not, here are four questions to help you decide:

1. **How often do I go to the dentist?** If you only need cleanings twice a year, dental insurance may or may not save you money.

2. **Do I have dental issues like cavities or need braces?** If you have ongoing dental needs, insurance might help cover those higher costs.

3. **How much is dental insurance compared to paying out of pocket?** Look at the cost of the insurance versus how much you usually spend on dental care each year.

4. **Do I have an HSA or FSA?** If you do, you can use those funds to pay for dental care with pre-tax dollars, which can save you money.

Getting Life Insurance

Nobody wants to talk about death, but it will happen to all of us one day — which is hard to imagine when you're still quite young. More importantly, we do not know when that day will happen, and this is why we get life insurance.

Life insurance is a policy that pays money to your family or someone you choose (called a beneficiary) if you pass away. It's like a safety net that helps cover expenses like funeral costs, paying off debts, or making sure your family can keep up with bills if you're not around.

I (Mykail) benefitted from life insurance, from an uncle that I have never met. My mother's brother died two years before I was born. However, he left a life insurance policy that gave my mother money to build our family home a year before I was added to the family. Without my uncle, my childhood home probably would have never existed.

There are two main types of life insurance: term life and whole life. Term life insurance lasts for a set number of years (like 10 or 20 years) and is usually cheaper. Whole life insurance covers your entire life but costs more.

Obtaining life insurance used to be a strict and invasive process. With more policy changes and technological advancements, the process has become a bit simpler. You'll need to decide what type of insurance you want. Once you know, you can start shopping around by comparing different insurance companies online or talking to an insurance agent.

Most companies will ask for basic information like your age, health history, lifestyle habits (like if you smoke), and how much coverage you need. You may need to go through a medical exam so they can assess your health. After that, the company will offer you a quote, which is the amount you'll pay for the policy (this is called a *premium*). Once you agree to the terms, you start paying the premiums either monthly or yearly, and your policy becomes active, giving you peace of mind that your loved ones are financially protected.

Choosing term life

When you are young, time and health are typically on your side. However, you might not have the money to afford an expensive policy, and this is why we encourage term life insurance policies. Term life insurance is a type of insurance that lasts for a set period of time, like 10, 20, or 30 years. If something happens to you during that time, the insurance company pays a lump sum of money to the person you choose, like a parent or sibling.

The reason it's called *term* is because it only covers you for a specific time. After the term ends, the insurance coverage stops, unless you renew it. Term life insurance is usually less expensive than other types because it doesn't last forever, and it's a simple way to protect your loved ones financially if anything unexpected happens during those key years.

Choosing whole life

A more expensive and permanent option for life insurance is whole life insurance. This is a type of insurance that covers you for your entire life, not just for a specific period like term life insurance. This means that as long as you keep paying the premiums (the cost of the insurance), your family or the person you choose will get a payout whenever you pass away, no matter how old you are.

TIP

One cool thing about whole life insurance is that it has a "cash value" part. Over time, a portion of the money you pay builds up like savings, and you can even borrow against it or use it later if you need to.

Whole life insurance tends to be more expensive than term life because it lasts forever and includes this savings feature. It's a way to make sure your loved ones are always financially protected, and it can also be used as a long-term financial tool for you. The major downside to this plan, however, is that if you cannot afford the insurance premium (due to loss of income or illness), the policy will lapse and you can lose out on the money in the policy.

REMEMBER Life insurance agents prefer to sell whole life policies because they get a bigger payout when they sell a whole life policy versus a term life policy. Be mindful of the type of life insurance you need and how much you can afford.

Looking at Disability Insurance

If you ever have an accident or get an illness that leaves you temporarily or permanently disabled, you will be glad that you are covered by disability insurance.

Depending on the policy, "disabled" can be defined in different ways, but it often covers physical disabilities, mental disabilities, and other health concerns like cancer, heart disease, auto-immune diseases, and sometimes pregnancy. If something unexpected happens, like breaking a bone or getting really sick, and you can't work for weeks or months, disability insurance makes sure you're not left without any money.

Disability insurance is a type of insurance that helps you if you get injured or sick and can't work for a while. Instead of you losing all your income, disability insurance will pay you part of your salary so you can still cover important expenses like rent, food, or other bills while you're recovering.

There are two main types of disability insurance: short-term (which covers a few weeks or months) and long-term (which can cover years, depending on the plan).

Going with short-term disability

If you get into a car accident and need a few months to heal, short-term disability insurance can step in to provide you with some income, so you're not completely stressed about money during that time.

Short-term disability insurance is a type of insurance that provides you with a portion of your salary if you can't work for a short period, usually from a few weeks up to six months. This could be because of an injury, surgery, or a serious illness that temporarily keeps you from doing your job.

It usually starts paying benefits after a short waiting period, like a week or two, and the amount you get is typically around 60 to 70 percent of your normal salary (depending on the plan you choose). It's a smart way to protect yourself from unexpected events that could impact your ability to earn money, making sure you can focus on getting better without financial worries.

Looking at long-term disability

If your injury or illness is a little more severe, causing you to be out of work for more than six months, you might need to opt-in for long-term disability. Long-term disability insurance is a type of insurance that provides financial support if you can't work for an extended period of time.

REMEMBER

Unlike short-term disability insurance, which covers you for just a few weeks or months, long-term disability insurance can pay you benefits for several years or even until you retire, depending on the policy. This way, you don't have to worry about how you'll pay your bills or support yourself if you can't work for a long time.

Typically, long-term disability insurance kicks in after your short-term coverage ends, so you might have a waiting period of several months before you start receiving benefits. The amount you get usually replaces about 50 to 70 percent of your salary.

Using Other Types of Insurance

Now that you know the most important types of insurance, let's discuss more optional (and some not-so-optional) types of insurance. Depending on the assets you own, like a car or house, you could be required to pay for insurance to protect those assets and others in case of injury or asset replacement. Just like health insurance, these other types of insurance require a set premium and have a deductible that needs to be paid before insurance kicks in.

Shopping for auto insurance

Auto insurance is a type of protection that helps cover the cost of accidents or damages involving your car. It's required by law if you want to drive or purchase a car, and the amount of coverage you need depends on where you live and what kind of car you drive. The good news is, you don't have to settle for the first offer you get. You can shop around to find the best price and coverage that works for you. Many companies let you compare rates online, so take some time to look at your options.

When it comes to paying for auto insurance, you can usually choose between paying monthly or semiannually. Paying semiannually (every six months) might save you a bit of money because some insurers offer a discount for paying upfront, but monthly payments are more manageable for most budgets.

While auto insurance is important and required, there are a few downsides to be aware of. For starters, insurance rates can be expensive, especially for teenagers, and you might end up paying more if you're a new driver. Also, if you get into an accident, your premium could go up, making your insurance more costly. Always make sure you know what's covered and what isn't to avoid surprises.

Buying pet insurance

If you have a pet that you love and care for, you might want to consider getting pet insurance. Pet insurance can help pay for things like vet visits, surgeries, and medications. It can be really helpful, especially since vet bills can get expensive quickly! You pay a premium to keep the insurance active, and then when something happens to your pet, the insurance will help cover part of the cost.

Pet insurance isn't required like auto insurance, but it can give you peace of mind, knowing you won't have to pay as much out of pocket if your pet needs medical care. Different plans cover different things, so it's important to look at what each plan offers. Some may cover only accidents, while others might include routine checkups and vaccinations.

Before deciding to get pet insurance, think about how often your pet needs to see the vet, how much you can afford to spend on their care, and what kind of coverage makes sense for your situation. Like with anything, you can shop around to find the best plan and price for your furry (or feathered) friend!

Purchasing homeowner's or renter's insurance

Getting insurance for the place you live is important. When you are a homeowner, insurance is required; however, as a renter, it depends on the rules of your landlord if insurance is required.

TIP

It might still be a great idea to get renter's insurance even if it is not required by your landlord.

Homeowner's insurance is a type of insurance that protects your home and belongings if something goes wrong, like a fire, theft, or natural disaster. It covers the structure of your house and your personal items, and may even help with liability if someone gets hurt on your property. Essentially, it's a safety net for homeowners to keep their investment secure.

On the other hand, renter's insurance is for people who don't own their place but are renting it instead. It doesn't cover the actual building (since that's the landlord's responsibility), but it protects your personal belongings inside the rental, like your furniture, electronics, and clothes, against risks like theft or damage. It can also include liability coverage in case someone gets hurt while visiting your rented space.

So, what's the big difference? Homeowner's insurance covers both the property and the belongings inside, while renter's insurance only covers the personal stuff inside a rented space. Let's say you're renting a house, and you have a laptop, some furniture, and a TV. If a fire damages your rented home, your renter's insurance would help you replace your laptop and TV, but it wouldn't cover any damage to the actual building. In contrast, if you owned that same house, your homeowner's insurance would cover both the damage to your belongings and the structure of the home.

Getting travel insurance

Travel insurance is an important tool to help you manage risks when you're going on a trip. It can cover a variety of issues, like trip cancellations, lost luggage, and medical emergencies. If you've ever planned a vacation, you know how much time and money goes into it. Travel insurance helps protect those investments by giving you some peace of mind in case things don't go as planned.

So, how do you get travel insurance? It's pretty easy! You can buy it online through travel insurance companies, or sometimes your travel agent can help you find a good policy. When you book your flights or accommodations, there's often an option to add travel insurance to your package. Just make sure to read the details of the policy to see what it covers.

Now, why is it important? Imagine you've saved up for months to go on a big trip, and then something happens (like getting sick or having a family emergency) that forces you to cancel. Travel insurance can help recover your costs, so you're not out a bunch of money. You should consider getting travel insurance if you're traveling internationally, going on a cruise, or planning a trip that requires significant financial investment. It's all about being prepared for the unexpected so you can focus on enjoying your adventure.

6
The Part of Tens

Chapter **22**

The Ten-Part Teen Tax Toolbox

E verybody has to file taxes. Yep, that's right, if you have a job or earning income above $14,600 (in 2024) then you have to do one very important job before April 15th. File your taxes. There are two possible outcomes either you will have to pay taxes or you will earn a tax refund from the government. Everybody's taxes are different. Depending on how you earned your income, the assets you have, and your overall lifestyle your taxes owed will be different than your friends or trusted adult.

Common Tax Forms You'll Need

Taxes come with paperwork, but don't worry, it's not as complicated as it sounds. When you start a job, you'll fill out a W-4 form to tell your employer how much tax to withhold from your paycheck. At the start of each year, your employer will send you a W-2 form showing how much you earned and how much tax was withheld.

If you're self-employed, you may need a 1099 form to report your income. The bank will send important tax documents if you have any other assets like a big savings account (that earned more than $10 in interest) or investment account (whether you gained or lost money).

Keep these documents organized because you'll need them to file your taxes by the deadline, which is April 15 (unless it falls on a weekend or holiday).

Taxable versus Non-Taxable Income

Not all income is taxed. For example, earnings from a part-time job or side hustle are taxable, but allowances or birthday cash are not. Scholarships may or may not be taxable depending on how they're used (tuition versus living expenses). Understanding what counts as taxable income is key to filing your taxes correctly.

You May Need to File Even If You're a Teen

If you made over $14,600 (in 2024) at a part-time job or gig, the IRS expects you to file a federal income tax return. Even if you earned less, filing could help you get a refund if too much was withheld.

Free Filing Tools Are Perfect for Beginners

Websites like IRS Free File and TurboTax Free Edition help you file your taxes step by step. These tools make it easy to enter your W-2 info, answer basic questions, and file your return online for free. There are also free services like VITA if you prefer to work with a tax preparer instead of doing a DIY tax prep.

Your Trusted Adult May Need to Help You File

If you're under 18 or still a dependent, your trusted adult may need to help you. For example, if you earned money while being claimed on their taxes, they'll need your income info to complete their return. Talk to them about how your income fits into their tax filing.

Refunds Are Real Money

If too much money was taken out of your paycheck, filing taxes could mean getting a refund. This is money you earned, so don't leave it on the table; file your return even if it seems small.

State Taxes Vary by Location

Not all states impose a state income tax, but many do. If you worked in a state that has a state income tax, you'll need to file a state tax return in addition to your federal one. Check the rules for your state to know what's required.

Keeping a Tax Folder

Staying organized makes tax season easier. Create a folder (digital or physical) for your W-2s, 1099s, pay stubs, and any other tax-related documents. Keeping track of receipts and expenses can also help if you're self-employed or eligible for deductions. This saves time and stress when it's time to file.

Understanding Tax Brackets

In the U.S., taxes are based on brackets, which means different parts of your income are taxed at different rates. For example, in 2024, if you earned $48,000, only part of your income was taxed at 22 percent. The first portion of your earnings falls into lower tax brackets (for example, 10 percent and 12 percent), and only the income over a certain threshold is taxed at the higher rate. This ensures you're not paying the highest rate on your entire income.

Adjusted Gross Income Matters

Your adjusted gross income, or AGI, is your total income for the year minus certain deductions, like student loan interest or contributions to a retirement account. Your AGI is important because it determines your eligibility for tax credits and deductions. Keeping your AGI lower can sometimes reduce your overall tax liability.

Chapter **23**

Creating a Win File: Your Ten-Part Personal Highlight Reel

A "win file," also known as a "brag file," is your personal collection of accomplishments, big or small, that show off your skills, progress, and strengths. Think of it as a digital time capsule of your proudest moments, ready to shine whenever you need it. Whether you're applying for a job or a scholarship, or you just need a confidence boost, a well-organized win file will have your back.

Discovering What Goes in a Win File

Anything that shows you're learning, growing, and achieving belongs in your win file. Here are a few examples to get you started:

>> Certificates and awards from school, sports, or extra-curricular activities

>> Screenshots of emails or messages praising your work or effort

>> Photos of projects you've completed, like a community garden or a mural

>> A log of personal wins, like completing a tough book, learning a skill, or acing a test

>> Leadership roles or volunteer experiences, even informal ones like organizing a family event

TIP

Don't overlook feedback from others, like kind emails from teachers or notes of appreciation from teammates or coworkers.

Going Digital for Easy Access

A digital win file is a must. Not only is it more secure than a shoebox under your bed, but it's also portable and easy to update.

Here's how you can organize it.

>> **Google Drive:** Create folders for categories like *Academics*, *Extracurriculars*, and *Feedback*. Inside each folder, upload scanned documents, photos, or screenshots.

>> **Notion software:** Use a database template to record achievements. Add fields for the date, category, and details.

>> **Evernote or OneNote software:** Create a notebook titled "Win File" and add entries as individual notes.

Here are some examples of folders you can add.

- » **Academics:** Include report cards, essays with high grades, or certificates from honor societies.

- » **Extracurriculars:** Upload flyers from events you helped organize, photos of your team, or awards.

- » **Feedback:** Save screenshots of glowing emails from teachers or thank-you notes from peers.

Finding Out How to Log Your Wins

Consistency is key. Try to update your file monthly, so no accomplishment gets forgotten. Here's an example of what an entry might look like.

Date: March 2025

Category: Extracurricular

Achievement: Organized a school-wide fundraiser that raised $1,200 for charity, exceeding the goal by 20 percent

Supporting material: Attached flyer and thank-you email from the principal

Don't Forget Personal Wins

Not every accomplishment comes with a certificate. Did you teach yourself to play a song on the guitar? Learn a new skill from YouTube? These personal wins show initiative and self-discipline, so add them to your file! Even hobbies like baking your first layered cake or building a PC are worth noting.

Looking at Long-Term Benefits

Your win file isn't just for now. Over time, it can evolve into a professional portfolio or a resource for writing resumes or college applications, or preparing for job interviews. Employers and admissions teams love specifics, and your win file will provide them.

Starting Small, Staying Consistent

Even if you feel like you don't have many wins to add now, start with what you have. Over time, your file will grow into a collection that reflects your unique journey and strengths. Trust us, future-you will thank you for this!

Collaborating with Mentors and Advisors

Your mentors and advisors can be an invaluable source of feedback and encouragement. Share your win file with them to get advice on how to frame your achievements and where to focus your energy for improvement. Their input can also help you identify wins you may not have considered.

Adding Multimedia Highlights

Photos and videos can bring your accomplishments to life. Did you organize a school event? Record a short video of it or capture impactful before-and-after photos of projects you've worked on. Multimedia makes your win file more dynamic and engaging, especially if you need to present it later.

Keeping It Professional

While personal wins are important, avoid adding overly casual items that might detract from the file's credibility. For example, a victory in a family game night might not belong here. Stick to wins that demonstrate growth, learning, or meaningful contributions to your community.

Preparing for the Future

Think ahead when organizing your win file. Include not only your achievements, but also notes on how these wins relate to your future goals. For instance, if you're interested in engineering, highlight STEM-related accomplishments prominently. This forward-thinking approach will make your file more purposeful and aligned with your aspirations.

Index

U.S. Department of Housing and Urban Development, 273
U.S. Department of Labor, 117, 183
utilities
 as an expense, 99
 needs *versus* wants, 101
 paying bills for, 267–269
 as a spending category, 48

V

vacations, dream, 283–287
values
 accounting for, 115
 knowing your, 220
Vanguard, 299, 305
VantageScore, 67
variable expenses, 46–47, 101, 268
variable interest rate, 82–83
vehicle identification number (VIN), 281
Venmo, 37
Verizon, 243
vesting schedule, 217
VIPKid, 136
vision insurance, 318–319
volunteer work, on resumes, 203
Volunteers in Service to America (VISTA), 160–162

W

W-2 form, 329
W-4 form, 329
waivers, fee, 179–180
wants, needs *versus*, 18–23, 47, 101–102

Watson, Emma (actress), 148
WayUp, 138
Wealthfront, 305
wellness programs, as a company benefit, 234
West Africa, traveling to, 285
West Asia, traveling to, 285
whole life insurance, 321–322
why, determining your, 18
win file, 333–337
windfall, 45
workforce
 about, 201
 interviews, 209–212
 job offers, 212–217
 negotiating job offers, 217–222
 networking, 206–209
 resumes, 202–206
workload, balancing with study schedule, 133–134
work-study programs, 131–134, 187

X

XY Planning Network, 308

Y

YouthRules, 236

Z

zero-based budget, 50–51, 125
zero-fault policy, 259
Zillow, 291

About the Authors

Mykail James is a financial educator, author, and the founder of an online financial education company, the Boujie Budgeter, dedicated to empowering young professionals with the skills they need to create sustainable wealth. With an MBA and over ten years of experience in the financial industry, Mykail specializes in helping first-generation graduates and early-career professionals develop strong financial foundations, improve their money management, and make informed financial decisions. Mykail is passionate about creating financial education workshops that consider diverse socioeconomic backgrounds, learning differences, and disabilities, ensuring that financial freedom is attainable for everyone.

Athena Valentine Lent is the founder of Money Smart Latina, where Latinas and finance meet. Not only has she recently been featured in *The New York Times* and *Business Insider*, but she is also the recipient of the 11th Annual Plutus Awards for Best Personal Finance Content for Underserved Communities. Once homeless in high school, Athena now annually connects over 1,000 high schoolers a year with higher education opportunities through her position at Jobs for Arizona's Graduates.

Athena first discovered the power of a budget in her early 20s. When she was in high school, personal finance was not something that she understood or that was taught in her family. After acing her budget, she was able to go on to complete an associate's degree in Criminal Justice from the College of Southern Nevada. She then pursued a dual bachelor's degree in Criminal Justice and Criminology from Arizona State University and a certificate in Counter Terrorism.

While serving the non-profit sector for 19 years, Athena became passionate about financial representation for the Hispanic community after finding out that other first- and second-generation Latinas lacked proper money management skills just like she once did. This passion led to her starting the popular website Money Smart Latina and advocating for issues such as the Latina wage gap and multigenerational housing.

Now Athena is an award-winning finance expert and the author behind *Budgeting For Dummies* (Wiley 2023). Her work has included speaking engagements with the former second gentleman Douglas Emhoff, Tamron Hall, and #WeAllGrow Latina. Her work can also be found on BuzzFeed, Prudential, Slate Magazine. Experian, T. Rowe Price, GOBankingRates, Insurify, and NJ.com. She also serves on the board of directors as an associate director for Credit Union West, which is one of the largest credit unions in Arizona.

When not working, she can be found reading a Stephen King novel with her leading man, a polydactyl cat named Harrison George.

Dedication

We would like to dedicate this book to the teens that we have been able to impact over the years, with a special dedication to the students of Jobs for Arizona's Graduates and the students in the Federal Trio Programs across the country. Thank you for allowing us to be your trusted adults while taking your first steps into money.

Authors' Acknowledgments

First, I, Athena, want to say thank you to my husband Josh Kalla. Your support over the past five years during my health crisis has not gone unnoticed. It's because of you that I get to write this book, teach personal finance, and do all of these great things. I love you and I'm so honored to be your wifey.

We'd like to thank my dream team from Wiley, Tracy Boggier, Tracy Brown Hamilton, and Marylouise Wiack.

Publisher's Acknowledgments

Acquisitions Editor: Tracy Boggier

Senior Project Editor:
Tracy Brown Hamilton

Copy Editor: Marylouise Wiack

Technical Editor: Markia Brown

Production Editor:
Saikarthick Kumarasamy

Cover Image: © vk_st/Shutterstock